Robert Franz: The Osterwald Liederbuch

Original Keys (Medium/High Voice)

Introduction by Graham Johnson OBE

Edited and typeset by Iain Sneddon

With a monograph by Victoria Edge on the biographies of Franz and Osterwald, their relationship and the genesis of the songs

Copyright © 2019 Iain Sneddon and the other contributors.

First Edition 2019

Lieding Publications
6 Oak Lane
London N11 2DP

www.lieding.co.uk

ISBN Number: 978-1-9162477-0-3

All rights reserved. This book or any portion thereof may not be reproduced or used in any manner whatsoever without the express written permission of the publisher except for the use of brief quotations in a book review or scholarly journal.

Contents

	Page Number
Introduction by Graham Johnson OBE	5
Synopsis of the research in German	9
The Osterwald lieder of Robert Franz: a Monograph by Victoria Edge	10
Notes and Translations	70
Discography	105
Ach wenn ich doch ein Immchen wär'	107
Kurzes Wiedersehen	112
Durch säuselnde Bäume	118
Herbstsorge	122
Wanderlied	126
Ach dass du kamst	129
Will über Nacht wohl durch das Thal	134
Ich lobe mir die Vögelein	137
Vergessen	141
Die Liebe hat gelogen!	147
Der Schnee ist zergangen	152
Der junge Tag erwacht	155
Da die Stunde kam	159
Treibt der Sommer seinen Rosen	162
Gewitternacht	164
Vom Berge	175
Und die Rosen, die prangen	179
Umsonst	182
Im Mai (*Nun grünt der Berg*)	184
Im Sommer	189
Und welche Rose Blüthen treibt	193
Um Mitternacht	198
Ständchen	207
Im Frühling	211
Nun hat das Leid ein Ende	216
Abends	220
Verlass' mich nicht!	224
Frühe Klage	231
Im Mai (*Musst nicht allein im Freien*)	234
Wenn ich's nur wüsste!	238

Lieber Schatz, sei wieder gut mir	241
Vergiss mein nicht!	244
Schöner Mai, bist über Nacht	248
Dort unter'm Lindenbaume	251
Ade denn, du stolze!	254
Die Harrende	259
Aufbruch	265
Erster Verlust	270
Bei der Linde	275
Nun hat mein Stecken gute Rast	278
Zu Spät	283
Sonnenwende	286
Mein Schatz ist auf der Wanderschaft	289
Du grüne Rast im Haine	294
Träume	300
Gleich wie der Mond so keusch und rein	304
Entschluss	307
In Blüthen	312
Aprillaunen	316
Dornröschen	321
Erinnerung	324
Entsagung/Albumblatt	328

Appendix

Notes on the Folksong and *Sechs deutsche Lieder aus dem 15. und 16. Jahrhundert*	330
Herziges Schätzle Du	338
Scheiden und Meiden	342
Far' hin!	346
Ich arme Mann	349
Dich meiden	352
Acknowledgements	357
Biographies	358
Index of Titles and First Lines	359

Introduction

By Graham Johnson OBE

Robert Franz and his music have had a long history of being rescued by admirers and well-wishers. There was a side of his nature that was quite content to wait rather passively for discovery and publication; he was certainly far from being his own best publicist. His own lack of "push" seems to have encouraged others, past and present, to step into the vacuum as his ambassadors and plenipotentiaries. His lieder came into print only as a result of the influential intervention of Robert Schumann; Felix Mendelssohn and Franz Liszt also played an important part in the launching of the music's renown. Franz repaid these three composers with dedications of books of songs; if there is something of the humble country cousin in his gratitude, he was to prove a more stubbornly independent provincial than these grander composers first imagined. He was always his own man and stuck to his last, particularly when it came to resisting well-meaning encouragement to write bigger works. Nevertheless the rescue work continued. When Franz was forced to retire from many of his performing duties as a result of the onset of complete deafness, poverty seemed the only outcome, and he seems not to have begged for help. Instead, his music spoke for him and for itself: almost magically there was a rallying call: a number of distinguished musicians arranged collections and benefit concerts to enable him to continue his life with some measure of financial security.

Franz the underestimated composer has always been something of a "cause", someone whose songs are worth defending, although the very idea of fighting seems inappropriate for music of such quiet subtlety and understatement. For long stretches of time his music seems to have been almost completely forgotten (the fate of composers who pour their lives almost exclusively into the rarefied task of making songs) and then a rediscovery of his substantial legacy (usually prompted by new recordings) has prompted sporadic re-evaluations and new surges of interest. It is true that Franz is no longer as famous as he once was (he was counted "the most significant song composer of the present time" in Mendel-Reissmann's musical lexicon of the 1860s) but he has always quietly resisted being demoted, and his music, free of kitsch and the desire to please commercially (the debilitating curse of hundreds of once ridiculously celebrated – and now completely forgotten – nineteenth-century song composers) has proved happily immune to the ravages of time.

The composer himself acknowledged the early influence of Schubert and Schumann, but the freshness and directness of his musical invention derives from a synthesis of the folksong and chorale traditions of central Germany. Bach was a lifelong lodestar, as was Handel (whom Franz knew as Händel of course) a fellow native of Halle. The Protestant economy (one may almost say thrift) of the piano writing does not preclude heated outbursts and, even in the quiet passages, there is a surprisingly romantic eloquence and ingenuity. It is easy to see how the intelligence, sincerity and humility of this music must have seemed to Schumann utterly enchanting, an antidote to the pompous musical forces that were inexorably leading to the eventual enthronement of Wagner. (It was Liszt who was happily capable of revering both Wagner and his antithesis Franz). The appeal of Franz lies in his very lack of overweening ambition, his lack of interest in being glorious and significant. The creation and manipulation of uncannily appropriate tonal analogues for different verbal ideas (characteristic of Schubert, Schumann, Brahms and Wolf) does not lie in his remit. Instead, Franz is the last great master of the strophic song – he learned a great deal from those modest lieder of Schubert (circa 1815-1816) that are, even now, all too easily overlooked. Franz had the knack of inventing accompaniments to fit the mood of the entire poem without attempting a fussily detailed response, line-by-line, or image-by-image. This overarching simplicity is the art that conceals art, and it is strongly reminiscent of another shy, enigmatic and reticent composer, Gabriel Fauré, thirty years younger, whose songs follow no one else's rules. The accompaniments of Fauré's *melodies*, like those of Franz, maintain an eloquent connection with the mood of the text *as a whole*, while avoiding becoming sidetracked by too much illustrative detail.

Victoria Edge and her talented team of two singers and pianists are the most recent in this distinguished roll-call of rescuers working with affection and determination to place this composer under the spotlight, however unwilling Franz himself may have been during his lifetime to occupy such a position. In this case, however, we have not only a new disc of songs, (many of them unknown to seasoned recitalists, let alone the general public) but also the republication of music that has long been generally unavailable and, attached to this song volume, a fascinating body of new research including a re-examination of various primary sources in Franz's hometown of Halle.

What seems to me particularly valuable about this project is that in concentrating on the settings of Wilhelm Osterwald, Victoria Edge opens several previously shut doors that lead down fascinating biographical corridors and byways. In my own case I must confess to having earlier underestimated the Osterwald songs, having preferred to perform Franz settings by more famous poets – Heine, Eichendorff and Mörike. Why did I shy away from Osterwald? Ignorance is no excuse, but I could find nothing about him in *Goedike*, that copious dictionary of nineteenth century German poetry, although the other valuable source, *Brümmer's* Lexicon, does contain an entry. I never succeeded in finding a copy of Osterwald's *Gedichte* for sale (in either the 1848 first edition or later editions) although it is possible to purchase, relatively easily, the poet's sagas and his later rather tub-thumping patriotic poetry in favour of Bismark's German unification in 1870. I found volumes of poetry by Otto Roquette, an equally obscure Franz poet (there are five Roquette settings) but Osterwald's lyrics remained elusive – at least this was the case some years ago, when I was collecting these things.

Since that time the accessibility of a great deal of hitherto unavailable printed material on the internet has given new impetus to Franz scholarship. In the contents pages of the third edition of his *Gedichte* (1873), now visible on-line, Osterwald lines up the titles of his poems with the corresponding Franz opus numbers. This not only indicates his pride in his connection with a musical celebrity, it celebrates a close collaboration, as if the poet wanted it to be known that poem and music had sprung together from a single inspirational source. In many years of handling volumes of poetry that have been set to music I have seen a few examples where the poet retrospectively acknowledges, usually with an asterisk, that this or that poem has been set to music by Beethoven (Matthisson), Schubert (Bauernfeld), Brahms (Allmers) or R Strauss (Henckel). But I have never seen such collaborations celebrated on a title page, signifying two friends and contemporaries working on a project together from start – like, dare one say it, "Rodgers & Hammerstein", or "Bill & Bob" as Victoria Edge affectionately terms her beloved subjects.

That Osterwald's *Gedichte* had their successful day during his lifetime is indicated by the fact that they were taken up by at least a hundred contemporary composers, a number of them almost certainly led to these poems because they were admirers of Franz's work. Names still to be found in modern musical encyclopaedias are Friedrich Kücken and the Dutch composer Léander Schlegel, and there is one much later setting by Max Reger. It is interesting that these three, loath to muscle-in on poetry already set definitively to music, chose to set Osterwald poems that had *not* already been set by Franz. Scores of others, some of them undoubted musical hacks, rushed in where angels feared to tread, and in attempting to compete with Franz they failed miserably. Surveying this list of names now, some of them briefly famous in their day, is a reminder of how fame, particularly among nineteenth-century song composers at the height of the lieder boom (c. 1860-1910), was often exceedingly transitory.

I now realize that the Osterwald settings should not be sidelined, any more than the Mayrhofer settings of Schubert should be ignored (unthinkable, this!) even if the only volume of poetry ever published by that Viennese master (Mayrhofer is now increasingly recognized as such after suffering years of disdain) was privately printed and also notoriously rare. Mayrhofer was second to Goethe as the poet most set to music by Schubert, just as Osterwald was second to Heine as Franz's chosen poet, but in both cases it was personal friendship that made the crucial difference. The friendship between Schubert and Mayrhofer stands at the heart of the composer's biography, and same is true of Franz and Osterwald. It also seems to me that not knowing at least a significant number of Franz's fascinating Osterwald settings (51 of them) is the equivalent of choosing to ignore the 53 Mörike settings of Hugo Wolf. It is true that Wolf composed many other marvellous lieder apart from those to Mörike texts (including those of the *Italienisches Liederbuch* which were arguably inspired by the one and two-paged miniaturist perfection of the majority of Franz's songs) but a real evaluation of Wolf's achievement is not possible without taking the Mörike "flavour" of Wolf's music into account. It might equally be argued that a full understanding of

Robert Franz is impossible without being aware of the Osterwald "flavour" that permeates some of the composer's most daring and individual songs.

We will never know everything about someone as discreet and reserved as Robert Franz, and by implication his friends. He will always be a mysterious figure who used his modesty and seeming lack of importance (as far as the big outside world was concerned) as a means of maintaining his closely guarded privacy. He was a shy and uncommunicative man, not widely travelled, just as capable of blinkered small-town acerbity as he was of gifting the world with musical utterances of heart-warming universality. His gruff manner and almost self-punishingly austere life-style make it clear that he had, in modern parlance, a number of "issues" that almost certainly stemmed from a spectacularly unhappy childhood. Whatever the details, whatever the constraints and repressions, and whether or not these recently encountered biographical doors are iron gates banged shut or closets gradually opening, the more one listens to this music the more clear it seems that the intimate alchemy binding these words and music together is potentiated by nothing less than love – however one chooses to understand that word. Irrespective of further biographical considerations, and on musical grounds alone, this symbiotic relationship places the Franz-Osterwald collaboration as one of the most fascinating in the history of the German lied and, until now, one of the most underestimated.

Graham Johnson
London, 27 July 2019

German Language Synopsis

«Bekümmert Euch um meine Lieder, darin steht's was ich gewesen bin!»

Im Jahre 1841 steckte die viel versprechende Karriere des 26-jährigen talentierten Musikers und Komponisten Robert Franz noch in den Kinderschuhen. In den vorangegangenen sechs Jahren hatte er gar nichts geschaffen. Später bezeichnet sein Freund Franz Liszt jene Zeit als Periode schöpferischen Brachliegens, die so viele Künstler einfach brauchen.

Doch im Jahr 1843 schrieb Franz voller Begeisterung an Robert Schumann über die außerordentliche dichterische Begabung seines engen Freundes Wilhelm Osterwald und vertraute Schumann an, er habe eine ganze Anzahl von Osterwalds Gedichten für Stimme und Klavier vertont. Von da an sollte Franz Zeit seines Lebens als Liedkomponist und Musiker hohe Anerkennung genießen.

Im Frühling des Jahres 1846 besuchte Franz mit seiner 17-jährigen Verlobten die Stadt Wien, wo er Franz Liszt zum ersten Mal begegnete und sich die beiden auf Anhieb gut verstanden. Osterwald schrieb ein ergreifendes Gedicht mit dem sinnigen und mehrdeutigen Titel «Zum Eingang». Der erste Teil, von Osterwald mit «Halle 1846» signiert, beschreibt dessen schmerzlichen Moment der Trennung mit dem Flehen, diese lange Nacht des schweren Abschieds nicht noch weiter zu verlängern. Nach seiner Eheschliessung im Jahr 1849 verließ Osterwald Halle an der Saale, wo er und Franz eine so musikalisch fruchtbare und fröhliche Zeit miteinander verbracht hatten. Der zweite Teil wurde 1872 in Mühlhausen fortgesetzt, wo Osterwald bis zu seinem Tod wohnte und arbeitete. Darin entsann sich Osterwald wehmütig seiner eigenen dunkelbraunen Haarpracht: Diese stellt ein auffälliges, in mehreren Liedern wiederkehrendes Motiv dar.

In seiner 1872 veröffentlichten Franz-Biografie, die großen Anklang fand, beschreibt Liszt einen «Moment tiefer Leidenschaft» und nennt ihn das einschneidende Ereignis im Leben des Künstlers, das sein kreatives Potenzial überhaupt erst hervortreten ließ. Liszt erwähnt jedoch weder den Zeitpunkt noch den Grund dieser Leidenschaft. Trotz physischer Trennung verband Franz mit Osterwald eine lebenslange Freundschaft. Im Jahre 1883 schrieb Franz an Osterwald, er freue sich über dessen Absicht, sein Komponistenleben in Worte zu fassen. Dennoch bestand Franz darauf, dass Osterwald diesen von Liszt beschriebenen Wendepunkt in seinem Leben nicht weiter ausführe - insbesondere, weil Osterwald der einzige Mensch sei, der über alle intimen Details Bescheid wisse.

Eine genauere Untersuchung der 51 verschiedenen Schauplätze der Osterwald-Gedichte, die hier zum ersten Mal gesammelt vorliegen, legt nahe, dass diese «tiefe Leidenschaft» zwischen Komponist und Dichter sehr wohl bestand, doch den gesellschaftlichen Konventionen jener Zeit - Anstand, Aufstieg und Familienpflicht - geopfert wurde. Aufgrund der Seltenheit der erhaltenen Textbelege dieser Beziehung gewinnt Franz' Aussage, an seinen Liedern solle man ihn erkennen, an neuer und tiefgreifender Bedeutung.

Rückblickend hoffte Osterwald noch im Jahre 1872, er und Franz mögen sich am Rande der Welt «auf grünem Rain» wiederfinden. Franz drückte ähnliche Gefühle aus und spielte rein musikalisch auf das Thema Heirat an. Verzicht, Geheimhaltung und Angst vor persönlichem Ruin sind der rote Faden, der sich durch diese faszinierenden, bewegenden und gefühlvollen Liebeslieder zieht, die in ihrer Kühnheit aus der Gattung «Deutsches Kunstlied des 19. Jahrhunderts» herausragen.

Victoria Edge © 2019
Übersetzung von Stephan Bächtold

THE OSTERWALD LIEDER OF ROBERT FRANZ: A MONOGRAPH

BY VICTORIA EDGE

Chapter One

«Die Wahrheit kann warten, denn sie hat ein langes Leben vor sich».[1]
The truth can wait, because it has a long life ahead of itself.

ROBERT FRANZ: BACKGROUND, CHARACTER AND DESTINY

On 12 June, 1814, Maria Philippina Schultesius (1781-1851), an educated, thirty-two-year-old spinster, became the wife of George Christoph Knauth (1757-1845), a previously unmarried, fifty-seven-year-old salt haulier, in the Church of St Moritz, Halle an der Saale. Church records show clearly that she came from a military family which was resident in Wettin, a small town north of Halle. There is an unexplained discrepancy here, as the Franz family tree gives the impression that the family had moved from Wettin and at that time were residents of Halle. Her widowed mother was in attendance at the wedding and remained in Halle until her death a year later. The same records also indicate some haste was involved in arranging the ceremony and the couple began married life in Brunoswarte 13, in the immediate vicinity of the church. On 12 August, 1815, also in the same, then Lutheran church, her son was baptized **Robert Franz Julius Knauth.** As it would be another sixty years before official birth registration was introduced, baptism records were considered sufficient. Robert Knauth's state that he was born at 03:30 on 28 June, 1815 in Neustadt 587, which is understood to be Brunoswarte 13. By 1818, George Christoph Knauth was in a position to purchase the freehold of this property, which up until then had been rented.

---

[1] From Schopenhauer's *«Über den Willen in der Natur»* which Franz quoted aloud to Waldmann, 1895 (XV). Pfordten, 1923 (110)

Robert Franz's birth house, Brunoswarte 13 (photograph W. Danz, 1956 – Stiftung Händel-Haus)

This dwelling, which was replaced by a block of flats in the 1970s, was close both to the place where Robert Franz was later to receive his secondary education and the heart of the city itself. It was here that Franz grew up with his parents and his only sibling, a sister, Emma Antonie Aurelie Knauth (born 1817), who, according to Franz's son-in-law, Robert Bethge, loved him dearly, but about whom little is known.

Robert Bethge (photograph Höpfner/Möller)

This includes any mention of whether she, like the Mozart and Mendelssohn sisters, had also been musically gifted. In 1840, she married Carl Friedrich Steiger, who became a pastor in Obergebra, some hundred kilometres west of Halle.

Bodenständig is a German word used to describe someone who does not travel far from home and it certainly applies to Robert Franz. Apart from a two-year sojourn to Dessau from **1835-1837** to study music theory with the composer J C Friedrich Schneider, and a few short trips, he was born, lived and died in Halle.

He held posts in its churches and the university, and was deeply rooted in its life. Franz shared with Beethoven the terrible fate of eventually becoming deaf, and he died just before the invention of effective hearing-aids. This would have severely restricted his opportunities to broaden his horizons and exacerbated his weak nerves. However, he was pleased to discover that his inner, musical ear was not impaired, but indeed enhanced by his affliction, even though he suffered considerable physical pain from acute earaches. The composer's references to the frequent corporal punishment meted out to him as a child, particularly blows to the head and ears, raise the possibility of injury induced hearing damage:

> «*Oft wußte ich nun dem heißen Drange eine zweite Stimme zu extemporieren nicht zu widerstehen, und zog mir in Folge dieses unerlaubten Privatvergnügens manche schallende Ohrfeige des Singmeisters zu.*» (Deutsche Musik-Zeitung: No. 45. Wien 3 November, 1860).

> "I often felt the strong urge to extemporise a second part and could not resist singing it. The consequences of this unauthorised private amusement were several resounding thick ears from the chorus master."

Franz thought that the cause of his deafness was a loud whistle from a steam-train, but there is no other record of these fleeting, sporadic sounds causing ear damage to by-standers, so perhaps it was the last straw for an already weakened ear-drum. The dates of the onset of Franz's deafness are inconsistent, but are all during the 1840s. Although this affliction deteriorated during his life, Franz's hearing loss did not entirely prevent him from holding conversations and many accounts bear witness to this; not least his late-life conversations over ten years with Waldmann, who also used the written word to communicate.

Robert Franz's life is easy to track; he was no restless spirit, like his favourite poet Heinrich Heine (1797-1856). A brief reference to taking possession of Heine's portrait[2] seems to have been a vicarious substitute for a personal meeting of the two men, which appears never to have taken place. Even so, the number of times Franz moved house within Halle is remarkable. Having finally left the family home on his marriage to Marie Hinrichs in **1848,** there followed no fewer than eight further moves. Despite the fact that there were known financial problems around **1869,** there could also have been difficulties created by the noise associated with music-making, rendering the Franz family unwelcome neighbours.

Franz first attended the *Bürgerschule* for his primary education. Even though singing hymns or folksongs and playing rudimentary keyboard accompaniments were normal evening pastimes in the home, Franz tells us that his mother is due the credit for his musical initiation. By this time, he was fourteen-years-old and she responded to Franz's request for a keyboard instrument by purchasing an ancient *Pantalon*, which neither of them had the faintest idea how to play:

> «*Dieses Spinenttartige Ding, nicht beledert, sondern bekielt und ohne Dämpfung*»,[3]

> "This spinet-like thing, not leather-covered, but quilled and without damping."

Having found a hand-written book of dances in a drawer of the instrument, at first, Franz worked out notation for himself, but his prodigious musical gifts were soon noted, and supported by local music teachers and clerics. Like so many prodigies, he quickly surpassed his tutors in skill and needed nurturing in the right hands. In his conversations with Waldmann, Franz divulges that his mother had a small pension and this was used to fund his musical education:

---

[2] Brief 47 an Senfft. 30 December 1869
[3] Deutsche Musik-Zeitung, Wien 3. November 1860, No.45. Here Franz seems to be customarily referring to the casing, rather than the action, which differs from that of the spinet

> «----Meine Mutter war eine prächtige Frau, sie bildete sich aus sich selbst weiter, hatte einen guten Kern und las aus eigenem Antriebe Goethe, Lessing, Scott u. A. Sie bekam als Hallorenkind aus einer Unterstützungskasse jährlich 48 Thaler, damit hat sie uns gekleidet, Schulgeld bezahlt, ----kurz, wie sie es ermöglicht auch für mich noch, als ich in Dessau war, meine Geldbedürfnisse zu bestreiten, das ist mir heute noch ein Räthsel.»

> "---My mother was a splendid woman, she educated herself further, had a good heart and read of her own volition Goethe, Lessing, Scott, among others. As a Hallorenkind she benefited annually from a support fund, receiving 48 Thaler, with which she clothed us, paid school fees, ----quite how she managed also to fund my financial needs when I was in Dessau, well that still remains a mystery to me to this day." (Waldmann, 1895, XIV)

A *"Hallorenkind"* denotes a child of a salt worker in Halle, but Maria Shultesius and her mother both declare that they and the late Grenadier Johann Schultesius, Maria's father, are inhabitants of Wettin at the time of her marriage in 1814. There is no known record of her father's involvement in any way with salt production or haulage in Halle. Even if one were to argue that Franz and his sister were the Hallorenkinder and not Maria, it is still difficult to see why she would require benefits, since her husband owned the freehold of the family home, as well as his own business in Halle.

Franz recalls:

> «...ich war ein richtiger Taugenichts und Straßenjunge, bei dem es schade um jeden Hieb war, der nebenbei fiel. Von Bescheidenheit kann bei mir auch nur in sehr beschränktem Maße geredet werden, weil ich stets eigenwillig meinem Kopf folgte und mich den Teufel um Schule und Haus kümmerte. Meine Mutter konnte mich allein nicht zwingen, da sie vom Vater in keiner Weise bei der Erziehung ihrer Kinder unterstütz wurde. Der ging in seinen Speditionsgeschäften früh 7 Uhr nach der goldenen Kugel (jetzt Hotel Mente) und kam todtmüde abends 9 Uhr wieder heim...meine Jugendzeit war vom derbsten Realismus erfüllt....» (Musketa 16).

> "I was a proper good-for-nothing and a street urchin; I deserved every clout aimed at me, even those that missed their target. I could hardly be thought of as modest in any way, since I was always led by headstrong impulses with a devil-may-care attitude to home and school. Because my mother was in no way supported in the upbringing of her children by my father, she could not single-handedly compel me to do anything. He went off at 7am every morning to his haulage business at the Golden Globe (now the Hotel Mente) and came home dead tired around 9pm. My youth was filled with the coarsest realism."

Not everyone in the extensive Knauth family in Halle was as hard-working and respectable as Franz's father, as can be seen from an interesting example in the town archives of Halle, when in 1837, assistance is required to deal with a wayward Knauth family in need of support.[4] (Use of the H in the records is inconsistent.)

> «*Der pensionierte Hallore Gottlob Knaut besitzt nebst seiner Frau beinah alle Untugenden. Er ist vor allem dem Trunke ergeben und die Salzwirkerbruderschaft konnte ihn nicht länger behalten, daher er vor 2 Jahren entlassen wurde. Damit er aber der Commune nicht zur Last fallen sollte, setzten sie ihn auf einen Antheil von 80 Reichsthaler jährlich.*
>
> *Er hat nur 2 ebenso schlecht erzogene Knaben von 23 und 18 jahren, um deren Ernährung und Erziehung er sich nicht gekümmert hat. Er ist überall dabei trotzig, ungehorsam und unverträglich, und wenn er nicht alles an den Schnaps verwendete, könnte er von jenen 80 Reichsthalern recht gut mit seiner Frau leben. Er ist 60 Jahr alt und noch stark und rüstig...*»

"Along with his wife, the Halloren pensioner Gottlob Knaut possesses almost every vice. Above all he is given to drunkenness and the Salt Workers' Brotherhood can no longer keep him as he was sacked 2 years ago. So that he should not however become a burden on the community, he has been allocated an annual allowance of 80 Taler.

He has 2 equally badly brought-up boys of 23 and 18 years, whose nourishment and rearing have been neglected by him. He is thoroughly defiant, disobedient and unbearable, and if he didn't spend everything on spirits, he and his wife could live perfectly well. He is 60 years old, strong and sprightly...."

For Robert Franz, experience of this side of life would have been absolutely normal.

---

[4] DMJ Genealogie, Berlin (2018) provided this example and all other previously unpublished genealogical facts, which appear in this monograph

Frankesche Stifungen c. 1882

Eventually, he was accepted into the *Waisenhausgymnasium* or *Frankesche Stiftungen* a short distance from Brunoswarte. In a newspaper interview of 27 October, 1860, he tells the *Deutsche Musik Zeitung* how his education was distracted by the music in his mind, «*wo ich ging und stand, klang es mir ruhelos im Kopfe herum.*» ("Whether moving or still, it rang around my head without rest.") So in **1835**, Franz declined to complete his education at the *Frankesche Stiftungen* and left without his final exams or Abitur in order to study music under Johann Christian Friedrich Schneider (1786-1853) in Dessau.

Friedrich Schneider

Eigenbrötler is a German word for someone who is utterly determined to do things their own way; quite literally bake their own bread the way they like it. This word perfectly describes Robert Franz, who seems to have had uncompromising ideas about his art. It is not difficult to imagine the clash of world-views between him and his elderly father, who deplored his only son's musical obsession and condemned it as a *Brotlose Kunst*, a breadless art, which was clearly not going to yield a financial profit to compare with that of the family's historical salt-processing operation or his haulage company. Christoph Franz wanted his son to study law but his mother offered the sympathetic and enabling environment for the music training which Robert needed, and she was able to persuade his father to comply.

Although Franz later came to view his period of study in Dessau as crucial to his skills in composing, at the time, he found that the discipline of music theory and harmony restricted his creativity, and he felt suffocated by it. Returning to Halle without having made much apparent progress, he only seemed to confirm his father's dire predictions of failure.

In **1841,** Robert Franz deputized for the organist Kurtze at St. Ulrich's Cathedral, and in **1844,** he was appointed his successor. This was to prove the mainstay of his profession for the rest of his working life. Since his youth he had played at services in every church in the city, often dashing from one to the other on the same day.

It is known that Robert Franz and Wilhelm Osterwald collaborated on a number of the songs under discussion in this monograph between **1837**, at the earliest, and **1846**. 1837 pre-dates any published works, but, for Franz, composition and publication are not connected. It can be claimed with some certainty that the texts were almost all written during this period.

Such was his growing reputation and innate talent that he began teaching music in the University of Halle in **1845.**

On **30 May, 1848,** Franz married his former pupil Maria Augusta Karoline Wilhelmine Bertha Friederike Henriette Hinrichs (1828-1891).

Marie Hinrichs (New York Public Library)

Marie Hinrichs, as she was professionally known, produced *Neun Gesänge Op. 1*, published by Breitkopf und Härtel, Leipzig, c. 1846, a feat of which her husband claimed to be very proud. Although the couple and their families were embedded in Halle, they travelled to Obergebra for the wedding, at which Pastor Steiger, Franz's brother-in-law officiated. They had three children: Maria Elisabeth (Lisbeth) (1849-1925), Georg (12 January, 1851 – 15 July, 1851) and Franz Heinrich Richard (1852-1900), a medical doctor, whose godfather was Franz Liszt.

Genesung (Recovery) Opus 5, No. 12[5] is exceptional, since its composition is actually recorded by Franz as "Halle, 1846". It was also published in this year. The poet is one of Franz and Osterwald's circle, Germanist (Karl) Julius Schröer (1825-1900), and he seems to be referring to Marie Hinrichs and her response to Franz's proposal of marriage. This poem mirrors similar sentiments expressed by Osterwald in his 1846 verses, *Zum Eingang* (To the Entrance). Also in 1846, Franz published his superb transcription of Schubert's quartet, *Der Tod und das Mädchen* (Death and the Maiden) D810, for piano duet[6], and all three of these works mark the turning-point in the relationship between Franz and Osterwald, and are discussed more fully in Chapter Six.

It is fortunate that Halle is the birthplace of Handel, who left there for good when he was 18 years of age. The museums are full of interest and musical history, and a joy to visit. Franz has his own exhibition in the affiliated W.F. Bach museum, but without Handel, all this might well have been lost in the mists of time. From **1842** until **1867,** Robert Franz worked tirelessly as *Dirigent* (conductor) of the Halle *Singakademie* and was appointed music director at Halle University in **1859.**

He reworked many masterpieces, including Handel's Messiah and Bach's St Matthew Passion which were published and performed. With little understanding of early music, his efforts were often disparaged and discarded, but not before his attempts to revive and bring attention to these works had succeeded. There is much for which to thank him in this sphere.

From about **1867,** the composer's deafness forced him to retire from both conducting and his duties as music director, and from the university. In **1873,** his financial worries were ended with life-long funding organized by his close friend and favourite singer, Arnold freiherr Senfft von Pilsach, and in **1885,** he was granted the Order of the Crown by the German Kaiser and made an *Ehrenburger,* thus bestowing upon him the Freedom of the City of Halle. In 1907 the *Halle Singakademie* was permanently renamed the *Robert-Franz-Singakademie* in his memory.

---

[5] Recorded by Graham Johnson and Robin Tritschler on their 2017 Hyperion disc. See the Discography.
[6] Goldstone and Clemmow, première recording, Franz Schubert (1797-1828): The Unauthorised Piano Duos, Vol.3. Divine Art Recording Group

Poignantly, a circular road, the Robert-Franz-Ring also holds Halle in its firm embrace.

Robert-Franz-Ring, Halle (photograph V. Edge)

Marie died on **5 May, 1891.** There is nothing to suggest that their marriage was anything other than contented. As one of his pupils, they had succumbed to the intimacy of private music lessons. From Schumann's engagement congratulations[7] it is possible to calculate that she must have been about sixteen-years-old when the relationship began, as she was engaged by the age of seventeen in **1846.** The thirty-one-year-old Robert Franz must have appeared to her to be an heroic figure and her constancy never wavered. He, in turn, never had anything but praise for her:

> «*Sie war eine großangelegte Natur, alle kleinliche lag ihr fern, grade und ehrlich.*»

> "She was a broad-minded woman of the world; trivia was of no interest to her, upright and honest."

These are the final words he had to say to Waldmann in their ten-year long conversations.

---

[7] Sasse, 177

Franz dedicated his Opus 23 to Marie. This was published in 1856 and appears with an anonymous verse, which seems to reveal a shared moment between the couple.[8]

Wir setzen uns da nieder	We sat down
Wol[9] in das grüne Gras.	In the green grass
Und sang hin und wieder	And sang now and again
Die alten lieben Lieder	The lovely old songs,
Bis uns die Augen nass.	Till tears filled our eyes.

Robert Franz died on **24 October, 1892** in his apartment in Luisenestraße.

(Photograph V. Edge)

---

[8] British Library: Robert Franz collected works
[9] As spelled

and He was interred three days later in the city's *Stadtgottesacker Friedhof* or cemetery.

Stadtgottesacker cemetery (photograph V. Edge)

Robert Franz and Marie Franz's gravestone (photograph V. Edge)

In 1903, a memorial was erected in his honour on the University Ring.

Robert Franz Memorial (photograph V. Edge)

Chapter Two

ROBERT FRANZ: PATRONYM, APTRONYM OR PSEUDONYM?

On 24 October, 1907 in Halle an der Saale, Franz's distinguished son-in-law Robert Bethge, husband of the composer's beloved daughter, Lisbeth (1849 – 1925), delivered a lecture on the composer Robert Franz to the town's *Volksbildungsverein* (Society for Education). He discussed at some length the controversy surrounding Franz's name, which was claimed by many critics to have been a pseudonym. (Bethge 6). Procházka offers one example, (74),

> «*Es wird häufig für einen guten Witz der Vorsehung gehalten(!) daß sie in «Robert Franz» die Taufnamen von Schubert und Schumann prophetisch in einander klingen ließ. In Wahrheit aber (sic!) war Rob. Franz nur ein Pseudonym. Fürwahr, die Vorsehung arbeitet gut und keiner bespöttelt sie ungestraft!*» [10]

> "It is frequently considered to be a good joke of providence(!) that the name "Robert Franz" comprised the sonorous Christian names of Schubert and Schumann. In truth though (sic!) Robert Franz was only a pseudonym. Forsooth, providence worked well and no one who mocked it went unpunished!"

Bethge's lecture states:

> «*Robert Franz wurde am 28. Juni 1815 als Sohn einfacher, aber sehr achtbarer Bürgersleute, des Bürgers Georg Christoph Knauth und seiner Ehefrau Marie Philippine geb. Schultesius, in dem noch erhaltenen, seinen Eltern damals gehörigen Hause Brunoswarte 13 geboren; in der Taufe erhielt er die Vornamen Robert Julius Franz. Wie ist er zu dem Namen Robert Franz gekommen? Seine Gegner haben seinerzeit die Mär aufgebracht, er habe die Vornamen der beiden ihm voraufgehenden Lyriker Franz Schubert und Robert Schumann eigenmächtig in sich vereinigt, um sich als den abschließenden Dritten in diesem Trifolium hinzustellen, der zugleich die Lyrik jener beiden in der seinigen zusammenfasse und vollende. Das ist der reine böswillige Unsinn: solches wäre seinem schlichten, einfachen, bescheidenen Sinn zuwider und geradezu unmöglich gewesen und hätte seiner Hochachtung vor Schubert und Schumann geradezu widersprochen. Die Sache ist sehr einfach und in sehr prosaischer Weise zugegangen. Sein Vater, Knauth, der ein sehr bedeutendes Speditionsgeschäft betrieb, hatte einen Bruder, der auch ein gleiches Geschäft hier betrieb, und bei der Gleichheit der Namen und der Geschäfte kamen oft Verwechslungen vor, aus denen Ärgerlichkeiten und Zwistigkeiten zwischen den Brüdern entstanden. Um dem ein Ende zu machen, kam der Vater unseres Robert Franz mit seinen*

---

[10] *(Ed. Hanslick «Zur Erinnerung an Rob. Franz» Neue Freie Presse 1892, No. 10 126, S73.)*

Geschäftsfreunden und Bekannten überein, daß man ihn Franz nennen möchte. Wie er auf den Namen Franz gekommen ist, weiß ich nicht. Genug, er wurde – lange vor der Geburt des Sohnes – im gesellschaftlichen Leben allgemein Franz genannt, während in den Urkunden der ursprüngliche Name Knauth weiter geführt wurde. So ist es gekommen, daß unser Meister von Beginn seines Daseins an Robert Franz genannt wurde. Wir besitzen noch ein Gedicht von einem seiner Taufpaten zu seinem ersten Geburtstag, welches dem kleinen <<Robert Julius Franz>> gewidmet ist. Als Robert Franz ist er dann aufgewachsen, als solcher hat er die Schule durchgemacht und Musik studiert, unter diesem Namen hat er gleich seine ersten Lieder herausgegeben und ist in der Welt als Robert Franz bekannt geworden. Erst 1847 hat er auf Drängen seines nachmaligen Schwagers Hinrichs Schritte getan, um dieser Duplizität der Namen ein Ende zu machen, und durch Allerhöchste Kabinettsordre vom 5. Juni 1847 ist ihm genehmigt worden, daß er den Namen Franz, wie er tatsächlich von jeher genannt war, auch rechtlich zu seinem Familiennamen mache, und so nennt er sich seitdem in aller Form Rechtens Robert Julius Franz.»

"Robert Franz was born to the unassuming but highly respected citizens of Halle, Georg Christoph Knauth and his wife Marie Philippine née Schultesius on 28 June, 1815, in the still preserved house then owned by his parents, Brunoswarte 13. He was baptised Robert Julius Franz. How did he come to be called by this name? His opponents have put about the fairy tale that he made his own the forenames of two of his predecessors in the art of song-writing, Franz Schubert and Robert Schumann, in order to attach himself as the third party in this trefoil, and equally to enfold and complete the lyrical work of both in his own. That is purely malicious nonsense: such an intention would have run counter to his modest, plain and simple nature as well as been quite impossible, and would have completely contradicted his enormous respect for Schubert and Schumann. The matter is actually very straightforward and easy to clear up in a quite prosaic fashion. His father, Knauth, who ran a very important logistics business, had a brother, who also ran a similar business here in Halle, and owing to the similarities in their names and businesses, this often gave rise to mix-ups and subsequent quarrels and annoyance between the brothers. In order to bring this to an end, the father of Robert Franz came to an agreement with his business colleagues and acquaintances, that he would be called Franz. How he came by this name I do not know. Enough, he was – long before the birth of his son – in society in general called Franz, whilst in official records his original name, Knauth remained unchanged. So it came about that our master was, from the onset of his life, known as Robert Franz. We own still a poem from one of his Godparents on his first birthday, which is dedicated to "Robert Julius Franz". As Robert Franz grew up, he was known as such through school and his music studies. He had his first songs published under this name and is known throughout the world as Robert Franz. Not until 1847, at the urging of his future father-in-law Hinrichs, did he take steps to end the ambiguity of his name. And by a Supreme Court Order of June 5, 1847, he was granted permission to use the name by which he had actually always been called and to make it his official family name, and so since then he formally and legally called himself Robert Julius Franz."

This version of events has been repeated by writers on Franz ever since and has acquired the status of fact. On examining its veracity, the question arises as to whether or not an artist's personal circumstances are relevant to their works. Osterwald (4) quotes Liszt in his *Lebensbild* of Robert Franz:

«*Führten aber nur die verschiedenen Phasen des geistigen Lebens dieses Resultat herbei?*»

"Don't the different phases of the intellectual life lead to the result?"

No one knows the extent to which art is influenced by the informed mind and every experience of any kind informs the mind. Franz's famous declaration, repeated by Osterwald (13), that:

«*Sie mag sich nur an die Lieder halten, das Übrige ist Nebensache.*»

"It (posterity) can stick to the songs, everything else is incidental",

is made by someone who did not want:

«*die liebe Nachwelt auch noch bis in alle Ecken und Winkel verfolgt werden[…]* »

"to be tracked down by the prying eyes of posterity".

Nevertheless, Robert Franz became a public figure who made public gestures in all kinds of ways, including his decade-long interview with Dr Wilhelm Waldmann, and these are described in countless letters with his patron Arnold freiherr Senfft von Pilsach, as well as many others. However, all researchers who engage with this composer come up against the fact that he rigorously controlled his image and the details of his life, which is why the impression is given that there is little of interest to discover and no motive for doing so.

In order to understand Franz's origins it is necessary to begin with his father, Georg Christoph Knauth. As already stated, in 1814, at the age of fifty-seven, he married Franz's thirty-two-year-old mother and it was a first marriage for them both. He was a salt haulier in the salt-producing town of Halle an der Saale and was part of a large extended family of Knauths, who had been active in this business for hundreds of years. It is said that Georg Christoph liked to be called by his second name (Krehbiel - vi) and was known as Christoph Franz.

His father was Johann Gottlieb Knauth (1723-1794) and his mother was Maria Regine Knauth, neé Riemer. Johann and Christoph were both salt hauliers and it seems logical to assume some kind of father and son business connection, which probably lasted until

Maria's death around 1780. At this time, his father remarried to Marie Dorothea Lutze and they had two sons, the first of whom they, quite astonishingly, named Christoph, thus providing Christoph Knauth with a new half-bother called Christoph Knauth, who was twenty-six years younger. Christoph the elder now had to contend with a step-mother who may very well have intended that Christoph the younger inherit their father's business. The latter's second brother was called Andreas Christian and when Christoph died in 1817, Andreas married his widow, Marie Dorothea née Deubel, who had been left with four small children. Marie died in 1825 and Andreas remarried to a widow, Johanne Strenz, in 1828 until his death in 1831.

The children of Andreas and Marie Dorothea included a Christian Gottlob Franz Knauth, a teacher at the *Frankesche Stiftungen*, which Franz had attended, and when he married Marie Sophie Pietsch in 1848, their wedding was planned to take place on 4 June in the Church of St Moritz in Halle. As it happened, Robert Franz and Marie Hinrichs had their own wedding planned for 30 May, 1848, but having had the banns read in the churches in Halle, the actual ceremony was held in Obergebra in Nordhausen, about a hundred kilometres to the west of Halle, and conducted by Franz's brother–in-law, Pastor Steiger.

Typically, his sister is only ever alluded to in passing by the likes of Bethge and Osterwald, and never by name. There is only a brief mention of the marriage «Trauung durch den Pastor Staiger» (sic) in records at hand. (Musketa, 1993, 318). Emma makes a brief appearance in a book by Friedemann Steiger, *Mein lieber Eduard: Die Briefe des Christian Friedrich Steiger an seinen Sohn (1859 bis 1868)*, (My dear Eduard: The letters of Christian Friedrich Steiger to his son (1859-1868)) where she arouses interest because she is generally considered to be the sister of Robert Franz.

Emma Steiger, maiden name "Knauth (genannt Franz)" (called Franz) lived with her husband in Obergebra which, in March 1851, also became the final resting place of Franz's mother. Franz's father, who had died aged nearly 89 in 1845, was interred in Halle, and the impression is still one of family tensions.

It is plausible that Franz's father adopted the name Franz informally, because it seems likely that he was not best pleased with the way his step-mother and by implication, his own father, had treated him. His grandfather and great-grandfather were both called Franz Knauth, and the name Franz was often chosen in the family. However, it was only used informally by Christoph Franz, his wife and two children. There remains the possibility that Robert Franz kept this name out of loyalty to his father, but far more questions arise about the choice of Franz as a second name for Robert, when he was also to be expected to use it as a family surname. Crucially, he was a late-born, first and only son, who would normally have expected to receive his father's name with pride.

A recognisable and trusted brand is a significant asset in business and the Knauth name was just that. Hence, it is unthinkable that Franz's father would have merely dropped it entirely and allowed his half-brother any such advantage. This is an industry with its own guild and apparel.

Member of the Salt Workers' Guild, Halle an der Saale, 1890
(INTERFOTO/Alamy Stock Photo)

Although Franz tells us the guild had little to do with music, its representatives appeared thus attired for funerals and festivals of all kinds.

Another fact that Bethge has wrong is the names of the composer which appear in baptism records as Robert Franz Julius Knaut.

Robert Franz's record of baptism (highlighted)

This means that had Franz had his name changed officially, it would either have been Robert Franz Julius Franz or the order would have been amended to Robert Julius Franz. Noticing that in 1993 all reference to this *"Allerhöchste Kabinettsordre"* has been dropped in the learned documents published by the Händel-Haus in Halle, a professional search was instigated. No trace of this document can be found and even if Franz's copy has been lost, which is perfectly likely, there appears to be no central record of it anywhere.

It is impossible to know with what rigour Franz's change of name document was scrutinized by Pastor Steiger, but throughout Franz's life, the composer was obviously worried about something, and this has puzzled researchers ever since. Here is an example which clearly relates to Franz's concerns that Osterwald might reveal some indiscretion. This is from a letter to Senfft (119/120) dated 8 December, 1871:

> «*Ihr Wunsch, eine Lebensskizze von mir aus der Hand Osterwalds zu besitzen, wird sich schwer erfüllen lassen. Einmal gehen ihm musikalische Fachkenntnisse gar zu sehr ab und dann fürchte ich mich auch, unter uns gesagt, vor seiner Indiskretion. Er würde gerade Dinge, an die ich nicht gerührt sehen mag, mit Vorliebe behandeln. Was dem Publikum über meinen Lebenslauf zu wissen frommt, findet es in Liszt's Aufsatz – alles Uebrige betrifft Privatbagatellen, die mit meinem Abscheiden ebenfalls vom Schauplatze verschwinden mögen: sie haben mit meiner künstlerischen Entwicklung nicht das Mindeste zu schaffen und können nur zu fatalen Mißverständnissen Anlaß geben ...*»

> "Your wish to own a sketch of my life composed by Osterwald is hard to fulfil. Firstly, his specialist musical knowledge is inadequate and I also fear, just between you and me, his indiscretion. He would just like to say things I would prefer not to see touched upon. What it serves the public to know about my biography can be found in Liszt's essay – everything else concerns private trivialities, which with my passing will likewise disappear from the public arena: they have absolutely nothing to do with my artistic development and can only give rise to fatal misunderstandings..."

The ellipsis implies that Senfft has been taken into Franz's confidence and that he would easily grasp Franz's point. One explanation for this might be the requirement for official papers to set up the pension, *Ehrenfonds,* which was provided for Franz in 1873 and masterminded by Senff himself. His devotion to and admiration of Robert Franz knew no bounds and it is entirely plausible that he would have condoned this apparent deception. Franz avoided foreign travel and one wonders if that was not for the same reason. If Franz had painted himself into a corner, the consequences of being unmasked could have had a devastating effect on his nerves, which plagued him until his death.

Osterwald studiously avoids any mention of the adoption of the name of Robert Franz in his beautifully-written, detailed and musically informed *Lebensbild* of 1886, even though Franz's claim to this surname had been the focus for vicious attacks from the cliques and critics, and was of biographical interest. As can be seen in the chapter on the collected Osterwald Lieder, set to texts which were probably all written before the poet left Halle, he and the composer appear to have developed a relationship which was not merely platonic. It seems unthinkable however, with his executive responsibilities in pedagogy, happy marriage and large family that Osterwald would recklessly implicate himself in any such rumours, but this is not the only example of Franz warning his friend of indiscretion, as will be shown later.

Pseudonyms were just as plentiful at this time as they are now; Franz's stubborn refusal not to leave it at that points to deep insecurity about his working-class origins, his background in trade, the fact that he justifiably believed himself to be equally as great a song composer as Schubert and Schumann, and that the names Robert and Franz really were his own. As a brand, it was irresistible.

It is not known whether Franz came to regret his decision to insist on his explanation for ceasing to use his family name. His fascination with the works of the mysterious travel writer and author, Charles Sealsfeld, who had quite literally escaped the cloistered life and fled Europe for America, may have been because he successfully assumed his new identity and achieved renown.

33

Franz Family Tree

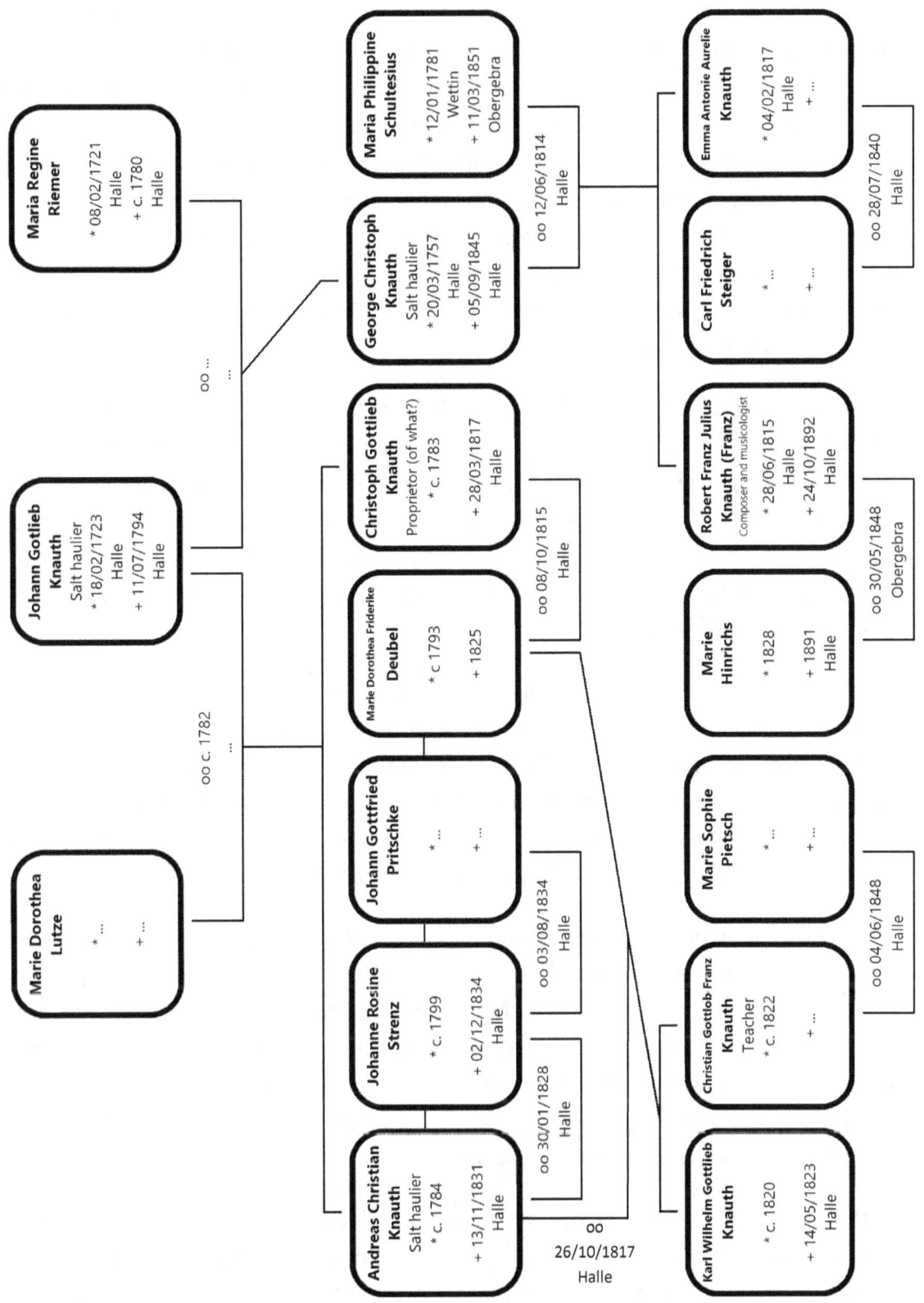

Chapter Three

WILHELM OSTERWALD: FAMILY HISTORY, PERSONALITY AND CAREER

(Karl) Wilhelm Osterwald was born on 23 March, **1820** in Bretsch bei Seehausen (Osterburg), a small town in the Altmarkt district of what was then Prussian Saxony, now Saxony-Anhalt. He was the son of Johann Nicolaus and Henriette Marie Osterwald, and his father was a choirmaster, organist and teacher in Bretsch. This, together with assistance from a benevolent cleric, enabled Johann to provide his son with an education sufficient to enter the grammar school in nearby Salzwedel. It was here that his love of botany was encouraged and fostered, and in **1834,** at the age of fourteen, he took up a place at the prestigious *Frankesche Stiftungen* in Halle an der Saale, some 220 kilometres to the south. His parents remained in Bretsch until their deaths, however, and Osterwald never lived there again.

As a pupil at the *Frankesche Stiftungen*, Osterwald benefited from a formal, classical education provided by teaching of the highest standard. He, in turn, was a model pupil, *ein Musterknabe,* immersing himself in learning, which remained his abiding passion for the rest of his life and also won the unqualified admiration of Robert Franz. It was at this point that Franz and Osterwald met for the first time and found instant rapport. (Procházka, 1894, 25, 26.) The musically prodigiously gifted Franz was not quite nineteen years of age.

From the outset, the lifelong relationship between these two men, one a lively, extravert poet, the other a secretive, controlling and introverted musician, who often found diplomacy and social skills hard to master, was characterised by opposing features together with that most irresistible force of attraction, inaccessibility to each other's talent, experiences and perceptions. Because this kind of fascination invites closeness and high regard, as in this case, it often leads to intense personal devotion.

Unlike Franz, Osterwald completed his education at the *Frankesche Stiftungen* and then went on to distinguish himself further. From 1840 – 1844 he read Philology at the University of Halle. He was always short of money, but both he and Franz revelled in the lively and stimulating environment prevailing in Halle at this time. Furthermore, it was during these years that Osterwald and Franz collaborated closely on Franz's emerging ability as a song composer and this convergence is considered to be a crucial factor in releasing Franz's creative powers.

In the eight poems composed by Osterwald in a collection entitled «*Bilder und Träume*» (Images and Dreams) 1843-1847, he writes in an almost cathartic way of the wrench of departing from a close male relationship. He treats of themes of social exclusion, «*Drei Deutsche*» (Three Germans), the callously arranged marriage of an older man to a despairing young girl, «*Eine Hochzeit* » (A Wedding), and ruptured male friendships, «*Einem Freunde*» (To a Comrade), (see Chapter Four), «*Demselben*» (To the Self-Same) and «*Frischauf*» (Let Us Away). This latter poem resurfaces in a revised form in 1873, entitled «*Zum Eingang*» (To the Entrance), and is analysed in full in Chapter Six. From the title of the group, which has echoes of Goethe's «*Dichtung und Wahrheit*» (Fiction and Fact), the implications are clear and it is up to the reader objectively to discern fabrication from factual experience in the warp and weft of the text.

Osterwald was always preoccupied with nature's reproductive systems, including his own, and Liszt's choice of the word 'juvenile' was certainly *un mot juste* when applied to Osterwald's frequent and overt sexual metaphors. He was also, in every sense of the word, a chauvinist. His jingoistic patriotism was boundless, but even this was exceeded by his smug belief in the superiority of the male sex. Those coming to «*Mannweiber*» (Male Female) from «*Allerlei*» (Farrago) 1842-1846, need to brace themselves for a sexist rant that is equal to any by Schopenhauer.

This stands in complete contrast to Franz, who referring to Schumann's famous song-cycle, declares to Waldmann (107):

> «*Ja, man nehme nur, Frauenliebe und Leben [...]. Eine Frau muß doch auch ihre Selbstständigkeit haben und soll nicht bloß an der Erde vor unsern Knien herumwinseln.*»

> "Yes, just take 'Women's Life and Love', [...]. A woman really must retain her independence and should not simply grovel on the ground at our feet."

Even so, Osterwald mocks clerics, «*Pfaffen*» (preachy parsons) with the valid point that without a bit of sinning, they would be out of a job. («*Mönch und Reiter*» (Monk and Horseman)). His *Weltanschuung* is frequently amorphous; raging at a loving God for restricting the freedom to love as one wishes, whilst retaining an unshakable belief in social responsibility. He is a master at portraying paradox and farce.

The verses Osterwald produced were also extremely popular with other composers during the 19th century, most notably Carl Bohm (1844–1920), a close friend of Franz, Otto Dresel (1826–1890), Max Reger (1873-1916) and Anton Rubenstein (1829-1894). Others, numbering at least a hundred, were more minor figures and dilettantes.

In **1845**, Osterwald began training as a teacher at the *königliches Pädogogium zu Halle* (King's School in Halle), which was followed by appointments in **1850** at Merseburg und Michaelis, in **1865** as Head of the Grammar School in Mühlhausen, Thüringen, and in **1880** he was given complete oversight of secondary education in the town.

During these years he produced the following works:

> 1848: *Gedichte*: comprising: *Sagen und Sagenartiges* 1843-1847, *Lieder*. 1839-1847, *Frühlingsfeier* 1845, *Bilder und Träume* 1843-1847, *Allerlei* 1842-1846, *Trips Trill, der Mann der That, Ein Fastnachtsmährchen* 1847

> 1849: Plays and sagas from the German medieval period. 1) *Rüdeger von Bechlaren*

1853: Poetry: *Im Grünen* and musical texts including 2 cantatas: 1) *Winfried und die heilige Eiche bei Geismar* (music: H.D. Engel, Merseburg) 2) *Frühlingsfeier* (music: G. Schreiber, Mühlhausen)

1854: Religious poetry: *Zur Häuslichen Erbauung*

1855: Epic poem: *König Alfred*

1862: Poetry: *Im Freien*

1867: Plays and sagas from German medieval period 2) *Walter und Hildegunde*

1870: Political writing: *Bleibt einig!* and contemporary poetry

1871: *Deutschlands Auferstehung*

1873: *Gedichte* (3rd edition), containing *Zum Eingang* and other references to Robert Franz

1886: *Robert Franz: ein Lebensbild*

In addition to these works, Osterwald produced a continuous stream of educational literature on the Classics and Middle High German literature, as well as studies of comparative mythology.

On 1 October, **1849,** Osterwald married the twenty-four-year old Marie Auguste Schröter in a private house, without ceremony, in Zörbig, a few kilometres north-east of Halle. The marriage was conducted by the Archdeacon M. Kästner.

Their first child, a daughter named Marie Henriette, came into the world on 25 July, **1850.** She was followed by a son, Ernst Wilhelm Hermann on 29 February, **1852**, then Franz Wilhelm Karl appeared on 15 June, **1853,** and Anna Wilhelmine on 9 November, **1854,** Franz Theodore joined them on 13 May, **1856,** together with Johannes Ernst on 17 August, **1858.** Three further sons, Ernst Wilhelm on 8 March, **1860**, Carl Wilhelm Alfred, on 10 January, **1862,** and Konrad Wilhelm on 22 March, **1864,** were also born to the Osterwalds.

Tragically, three of their sons fell victim to the high rate of infant mortality prevalent at this time. A glimpse into the records provides researchers with a picture of how terribly hard life must have been for mothers in these, not unusual, circumstances. Not only was Marie Osterwald still recovering from the very recent birth of Johannes, on 28 August, **1858**, their firstborn son, Ernst Wilhelm Hermann, succumbed to dysentery at the tender age of six and a half. Then, with her previous confinement just five months away, Ernst Wilhelm died from infant diarrhoea at the age of five months on 29 August, **1860**. The last of their sons to be lost in infancy was two-year-old Carl Wilhelm Alfred, from measles on 16 May, **1864**, when Marie was only two months away from giving birth for the final time to Konrad. Of their seven sons, four survived to adulthood, together with their two daughters.

It is worth stopping to consider the struggle it must have been to raise such a large family without running water, refrigeration, modern medicine and conveniences of all kinds. The August heat was obviously dangerous and efforts to maintain hygiene would have been a constant battle. Moreover, Osterwald was never particularly wealthy and domestic help would probably have been minimal. Marie's father was deceased at the time of her marrying and nothing is known of her mother. In **1852**, her mother-in-law only stands as godmother to Ernst by proxy. The old adage that behind every successful man there is an exhausted woman would not have been out of place here.

Nevertheless, by all accounts, this was an extremely close marriage, and both Marie and her distinguished husband devoted themselves to their family. She lived to the age of sixty-one, dying at home in St Petri 95b on 15 March, **1887**, just eleven days before her beloved husband, who followed her on 26 March, **1887**, aged sixty-seven, after succumbing to a severe lung infection.

In **1871,** Professor Dr. Karl Wilhelm Osterwald was further honoured with *"Dem Adler zum königlichen Hausorden von Hohenzollern"* (The Royal House Order of Hohenzollern). The high status, respect and affection he enjoyed are confirmed in his obituaries.

> *«Er strebte in erster Linie an, der väterliche Freund seiner Schüler zu werden, dann erst ihr Lehrer. Er wollte den ganzen Menschen kennenlernen und für sich haben, um einen jeden nach seiner Individualität fördern zu können».* *(Henning)*

> "Above all he strove to be the paternal friend of his pupils, and then their teacher. He wanted to know and identify with the whole person, in order that he could foster each one according to their individuality."

A memorial was erected in his honour in **1889** in the woods on the edge of the town of Mühlhausen and ceremoniously unveiled during a School Festival.

Plaque on the Osterwald Memorial (photograph V. Edge)

Osterwaldstraße - Mühlhausen (photograph V. Edge)

A further honour followed in **1934**, when the street between *Goetheweg* and *Vogteier Platz* was named *Osterwaldstraße*.

Robert Franz and Wilhelm Osterwald remained close for the rest of their lives and Franz was badly shaken by the death of his friend. His essay, *dem Andenken Osterwalds*, which Franz explained, illuminates the nature of their relationship, as well as extolling his friend's gifts as a writer, in order to raise public awareness of his existence, appears to be lost. Franz explains in his letter to Senfft of 24 May, 1887:

> «*Für die Musik sind die Gedichte Osterwald's eine wahre Fundgrube.*»

> "For music the poems of Osterwald are a real treasure trove."

It is left to us to speculate why neither Franz, nor Osterwald, nor their spouses stood as godparent at any of their twelve children's baptisms. There is every apparent reason why they should have done, and their absence is a remarkable and conspicuous omission.

Chapter Four

«Bekümmert Euch um meine Lieder, darin steht's, was ich gewesen bin!» [11]
"Concern yourselves with my songs; what I have been is there."

THE OSTERWALD LIEDER OF ROBERT FRANZ

Karl Wilhelm Osterwald (1820-1887), the poet of these fifty-one songs, or *Gesänge*, as Franz often called them, and the close former school friend of the composer, like Franz, belonged to a group of culturally sophisticated academics and musicians in Halle. These were vibrant and heady times, particularly in the early to mid-1840s, and they were famously influential in the promotion and advancement of the arts:

> *«Aus diesem Kreise tritt uns zum erstenmal die sympatische Charactergestalt von Franz' Lieblingsdichter Wilhelm Osterwald entgegen, mit welchem später den Meister das Band inniger Freundschaft verbinden sollte. Geboren am 23, Februar 1820 (zu Bretsch i.d. Altmarkt) also um fünf Jahre jünger als Robert Franz, traf er mit letzterem bereits als Schüler des Waisenhausgymnasiums zusammen und schon damals fanden sich die Musen beider zu gemeinsamen künstlerischen Versuchen. Das reichbewegte Universitätsleben in Halle, an dem Franz, wie wir sehen werden, so eigenartigen Anteil nahm, verband die gereisten, einander geistesverwandten jungen Männer in so inniger, übereinstimmender Weise, daß unser Meister in seinen Briefen an den Freund nie ohne Rührung jener gemeinsam verlebten **«alten lieben Zeit»** gedachte.»*
> (Procházka, 1894, 25, 26.)

> ***Erinnerung***
>
> *Die Sterne Flimmern und prangen selig in stiller Nacht,*
> *in Schmerzen aber und Bangen mein klopfend Herze wacht.*
> *Am Monde vorüber gleiten die Wolken im luftigen Lauf,*
> ***die alten, die seligen Zeiten*** *steigen wie Geister herauf.*
>
> *Sie ziehen vorüber und neigen wehmüthig has Haupt mir zu,*
> *schweig' stille mein Herz, o schweige, lasse die Todten in Ruh!*
> *Ein Stern fällt zitternd und schnelle hinab in das dunkle Moor,*
> *Die Nacht aber bleibet helle und prangt so schön wie zuvor.* [12]

---

[11] Franz to Waldmann 1895, VIII
[12] Erinnerung, Opus 51, No. 10. 1879

Frühe Klage

Aus der Ferne schallen Gesänge, froh von zittern der Luft gewiegt;
Müsset verwehen, liebliche Klänge, luftig und leicht wie die Jugend verfliegt.
Kränze im frischen Frühling gewunden, welken, noch ehe der Mai verblüht;
ach! und ehe der Lenz geschwunden, schleichet die Sorge zum jungen Gemüth.

Zieht vorüber, frohe Lieder, macht mir das Herze nicht enge, nicht bang,
alter Zeiten *gemahnt ihr mich wieder – leise verhallend schwinde der Klang.*[13]

"From this circle we meet for the first time the sympathetic figure of Robert Franz's favourite poet Wilhelm Osterwald, with whom the master was later to develop an intimate bond of friendship. Born on 23 February, 1820 (at Bretsch i.d. Altmarkt), thus five years younger than Robert Franz, he had already encountered the latter as a pupil of the Grammar School in Halle, and even then the muse had sought them both out for mutual artistic experiments. The bustling university-life in Halle, in which, as we will see, Franz took part so idiosyncratically, bound the mature, like-minded young men together in such an intimate and agreeable way, that our master, in his letters to his friend, never failed to mention the time shared together, **those blissful old days,** without emotion."

The piano part for **Remembrance** repeatedly emphasises the Perfect Fourth motif from Wagner's Bridal Song in *Lohengrin*.

Remembrance:

The stars flicker and shine blessedly in the silent night;
In pain though and fear my pounding heart awakes.
The clouds glide across the moon in their airy train;
The **old blissful times** rise up like spirits.

---

[13] Frühe Klage, Opus 22, No. 4. 1855.

They pass by and incline their heads sadly towards me.
Be silent my heart, be silent; let the dead rest in peace!
A trembling star falls swiftly earthwards into the dark fen.
The night though remains bright, as beautifully resplendent as before.

Early Lament:

From a distance songs resound, happily rocked by the trembling of the wind.
They must die down, lovely sounds, airily and lightly as youth flies.
Garlands wound in early spring wither, even before May is out.
Ah, and before spring has vanished, cares creep into my youthful spirit.

Here Franz conceals 'quasi recitative', from the piano only, the unmistakable melody of Mendelssohn's Wedding March from *A Midsummer Night's Dream;* a work mentioned by him in conversation with Waldmann.

Move on happy songs; make my heart neither closed nor afraid.
You remind me again of **old times** – may the resounding tune softly fade away.

These musical references to marriage could refer either to the closeness of the relationship between composer and poet or foreshadow future plans which will significantly change the status quo:

«Daß Osterwald mit 51 Liedern vertreten ist, also beinahe einem Fünftel, ist durchaus nicht in der Freundschaft allein begründet, die ihn mit Franz verband, vielmehr in der «in jeder Hinsicht wahlverwandten Natur» (Procházka) der beiden Poeten; «durchaus jugendlich» nennt ihn Liszt, «mit vorwiegend weiblicher Anschauung, weiblichem Empfinden». Die von seltenem Wohllaut und natürlicher Grazie getragenen Gedichte schlagen mit Glück einen frisch volkstümlichen Ton an und weisen zudem fast alle eine ebenso meisterliche als feinsinnige Pointierung auf.» (Procházka.) So konnte Franz von ihm rühmen: «Für die Musik (sind die Gedichte Osterwald's) eine wahre Fundgrube»[14] *[...] «denn*

---

[14] *RF, AP 24/5/1887, Brief 325*

seine Verse machten durchaus den Eindruck, als ob sie spontan von mir komponiert wären. Selten wird man wohl ein Talent finden, das sich so anzupassen verstand» Pfordten (97).

(«*Selten wird man wohl ein Talent finden, das sich so anzuschmeigen verstand wie das meines lieben Freundes.*»[15])

"That Osterwald is represented with fifty-one songs; that is almost a fifth (of the total number), is by no means based on his bond of friendship with Franz alone, rather far more in every respect on their strong affinity for one another. So very youthful, Liszt called him, with predominantly feminine notions, feminine feelings. These poems, characterized by innate musicality and natural, measured grace happily struck a fresh, traditional tone and could accommodate almost all the equally masterly and sensitive musical emphasis. And so, Franz declared, "for music the poetry of Osterwald is a real treasure trove, because his verses give the impression that they were quite spontaneously composed by me. Only rarely does one find a talent that understands how to nestle up close, like that of my dear friend."

Liszt actually wrote:

«*Osterwald ist als Dichter eine dem Franz'schen Geist verwandte Natur darin, daß er durchaus jugendlich ist.*»

"Osterwald as poet has a natural affinity with the mind of Franz, in that he is quite juvenile." (Liszt, 1872, 21.)

This is borne out in the song texts, which are often humorous, suggestive and mischievous. That Franz and Osterwald had an irresistible *Goethe'schen* affinity for one another in the sense of *Die Wahlverwandtschaften* or Elective Affinities is beyond doubt.

Osterwald wrote his *Lebensbild* of Robert Franz in 1886, often referring to himself in the third person, and always last in the list of poets Franz favoured. However, we are permitted one small glimpse into their life at this time:

«*Robert Franz, den seine Vorbildung vollständig befähigte, sich an diesen Debatten nicht bloss passiv zu beteiligen, wurde durch dieselben doch keineswegs von seiner Kunst abgezogen, vielmehr regte gerade das lebhafteste Gespräch über irgend ein Zeitthema den Musiker in ihm mächtig an und drängte ihn, abends in seinem bescheidenen Hinterstübchen, (In Brunoswarte 13.) wohin nach den Spaziergängen der eine oder der andere der Freunde ihn begleite, sich*

---

[15] *R F, A P, 24/6/1887, Brief 326* (Pfordten's source is the same as the corrected version, above, and it seems reasonable to assume that the change from "*anzupassen*" meaning to fit/suit to "*anzuschmeigen*" to nestle or cling to, is his.)

ans Klavier zu setzen, irgend eine Melodie anzuschlagen, die ihm unterwegs während unsers Gesprächs in den Sinn gekommen war, wo sich, wenn ich dabei war, zuweilen wohl auch ein unter dem Eindruck seiner wunderbaren Musik entstandener oder entstehender Text gesellte.» (Osterwald, 1886, 6.)

"Robert Franz, since his educational background enabled this, did not simply take part in these debates passively, neither was he distracted from his art by them. Far from it, these current affairs aroused the musician in him and urged him to return to his modest little room at the rear of his family home, (In Brunoswarte 13.) during the evenings, after a stroll accompanied by one or other of his friends, to sit at the keyboard and strike up some melody, which had come into his mind during our discussion; whereby I, when I was there and influenced by his wonderful music, would occasionally join in with a finished or developing text."

This then is the collaboration which sets these works apart from Franz's settings of other poets. The two men co-operate and contribute ideas to reach their shared aim. Franz's music ceases to be a wordless syntax because Osterwald's inspired skill as a philologist and classicist is placed at his disposal. They use this medium to express intimate and deeply-felt emotion, often using erotic imagery, as in *Dornröschen*, Sleeping Beauty, (Opus 51, No. 3) and even the homoerotic sentiments of *Um Mitternacht,* At Midnight, (Opus 16, No. 6). Günter Hartung states:

«*sie gaben, gerade wegen ihres Mangels an Subjektivismen, «der Musik volle Freiheit im Ausdrucke».»[16].*

"Because of their lack of subjectivity, they give the music complete freedom of expression".

Just four of these fifty-one songs are not highly subjective, so that seems an extraordinary observation to make. They are rather lightly dismissed by Hartung in the same chapter as *"Diese studentischen Liebespoesien",* "this student love poetry". However juvenile, these were both fully grown men.

Nevertheless, before Osterwald was given approval by Franz to portray the composer's life in words in his *Lebensbild* of 1886, Franz strongly urged him to write with care:

[17]«*Willst du der Periode, die wir in den vierziger Jahren gemeinschaftlich bestanden, und die, einzig in ihrer Art, auf unser späteres Verhalten den größten Einfluß ausgeübt hat, unter Vermeidung allzu persönlicher Details eingehender Erwähnung thun, so würde das nur meinen eigenen Wünschen entsprechen – des Lehrreichen und Interessanten enthält sie genug! Dazu kommt noch, daß diese Zeit – Liszt berührt sie nur im Vorübergehen – bisher niemals in Betracht gezogen*

---

[16] Sasse, 1986, Schriften des Händel-Hauses • 9 (53)
[17] This paragraph also appears in Sasse, Schriften des Händel-Hauses in Halle. 4. 1986, 14 von Edwin Werner

wurde, obschon sie den eigentlichen Wendepunkt meiner Beziehungen zur Kunst bildet. Du bist der einzige, der über die ästhetische Seite derselben intimeren Bericht erstatten kann.» (Procházka, 1894, 25, 26.)

"Will you avoid mentioning in any depth the all too personal details of the period which we both shared in the 1840s, and which uniquely in their way, exercised the greatest influence on our later conduct. That would comply with my wishes. The academic and interesting will suffice! Because this period – Liszt only touches on it in passing – up until now has never been considered, even though it formed the actual turning-point of my relationship with the arts. You are the only one who can give an intimate report on the aesthetic side of this".

One unavoidable conclusion to be drawn is that Franz was economical with the truth. It seems to be a personal ambition of his to conceal his life from the prying eyes of posterity, whilst a part of him still fervently hopes to be unmasked. This extreme ambiguity of secrecy and discovery, so typical of illicit love affairs, is laid bare in the very places he tells us to look – the songs.

Here is what Liszt did touch on in passing in his biography of Franz, and Osterwald did not resist the opportunity to quote from it in his *Lebensbild* (4/5).

Seeking the moment of creativity unleashed in Franz, Liszt writes:

> «*Der Augenblick in welchem Franz sich auf's Neue zur Composition angetrieben fühlte, war nicht blos in der Geschichte der Entwicklung seines Talentes von Wichtigkeit; er traf mit einem Moment tiefer Leidenschaft zusammen, welche rüttelnd an allen Fibern seiner Seele auch die poetischen Saiten zu neuen Schwingungen erregte. Er liebte mit aller Hingebung, wie sie nur in seiner reinen edlen Nature keimen konnte. Er träumte von einem Glück. . . leise berührte ihn sein Flügel . . .und dann entfloh es! Diese Katastrophe seines innern Geschicks entschied seine völlige Reife. Er brach mit allen Lockungen schwankender Wünsche, schwankender Hoffnungen; der Schmerz stählte und concentrirte seinen Geist und gab ihm jene Weihe, jene Energie, die der Seele ihre ganze Freiheit lassen, um mit allen Kräften diese Freiheit zu bestätigen. Mit diesen neuerweckten Kräften fühlte er sich berufen, seinen Platz unter den Männern der That einzunehmen, Im Namen seiner innern Begseisterung seine eigene Sprache zu sprechen.[...] und schrieb nur, um den ihn bewältigen Gefühlen einen Austrom zu verschaffen ---per sfogarsi.» (Liszt, 1872, 46/47.)*

> «*Ach! nimmer rufest du zurück, was einmal dir entschwunden*, **denn leichtes Schwingen hat das Glück und weilet kurze Stunden.**» *Verlass' mich nicht!* (Opus 21, No. 6.) «*Seinem Freunde Wilhelm Osterwald zugeeignet vom Componisten.*»

"The moment in which Franz felt himself driven to compose anew (pre 1843), was not of importance simply in the history of the development of his talent; it coincided with a moment of deep passion, which shook every fibre of his soul and stimulated those poetical strings to new vibrations. He loved with complete abandon, such as which could be aroused only in his pure, noble nature. He dreamed of happiness . . . it gently touched him with its wings . . . and then it flew away! This catastrophe of inmost fate was decisive in his complete maturity. He broke with all wavering desires, all uncertain hopes; the pain steeled him and concentrated his mind, and gave him that opening, that energy, which by its power frees the soul to confirm its freedom. With this new-awakened strength he felt himself called to take his place among men, to take on the task, in the name of the inner drive to speak his own language. [...] and wrote only, in order to create an outpouring of overwhelming feelings. --- To let off steam."

"Oh, you can never reclaim what has once escaped you, **for happiness has light wings and does not tarry long."** Do not forsake me! (Osterwald Lied Opus 21, No.6) "Dedicated to his friend Wilhelm Osterwald by the Composer."

Liszt's choice of the phrase, "catastrophe of inmost fate" is remarkable. The implication is one of permanent disaster, relating to the psyche of Franz himself, not merely a disappointment in love.

Franz's biographers write of a failed relationship with one of Franz's singing students, Luise Gutike, daughter of a respected medical practitioner in Halle. Franz clearly knew and socialised with the family, which he refers to briefly in letters to Schumann. She is described by Franz and Osterwald's mutual school friend, Theodor Held (1822–1908) (Procházka, 64), as captivating, as though Raphael had painted innocence itself, with an inextinguishable expression of the utmost purity framed by her blond hair. Her beautiful complexion, with its rosy tint, as well as her entire, angelic presence and grace of movement made a lasting impression on Held and his school friends.

The reason given for the break-up of the relationship is «*Jener ersten "heimlichen, stillen Liebe"*», That first "secret, silent love" to which Franz originally dedicated his Opus 1, but later revised to Luise Gutike. (Ibid.) Procháska tries to explain this away as signifying Franz's first love being for music which came between them. (Ibid.) Music may be many things, but silent it is not. Pfordten (10) is even more dismissive:

«*Mehr brauchen wir eigentlich gar nicht zu wissen.*»

"More (about this failed relationship) we simply do not need to know."

Doch heimliche, stille Liebe wacht... Osterwald Lied, *Um Mitternacht* (Opus 16, No.6)

But secret, silent love keeps watch... Osterwald Lied, At Midnight

At about the same time, Franz writes excitedly to Robert Schumann:

> «*Ich habe in der neueren Zeit in Halle einen Dichter (Wilhelm Osterwald) entdeckt, der an Ächtheit der Empfindung Alles übertrifft was ich kenne. Mehrere seiner Poesien habe ich componirt u. werde sie Ihnen gelegentlich mitteilen. Sie sind insgesamt vom weichsten Duft überhaucht, u. geben der Musik volle Freiheit im Ausdruck. So schnell als ich nur kann, erhalten Sie einen langen Brief.*» *(Musketa, 168.)*

> "I have recently discovered a poet (Wilhelm Osterwald) in Halle, who surpasses all I know in authenticity of expression of feeling. I have set several of the poems and will duly impart them to you. They are generally imbued with the gentlest fragrance, and lend the music complete freedom of expression. You will receive a long letter as soon as I can manage it."

There is no ambiguity in Franz's instructions to Osterwald as to the restrictions he should observe when writing his *Lebensbild* of 1886. «*Du bist der einzige*» / You are the only one *(who can report on the aesthetic side of this)* implies a high degree of intimacy between the two men. Liszt makes no mention of a female love interest or of Luise Gutike herself in his biography. Indeed the most superficial glance at records raises serious doubts about the veracity of this version of an alleged cataclysmic event, not least the very act of retrospectively revising the dedicatee of Opus 1 to Luise Gutike. If she had caused Franz's "catastrophe of inmost fate" by jilting him, it poses the question as to why he would wish to remind himself of this for the rest of his life. Rather it seems to be a cosmetic device to deflect attention away from someone else. Perhaps, posterity should take this *cum grano salis*, as Franz, rather appositely, often said, especially as she appears to be godmother to the Franz's third child.

All but twelve of these poems were published in 1848, so extant during the years previously. That is not to say that they were not all written during this period, the form and content suggest they were, with Franz releasing the settings randomly over the rest of his lifetime and dispersing them throughout the other works he published. The editions and collections are fairly arbitrary and a properly catalogued set of volumes is long overdue. Information on publishers can be found in the archives of the Handel-House Museum in Halle, to which an enormous debt of gratitude is due for its exemplary efforts to preserve everything connected with the composer.

In spite of Franz's exhortation to look at <u>all</u> his songs, for some reason, this has never seemed to include the Osterwald settings, which up till now, have received scant attention, if not neglect from Lieder artists. Further examination of Osterwald's *Lebensbild* of Franz leads us to a significant contradiction:

> «*Die grosse Mehrzahl meiner Kompositionen hat Jahre lang im Pulte gelegen und erfuhr an sich bei Gelegenheit Abänderungen der durchgreifendsten Art, in welchen die ursprüngliche Form kaum noch wieder zu erkennen war. Dabei habe ich allerdings eine energische Entwicklung durchgemacht; an der Reihenfolge meiner Werke wird man sie jedoch nicht erkennen. Auch war ich niemals eitel genug, Tag und Stunde des Schaffens zu verzeichnen, damit dasselbe von der*

> *lieben Nachwelt auch noch bis in alle Ecken und Winkel verfolgt werden könne. Sie mag sich nur ruhig an die Lieder halten, das Übrige ist Nebensache.»* (Osterwald, 1886 (13).)

> "The great majority of my compositions had lain in my desk and occasionally found themselves subjected to radical changes, in which the original form was hardly recognisable. At the same time, however, I underwent a decisive development; that the sequencing of my works will, of course, be unrecognizable. Also I was never conceited enough to record every date and time of my creativity, just to have posterity search high and low in every corner of my life. Let them stick to the songs, everything else is irrelevant."

This deliberate attempt to muddy the waters is characteristic of Franz, who exasperates researchers with his insistence on controlling everything – usually by conversation or letter. Furthermore his totally uncompromising stance on his artistry, however justified, was a significant conceit and takes this claim well into the realms of irony. Nevertheless, the contradiction, which is emphasised by Bethge, as follows, is obviously between concealment of artistic motivation and a clear invitation to investigate further.

His beloved daughter Lisbeth's husband wrote in his *Lebensbild* (Bethge, 1908 (29)) of his father-in-law:

> *«Es ist viel über ihn geredet und geschrieben worden, und es wird noch viel über ihn gesagt werden. Das Beste aber, was wir tun können, ist, daß wir nach seinem eigenen Worte handeln: "Wer etwas von mir wissen will, der mag mich in meinen Liedern suchen und kennen lernen".»*

> "A great deal has been said and written, and there still will be much said about him. But the best thing we can do is to act according to his own words: "Whoever wants to know anything about me may seek and acquaint themselves with it in my songs"."

It is certainly true that a great deal has been said and written about Franz, but to summarize, he wrote overwhelmingly *Gesänge für eine Singstimme mit Begleitung des Pianoforte*, songs for solo voice with piano accompaniment, numbering 279 in total and offering many examples of perfection in small form; musical miniatures. Franz himself discusses this in conversation with Waldmann, 1895 (61-62):

> *«Bei mir giebt die Begleitung gleichsam die Situation wieder, die der Text ausspricht, - die Melodie muß dagegen das Bewußtwerden der Situation zur Geltung bringen. So sind alle meine Lieder enstanden. Sie sind für Mezzosopran geschrieben – zwei Oktaven Umfang, - da läßt sich schon etwas ausführen. Alle Ausgaben für tiefe Stimmen, mit denen habe ich nichts zu schaffen.*

> *Als junger Mann habe ich in meiner ersten Herzensneigung viele dieser Sachen komponiert. Als dann später sich dies Verhältnis zuschlug, habe ich doch in*

> *dieser Form - Mezzosopran – weiter komponiert, in die ich mich nun einmal hineingelebt hatte.»*

> "My intention is to have the accompaniment represent as it were the events which the text verbalises, - the melody must on the other hand and in contrast, set off to advantage conscious awareness of the events taking place. Thus have all my songs come about. They are written for mezzo-soprano, - comprising two octaves, - since that enables something meaningful to be performed. All editions for low voice, with those I have nothing to do.

> As a young man I wrote many of these pieces when experiencing the pangs of first love. When later this love affair took a turn for the worse, I still continued composing in this mezzo-soprano style in which I had immersed myself."

Interestingly, an article by Günther Hartung (Musketa, (41, footnote 73)) makes a remarkable claim which does not bear scrutiny:

> *«Auf so gelegten Fundament geschah Ende 1842, ausgelöst durch eine leidenschaftliche "erste Herzensneigung" der Durchbruch zum eigenen Schaffen...»* (Ibid.)

> "On such a foundation the breakthrough to his own creativity occurred at the end of 1842, triggered by passionate "first pangs of love"."

The aforementioned footnote 73 states:

> *«Waldmann (1) 1895, S.62 – Es handelte sich um die Liebe zu der geistig und musikalisch hochbegabten Gesangsschülerin Luise Gutike, Tochter eines angesehen Artzes, die über eine bezaubernde Singstimme verfügt haben muß.»*

> "It concerned the love for the intellectually and musically extremely gifted singing student Luise Gutike, daughter of a respected doctor, who must have had mastery of an enchanting singing voice."

This is pure speculation on the part of its author, as the conversations with Waldmann make no mention of Luise Gutike, or her relationship with Franz. In the extract, they are discussing only the music and the passage is continuous, as shown above. In order to give the impression of a passionate affair between Robert Franz and Luise Gutike, Hartung has appended his own inference as fact.

The question of gender in the Osterwald songs is intriguing. Franz shared with Wagner the firm opinion that the melody represents the female and text represents the male. (Musketa (41)) Liszt makes a strange observation (21) that in the Osterwald songs:

> *«Die ersten sind mit wenigen Ausnahmen die einzigen, wo nicht weibliche Anschauung, weibliches Empfinden der Kern der Bewegung ist.»*

> "The first ones are, with few exceptions, the only ones without a female point of view or female feeling at the heart of their motivation."

At first this might appear the case, but again it does not withstand scrutiny. A scant five appear to be a female addressing or referring to a male, sixteen appear to be a male addressing or referring to a female, and thirty appear to be gender-neutral.

Pfordten (46) also comments on the mezzo-soprano register, explaining that Franz certainly did not rule out the male voice when the text suited it, but as Franz had explained to Waldmann:

> «Im übrigen gehört das Lied der Lyrik an, und die Lyrik ist in ihrem Empfinden geschlechtslos.»

> "Incidentally, song belongs to lyric poetry, and lyric poetry is by its nature without gender."

Pfordten (Ibid) does not hide his view that this is a somewhat idiosyncratic position to take, but it is one shared with Handel and entirely characteristic of the composer's firmly held beliefs. He also credits Franz with expert knowledge of the workings of the human voice and its capabilities, which raises doubt as to whether he really did write for a mezzo- or low- soprano, as he also called it. The range is unarguably from about A below middle C to no higher than top A, which is the register for a lyric tenor and one that many mezzo-sopranos find has an uncomfortably high tessitura. Franz also believed that A, not C, is the first note[18]. Under the circumstances, speculation that Franz wrote these songs for Osterwald's voice does not seem too far-fetched. Franz's own voice was not adequate for professional work and as a life-long, enthusiastic smoker that was probably just as well.

Transposition was anathema to Franz. He entered into protracted and detailed polemics on this topic, and would never accommodate the vagaries of the human voice. He could no more understand the justification for transposing his songs than doing the same to a Beethoven symphony and his arguments, although uncompromising, give much food for thought on a practice which modern singers take for granted. There is a letter from Senfft in 1874 (200) where the singer remonstrates with Franz over this point:

> «Die Alternative: «Singe es in der Original-Tonart oder gar nicht», finde ich hart.»

> "The alternative: "sing it in the original key or not at all", I find harsh."

Once he had sold his work, Franz had no further rights over it, which explains why there are many volumes for low voice. His work was never transposed up, as far as is known.

---

[18] Waldmann (91) and Procháska (51)

Between 1842 and 1845, Franz produced thirty-five songs, averaging about a dozen a year, which he appears to have done until 1858 (Musekta (18)). Enjoying his new-found success and *Liederfrühling,* on 30 July, 1843, he writes Robert Schumann a cheerful letter, referring twice to the Gutike family and cordially inviting, if not urging him to meet up with them and other friends in Halle (Ibid). It is hard to understand how Franz's fallow period from 1837 until the beginning of the forties, followed by a crisis of love and a breakdown which released his creative powers, relate to the contents of this letter. The trip to the Tirol, Salzkammergut, and Italy to cure his shattered nerves is reported by Procházka (65) to have taken place in 1843, when he appears most engaged in composing his songs:

> «*Ich bin im Laufe des letzten Halbjahres ein Komponist geworden; wie das gekommen ist, weiß ich selber nicht...*» (letter to T Held, Procházka (33)).
>
> "In the course of the last six months I have become a composer; how that has come about I do not even know myself."

There does not appear to be any detailed account of Franz's singular trip abroad; who accompanied him and what happened that was of such significance that it helped to transform Franz into a composer are crucial questions, which remain unanswered.

Older articles such as Apthorpe's, 1902 (xvi-xvii) speak very highly of Franz's songs. He explains the centripetal, as opposed to the Wagnerian centrifugal, nature of them and praises their ability to give outward expression to inward thought and feeling. Even though the melodies are accommodating and singable, he emphasises the intimate connection between the piano and voice, as Franz described to Waldmann above, and calls it "not quite solo-singing" but more "concerted performance". He goes on to say, "Franz's broad modern treatment of the pianoforte, and the essentially polyphonic structure of his accompaniments, present tasks to which the ordinary professional accompanist is hardly grown; they require a finished pianist and musician".

Krehbiel is equally enthusiastic and admiring and quotes Franz speaking to Waldmann, "I composed feelings not words". That is such a small statement about a metaphysical gift only bestowed upon a few. Franz knew what it was to be a suffering artist, compelled by what he perceived to be an outside force, which Goethe called the *Daemonic*. Osterwald (8) tells us that Franz concerned himself with the study of partials or micro-tones – *die Aliquottöne* and other musicological mysteries in order to perfect his work. While he struggled against chronic deafness for most of his adult life, his inner musical ear, to his delight and relief, did not fail him. Even so, his diligence and years of intense study took their toll on his already weak nerves, and he gradually lost the use of his right hand towards the end of his life.

By 1993 and Gorrell's chapter on Franz, the reader finds that Franz has been relegated to a chapter called "The Supporting Cast", (Gorrell, 1993, 232-236). She praises the skill and careful workmanship of Franz's songs, but condemns the "sameness and lack of passion" most of them demonstrate. Claiming that there is very little variety in his overall production, she writes that "the accompaniments are within the capabilities of an accomplished amateur". "Word painting is not a significant feature in either the accompaniment or the vocal line." She finishes by advising, "Franz's care setting text and his moderate interpretive demands are also important considerations for students in their early studies. But even the mature artist can find value in occasionally programming Franz's songs, as points of vocal and emotional calm." Perhaps, she is unaware that Lotte Lehmann would devote entire recitals to the works of her highly esteemed Robert Franz, a composer she considered most worthy of her artistry. Her farewell recital recording, released in 1978, includes several Franz lieder.

In Letters of Robert Franz, published on 1 April, 1921, William Barclay Squire writes in his preface:

> "That Franz was, and still is, never appreciated at his full worth, is quite true; but the reason is not far to seek, and various passages in his letters show that he realized it himself. His songs are too intimate to produce their full effect on the general public, and moreover they require a perfection of performance in which the shares of both singer and accompanist shall be fused with a degree of sympathy that is rarely attainable. The admirable article by E. Dannreuther in Grove's Dictionary says the last words on Franz's songs, and is as true now as when it was written. They will probably always remain caviar to the multitude; but, in the history of music, they will keep for Franz's name a place by the side of those of Schumann, Schubert and Wolf."

Osterwald writes:

> «...so will es auch mir mehr und mehr scheinen, als werde der Franz'schen Muse ihr Recht bedeutend verkürzt, wenn man sie ausschliesslich aus dem Gesichtspunkte des weltlichen und geistlichen Volksliedes betrachten wollte. Unzweifelhaft erträgt, ja fordert dies ein Viertel seiner Lieder, in dem der echteste Ton des deutschen Volksliedes angeschlagen ist, aber der Rest, in dem sich der Franz'sche Charakter als künstlerischer Ausdruck seiner Persönlichkeit, die sich mit dem Ideengehalt ihrer Zeit erfüllt und gesättigt hat, passt nicht in den Rahmen dieser Betrachtung.» (Osterwald, 1886, 9.)

> "...And so it appears to me more and more, as though Franz's muse would become significantly limited, if one viewed his work exclusively from the point of view of hymns and folk songs. Undoubtedly, they contribute, or could claim to do so, to a quarter of songs which strike a tone of German folk music, but the rest, in which the character of Franz expresses its personality artistically and which fulfil and satisfy the ideas of their time, does not fit into the frame of this observation."

There is infinite variety in Franz's songs and the best way to verify this is to take his advice and study them. That is not to say he developed any kind of progressive style;

something for which he was roundly condemned by critics who, Franz felt, would always sacrifice beauty for novelty.

By extracting the individual Osterwald love songs and forming them into a collection, a light is thrown on this period for the first time. Some topoi are so obvious that they are laboured to the point of parody, and the best example of this is the continual reappearance of the month of May, which features about twenty times and gives the impression of being some kind of cypher. It could be argued that these lyrics are characterized by every pathological symptom of romantic love within the range of human experience.

The symbol of the rose emerges in one form or another eighteen times in the Osterwald Songs and it is not fanciful to believe that it had great significance in this relationship. One of the twelve poems not published until 1856 was Opus 26, No. 2, *In dem Dornbusch blüht ein Röslein*, (In the thorny bush a little rose blooms), the wordless music for which Franz provided Osterwald for completion, although it is not known when. He was delighted with the rather flirtatious result and full of praise for Osterwald's skill. At the same time Opus 26, No.1, *Wenn ich's nur wüsste!* (If only I knew!), was also completed in this way, with its poignant lines:

«*ob er so immer war, da er mich küsste!*»

"If only I knew whether he has remained the same since he kissed me!"

The symbol of the reoccurring dark head makes an appearance in this song, as it does in five others. All hair is, like that of both artists, curly, brown or dark, (Opus 4, Nos. 9 and 12, Opus 7, No. 1, Opus 26, No. 1, Opus 31, No. 2 and Opus 43, No. 6), never the stereotypical golden hair of Teutonic maidens attributed to Luise Gutike. With one exception, the word Frau or Fräulein is avoided completely, with a preference for Mädchen, Maid and variations thereon, often concealing Mai/May, once again. «Frau Mutter» appears in the apparently rather frivolous, *Mein Schatz ist auf der Wandershaft*, (My sweetheart has been on his travels), Opus 40, No. 1. This title is almost identical to the first line of other settings which are known as *Heimlicher Liebe Pein* (The Torment of Secret Love) and are versions of a poem from *Des Knaben Wunderhorn* (The Boy's Magic Horn) collected by Ludwig Archim von Arnim (1781-1831) and Klemens Brentano (1778-1842). The themes of an unsuitable relationship, malicious gossip, parental disapproval and frustration are very similar.

The allusions to enforced secrecy and a sense of lack and loss abound, with vivid concepts like fear of abandonment, ruination and temptation from serpents, symbolizing the female, making their presence felt. The unusual frequent choice of the verb "*treiben*" seems to be some kind of *double entendre,* as it is a very informal way of implying sexual intercourse. (*Es mit jemandem treiben.*) Most crucially, lovers often refer to "*Mein Kind*", "My Child" which is certainly an old-fashioned term for "my pretty maid", or "sweet maid". However, it also has strong connotations of sacrifice, bearing in mind Biblical and mythical examples. Sacrifices are generally made to ensure a better future and perhaps, that is what happened.

Graham Johnson has indicated the potential significance of the Osterwald/Franz version of *Die Liebe hat gelogen!* (Love has Lied), Opus 6, No. 4 as a possible reference to verses of the same title, set by Schubert and written by the only poet from this time known to have been homosexual, August von Platen-Hallermünde (1796-1835). Certainly the accepted sentiment that love shared physically between two men has no place in this world, could mean that love must have lied to them, just as dreams of youth lie in *Gewitternacht* (Stormy Night) Opus 8, No. 6, and hope lies in *Bei der Linde* (By the Lime Tree) Opus 36, No. 4. Heine had unmasked Platen as a homosexual in 1830 and much later, Franz claims to find his syntax unnatural for the German language. Even so, he sets Osterwald's versions of Platen's titles *Die Liebe hat gelogen* and *Erster Verlust* (First Loss) Opus 36, No. 2. In the latter, it is spring which has lied, with a false promise by an external force at a fundamental point in the relationship. The original title of the poem was *Des Mädchens Klage* (Maiden's Lament) and was one of twenty-one titles changed, this one seemingly to hint at that *erste heimliche stille Liebe*.

Platen's *Ihr Vögel in den Zweigen schwank, Wie seid ihr froh und frisch und frank*[...] (You birds tottering in the branches, how happy and lively and open you are) which bears a strong resemblance to Osterwald's *Ich lobe mir die Vögelein, die auf den Zweigen springen* [...] *will singen frank und frei wie ihr*[...] (I cherish the little birds, hopping among the branches [...] I want to sing openly and freely like you...)(18) is heavy with innuendo. Understandably, given the moral climate at the time, fear of being discovered, unmasked or ensnared features strongly in these songs, which every so often admit to the darkest, covert concupiscence.

Osterwald's verses from *Bilder und Träume*, discussed in Chapter Three, include the following poignant sentiments from one man to another. The disillusionment in love is neither subtle nor understated.

Einem Freunde

Viel Sträuße sollt' ich heute winden,
Die Blumen hast du ja so gerne,
Doch in des Winters Wachtkaserne
Sind Blatt und Blumen nicht zu finden.
Hätte ich den Zauberstab in Händen,
Die kalten Welten aufzutauen,
Die Himmel ließ' ich heute blauen,
Um blauen Veilchen dir zu senden.

Die Düfte blühnder Fliederlauben,
Sie sollten buhlend dich umfließen,
Und du in deine Arme schließen,
Den lang, ersehnten Liebesglauben.
Doch Freund, ich kann die bunten Träume
Nicht in das Licht des Tages bannen —
Kein ander Grün, als dunkle Tannen
Und aufgesparte Weihnachtsbäume

Die andern sind mit Schnee behangen,
Und statt der linden Frühlingsdüfte
Ziehn Winternebel durch die Lüfte –
Nicht Zeit ist's Blumen zu verlangen!
Die Welt darf andre Sträuße fodern,
Als die ein Liebender gewunden,
Frisch auf! die Klingen sind gebunden,
Los denn! die blanken Hieber lodern!

Schon dröhet laut des Kampfes Kunde,
Komm, laß die Basen, laß die Vettern,
Komm, eh die Singsbrommeten schmettern,
Noch kommen wir zur rechten Stunde.
Laß dir noch eins in's Auge sehen,
Dann mag das Banner muthig fliegen,
Und gilt es sterben oder siegen,
    Wir wollen zu einander stehen.

To a Comrade

Today I should tie many posies,
Flowers please you so,
But in winter's military barracks,
Leaf and blossom are nowhere to be found.
Had I a magic wand in my hand
To thaw out the cold world,
I'd have the skies turn blue today,
To send you blue violets.

Fragrant blossoming lilac leaves
Should woo you in their embrace,
And you should enfold in your arms
The long-desired faith in love.
But friend, I cannot cast the spell
Of such colourful dreams onto the
Light of day – No other green than dark pines
And spared Christmas trees.

The rest are covered in snow,
And instead of the mild scent of spring,
It is winter fog that hangs in the air –
It is no time to yearn for flowers!
The world may ask for different posies,
From those tied by a lover,
Let us away! The swords are sheathed,
To battle! the bright blades are blazing!

The air resounds with the call to battle,
Come, let us leave our cousins,
Come, before the bugles sound,
We might just make it in time,
Let me look into your eyes once more,
Then let the banner bravely fly,
And in death or victory,
    Let us stand together.

Chapter Five

THE WIDER CONTEXT

Franz's songs were extremely popular and successful until around 1920, when they lost popularity, first in Germany, and then in Britain and North America. There is no doubt that the First World War drove a stake through the heart of *Hausmusik* and German language musical texts in many countries. That, and the appearance of television and film, which has taken people away from the piano at home; but it does not really explain why the Lieder of Schubert, Schumann, Brahms, Mendelssohn, Wolf, Wagner and others, with whom Franz was directly or indirectly connected, have retained their popularity, while his has waned. Modern singers neither know nor care about the artistic spats that are supposed to have made Franz so controversial in his heyday. He can certainly do without preposterous claims that his work lacks variety, since the infinite and astonishing diversity of his oeuvre is so immediately conspicuous.

Because it is impossible to ignore the Dionysian/Apollonian concepts and themes of instinct and carnal desire versus contemporary social responsibility in the Osterwald texts, it is not surprising to learn that Thomas Mann was a great admirer of Franz. Although, August von Platen has been suggested as a more logical and apposite inspiration for the central character *Gustav von Aschenbach* in "*Der Tod in Venedig*" (The Death in Venice) of 1913, especially since August is virtually an anagram of Gustav, Robert Franz himself cannot be ruled out:

> «*So sieht es noch Thomas Mann in der Lebens – und Zeitalterbilanz seines Doktor Faustus, wo er von der «glorreichen Kultur des deutschen Kunstliedes» spricht, «welche nach leidlich trockenen Vorspielen in Schubert wunderbar entspringt, um dann durch Schumann,* **Robert Franz***, Brahms, Hugo Wolf und Mahler ihre national durchaus unvergleichlichen Triumphe zu feiern.»*[19] (Musketa, 1993, 35, G. Hartung.)

> "That is how Thomas Mann saw it in the Life and Times of his Doctor Faust, where he speaks of the 'glorious culture of the German Art Song', whereby, after the wonderful emergence of fairly dry overtures in Schubert, it then became an incomparable national triumph celebrated through Schumann, **Robert Franz,** Brahms, Hugo Wolf and Mahler."

Many people remain sceptical about Gustav Mahler, a photograph of whom was found on a newspaper clipping as number 23 in Mann's notes for *Der Tod in Venedig*, being the model for *Gustav von Aschenbach*. The only hint Mann ever gave was in September 1910, two days after the occasion of Mahler's last concert in Munich, when he sent a letter of homage to the composer, together with a copy of his novel *Königliche Hoheit*, in which he mentions *die «Maske Mahlers»*[20]. This expression is ambiguous and in

---

[19] Mann Thomas: Ges. Werke in 12 Bänden – Berlin; Weimar : Aufbau 1965. – Bd.6, S. 107
[20] *Article, 25 March 2018, Hans Rudolf Vaget, Süddeutsche Zeitung*

keeping with the many-layered nature of *Der Tod in Venedig*, the very title of which could be taken to mean Aschenbach himself, or the cholera epidemic. If it were the case that Mann had identified the concepts central to his novel in Franz's work (teasing young boys do appear in *Um Mitternacht*), Robert Franz might well have been his inspiration, and the newspaper cutting a complete red herring. Here is his description:

> *«Gustav von Aschenbach war etwas unter Mittelgröße, brünett, rasiert. Sein Kopf erschien ein wenig zu groß im Verhältnis zu der fast zierlichen Gestalt. Sein rückwärts gebürstetes Haar, am Scheitel gelichtet, an den Schläfen sehr voll and stark ergraut, umrahmte eine hohe, zerklüftete und gleichsam narbige Stirn. Der Bügel einer Goldbrille mit randlosen Gläsern schnitt in die Wurzel der gedrungenen, edel gebogenen Nase ein. Der Mund war groß, oft schlaff, oft plötzlich schmal und gespannt; die Wangenpartie mager und gefurcht, das wohlausgebildete Kinn weich gespalten. Bedeutende Schicksale schienen über dies meist leidend seitwärts geneigte Haupt hinweggegangen zu sein, und doch war die Kunst es gewesen, die hier jene physiognomische Durchbildung übernommen hatte, welche sonst das Werk eines schweren bewegten Lebens ist.»* (Thomas Mann, Der Tod in Venedig 76, OUP 1971.)

"Gustav von Aschenbach was of medium build, with dark brown hair and clean-shaven. His head appeared a little too big in proportion to his almost dainty form. His receding hair was brushed back, full at the temples and greying, and it framed a high brow, almost scarred with furrows. His rimless gold glasses cut into the bridge of his sturdy, roman nose. His mouth was large, often slack, often suddenly thin and tense; his cheeks sunken and lined, there was a slight cleft in his well-formed chin. Significant fate had played its part in the formation of this suffering face, which was usually tilted to one side, and yet it was art, not a hard life, that had shaped this face."

There are no likenesses of Robert Franz wearing glasses, but the photograph which follows appears to fit the description Mann gives of Aschenbach. Of course, this is pure speculation, but as Mann never confirmed nor denied that Aschenbach was based on Mahler, we are at liberty to suggest other possibilities. One thing is certain; Thomas Mann would never have embarrassed Robert Franz – even posthumously - by implicating him in any way and he deliberately deflected attention on to a man who was indisputably heterosexual. On the side of Franz's memorial in Halle is the word Bach – and yes, he was a heavy smoker; so perhaps Mann conflated the two since serious writers are not without a sense of humour.

Robert Franz (Stiftung Händel-Haus)

Chapter Six

THE SACRIFICE

In 1846, the year Osterwald left Halle, Franz became engaged to the young Marie Hinrichs, an aspiring lieder composer herself. Notably, he published his superb transcription of Schubert's quartet, *Der Tod und das Mädchen* (Death and the Maiden) D810 for four hands, one piano. The last line of Schubert's famous Lied setting of Matthias Claudius (1740-1815), D531 «*sollst sanft in meinen Armen schlafen!*» ([thou] shalt gently sleep in my arms) brings to mind «*ein warmer Arm dich hält mit sanftem Druck umfangen*» (warm arms can gently hold you in a firm embrace) from the aforementioned *Verlass' mich nicht*, Opus 21, No. 6, where Death also appears at the end with the words, «*Da kalter Tod die Blumen bricht im Herzen und im Hagen*» (Since cold death breaks the flowers in my heart and in the groves).

The impression given by the composer's decision to arrange this particular work without syntax is one of adieu to the maiden with black-brown hair (Opus 31, No. 2, *Ade denn du stolze*, Farewell then, you haughty maid). This idea is emphasised by the almost unbearably moving *Abends* (In the Evening), Opus 20, No. 4.

Franz no longer seemed to feel the need to keep the following work hidden away from the prying eyes of posterity, for he gives the year and place of his composition *Genesung* (Recovery) Opus 5, No. 12 as Halle, 1846. The poem was written by a member of Franz and Osterwald's close circle of friends, (Karl) Julius Schröer (1825-1900). (Procháska, 1894, 25.) The vocabulary and *Stimmung* or mood is strikingly similar in verses two and four to *Um Mitternacht*, which certainly existed as a poem before 1848, and which Franz did not release until 1856. *Um Mitternacht*, with its furtive longing and homoerotic allusions, may well have served as a basis for renunciation and transformation in references familiar to both poet and composer of *Genesung*.

Und nun ein End' dem Trauern,	And now an end to grieving
dem Schauern in den Mauern,	To shuddering within the city walls
und nun ein End' den Thränen,	And now an end to tears
und nun ein ander Lied!	And now another song!
Was dulden und was Tragen!	What suffering and what a burden!
Das klagen und Entsagen,	The weeping and renunciation,
das Sinnen und das Sehnen	The brooding and the yearning
bin ich endlich müd'!	Finally tire me out!
Ich fühl' mich neu geboren!	I feel myself born anew!
Ich habe' sie mir erkoren,	I have chosen her for myself,
ich habe sie gefunden	I have found her
und habe neuen Muth!	And have new courage!

Will ringen ohne Zagen,	Wanting to strive unhesitatingly
will jagen, wetten, wagen,	Wanting to hunt, risk, dare,
bis dass sie überwunden	Until she is conquered
an meinem Herzen ruht!	And rests upon my heart!
Und wenn es wird gelingen,	And when it is accomplished,
da will ich Lieder singen!	Then I will wish to sing songs!
Will singen Herz an Herzen,	Wish to sing from heart to heart,
Will singen für und für.	Wish to sing forevermore.
Doch sollt' es nimmer glücken,	But should this not succeed,
da schlag' ich es in Stücken,	Then I will smash to pieces
mein Saitenspiel voll Schmerzen,	My soul of music full of pain,
Und schweige für und für!	And be silent forevermore!

(Translation by V Edge © 2019)

There is an unconcealed attempt at optimism by someone whose feelings have been badly wounded and who seems to have had enough of living in the shadows in fear of town gossip. Like Osterwald in the following two-part poem, *Zum Eingang*, there is no question about the path Franz's life will take if he is accepted by his chosen one.

The first part of this poem was initially published as the final item in the above-mentioned group «*Bilder und Träume*» as «*Frischauf*». In the first version, there are five changes to the order of the verses and there are three additional strophes, two of which, protest strongly against French influence and female emancipation. The third, final verse is revised and inserted at the end of the second part of the 1873 version.

> «*Euch aber, wack're Jungen*
> *an die mein Gruß ergeht,*
> *Euch sei dies Lied gesungen*
> *zum fröhlichen Valet.*»
>
> "To you, upright lads,
> whom I salute,
> this song is sung,
> to the cheerful servant."

Zum Eingang can mean "To the Beginning", which echoes the last line of the first part, "To the Entrance", or "In place of the Introit". It is used apropos of apparently nothing immediately obvious as the introduction to *Gedichte von Wilhelm Osterwald (Leipzig, Verlag von F E C Leuckhart (Constantin Sander) 1873)*. Osterwald pays homage to Franz thus:

> «*Die von Robert Franz componierten habe ich in dankbarer Würdigung der Ehre, die ihnen der größte musikalische Lyriker der Gegenwart erwiesen hat, mit der Opuszahl der Compositions bezeichnet.*» (Ibid.)

> "Those composed by Robert Franz I have, in grateful acknowledgement of the honour, which he, as the greatest lyrical composer of our times, has paid them, marked with the opus numbers of the compositions."

In Part One, Osterwald cannot hide his bitterness as he speaks of the poet in the form of the nightingale, then in an effort to be more cheerful, makes a mischievous «*lose*» reference to *Nun hat das Leid ein Ende* (Now suffering has an end), Opus 18, No. 3. The pull back to the weeping rose is almost irresistible but it seems that he has no choice but to leave. The "Singer" and he must leave this life, and Osterwald makes a heart-wrenching plea not to make the long night any longer than it is already. This echoes Franz's weariness at being forced to live in the shadows. In verse seven, Osterwald uses the metaphor of a ship finding safe harbour to hint at heterosexual intercourse and family life. He then launches forth with heavy irony, bordering on sarcasm, with "the temple to German men and women, where cool reason rules the heart of man. Here, where the courtship of a woman is purified by chastity". The temple is an obvious reference to Greek love, which was considered to be a higher form of personal devotion shown by one man to another. It seems astonishingly bold to us in isolation, but published in a collection of Osterwald's poetry in 1873, maybe not.

In a society where men were expected to sow their wild oats before they married chaste virgins, there was bound to be a shortage of available women, and those who were prepared to engage in fornication were often a serious health risk to men.

In the final, ninth verse of Part One, the deliberately odd choice of *bestellen* betrays a clear reference to *bepflanzen/befruchten* (to plant or inseminate). *Man bestellt den Acker* (One sows a field). This reveals a clear intention to make a marriage of reason and to procreate. The *Introitus* also means the entrance to the female reproductive organs.

Osterwald composes the six verse, second part of *Zum Eingang* in Mühlhausen in 1872:

> «*Vor sechsundzwanzig Jahren dies Lied zuerst erscholl, als mir die Locken waren noch braun und kraus und voll;*»

> "Twenty-six years ago, this song first rang out, when my curly locks were still brown, and frizzy and full;"

Mutual school and life-long friend Theodor Held writes of Franz:

> «*verklärt durch [...] blaue Augen und umrahmt von glatt anliegendem, dunklem Haar, das erst in den letzten Jahren anfing, in des Alters Grau zu spielen.*»

> "Transfigured [...] by blue eyes and framed by smooth, flat, dark hair, which did not begin to go grey until well into old-age." (Procházka 28, 29.)

As mentioned above, the appearance of apparent females with dark hair is quite exceptional in 19th century German romantic Lieder, which customarily portrays the female ideal as having hair as golden as Heine's *Lorelei*. Certainly, if Franz had wished to portray the females in his songs as having golden hair, Osterwald would have obliged, but to reiterate, Franz considered the music to be female and the text to be male. There has to be a reason why the love object in these works has dark hair and it does not take a great leap of imagination to deduce it. Because this is so uncharacteristic of the genre, it gives the distinct impression of male/female role-play in the songs' texts.

The call, *Frischauf!* (Let us away!) is repeated throughout Part One, but does not reappear until the end of the work itself. Part Two reassures the writer that the sacrifice has been worth it, although Osterwald does not mention his wife and nine children, instead he mentions his successful career. He refers to German politics, which differed from those of the liberal, progressive Franz and hints that Bismarck's Germany is wrong about the performance of song being effeminate. Franz loathed Bismarck as can be seen in a letter to Senfft:

> «Die außerordentliche Perspektive, welche Sie mir hinsichtlich unseres preußischen Kometen (v. Bismarck) eröffnen, könnte mich fast erschrecken. Denke ich mir den Mann mit modern-musikalischen Träumereien im Herzen und dem blutigen Fanatismus auf den Lippen – dann hört wirklich alles auf! Im Menschen schlummern doch seltsame widersprüche!» (Senfft, 1863, 11.)

> "The extraordinary perspective, which in respect of our Prussian comet (v. Bismark) you reveal to me, could almost shock me. If I think of the man with dreams of modern music in his heart and such bloody fanaticism on his lips, - then that really is the limit! The strangest contradictions slumber within men!"

The final revised paragraph now speaks of the abiding hope that we *"wir"* will be reunited "somewhere on the verdant margins". «Noch Eine [...] wandelt die Welt zum Raine, auf dem's zu der Liebsten geht.» (There is another who travels the world to its margins, which lead to the beloved.)

The margins of society are for people who live outside socially accepted norms and are referred to in *Aufbruch* (Departure or Breaking Out) Opus 35, No. 6. The call, *Frischauf!* will be recognizable to them both and "shall always be sung by one to the other". *Zum Eingang* is shown in full as follows:

Zum Eingang

Ich sah die Rose weinen	I saw the rose crying
An einem Abend spat[21],	Late one evening,
Als aufgehört zu scheinen	When the lovely sun
Die schöne Sonne hatt':	Had ceased to shine:
Es zitterte und zagte	The dew in its petals,
In ihrem Kelch der Thau,	Trembled and shivered,
Daß droben nimmer tagte	That above would never dawn
Ein Himmel klar und blau.	A clear blue sky.
Ich hört' in trüben Tagen	I heard in gloomy days
In einem dichten Hag	In a wooded copse,
Die Nachtigallen schlagen	The nightingales singing
Wehmüthiglichen Schlag:	A melancholy song:
Wie daß nun alle Rosen	How now all the roses
So gar verblühet sein	Are so completely faded
Und wilder Stürme Tosen	And the raging, wild storms
Kein Leben ließe gedeihn.	Allow no life to flourish.
Geduld, du junge Rose!	Patience you young rose!
Dein Klagen schlummert ein,	Your complaining will abate
Wenn leise dich und lose	When gently and mischievously
Aufweckt der Morgenschein,	The sunrise awakens,
Geduld, ihr Nachtigallen!	Patience, you nightingales!
Geduld bis über's Jahr,	Patience until the year is past,
Da neuen Lenzes Wallen	Then a new wave of spring
Bringt neue Rosen dar!	Offers up new roses!
Ich sah des Stromes Welle	I saw the surging wave
Mit Zagen weiter ziehn,	Fearfully pull away,
Sie sprach: so gern zur Quelle	It spoke: so much back to my source
Möcht' ich zurückefliehn.	Do I want to flee.
Sie wankete und weilte,	It wavered and tarried,
Als ob nun aller Fluß	As though now all the river
Umsonst von dannen eilte	In vain hurried from there
Und fände keinen Schluß.	And found no end.
Ich hör' auch Sänger singen	I also hear singers singing
Mit einem trüben Muth,	With a gloomy air,
Wie daß in allen Dingen	As though in all respects
Die Welt sei nimmer gut.	The world can never be good.
Daß todt sei alles Leben	That all life be dead
Und ringsum schwarze Nacht,	And all around black night,
Und daß wir es nun eben	And that we are simply
Annoch zu nichts gebracht.	Brought to nothing.

---

[21] Osterwald omits the Umlaut in his original copy, presumably for scansion

Frischauf, du zage Welle!
Ist steinig auch die Bahn,
Du kommst gewiß zur Stelle
Zum weiten Ocean.
Frischauf auch ihr, o Sänger,
Frischauf zu dieser Frist!
Und macht die Nacht nicht länger,
Als lange sie schon ist.

Frischauf! und laßt das Sorgen
Und laßt das Jammern sein,
Ein frischer freier Morgen
Zieht auch für uns herein.
Ob unser Schiff auch schlagen
Der wilden Wogen viel,
Es wird ja doch getragen
Zu einem sichren Ziel.

Dahier in Volkes Mitte,
Hier laßt uns weiter baun
Den Tempel deutscher Sitte
Bei Männern und bei Fraun,
Hier, wo des Mannes Sinnen
Beherrscht Besonnenheit,
Hier, wo des Weibes Minnen
Durchläutert Züchtigkeit.

Frischauf! und laßt das Klagen
Und habet frohen Muth;
's ist wie zu allen Tagen
Die Welt auch heute gut.
Frischauf! der Ruf, Gesellen,
Sei euch und mir gethan,
So wollen wir's bestellen
Und fröhlich fangen an.

Halle, 1846

Let us away, you timid wave!
If the road is indeed stony,
You will surely come to the place
To the wide ocean.
Let us away with you, oh singer,
Let us away at this time!
And make the long night no longer,
Than it already is.

Let us away! And let the cares
And let the misery be,
A fresh, free morning
Also dawns for us.
Even though our ship be beaten
By the wild surge,
It will surely be carried
To a safe harbour.

Here in the centre of the nation,
Here let us continue to build
The Temple of German customs
Among men and among women,
Here, where reason rules the
Senses of men,
Here, where the courtship of women
Is purified by chastity.

Let us away! And leave off complaining
And be of good cheer.
It is as it is every day;
The world is also good today.
Let us away! The call, companions,
Has come to you and me,
So we will prepare to answer
And cheerfully begin.

Vor sechsundzwanzig Jahren	Twenty-six years ago
Dies Lied zuerst erscholl,	This song first rang out,
Als mir die Locken waren	When my curly locks were
Noch braun und kraus und voll;	Still brown and frizzy and full;
Die Doppelzahl der Jahre	Twice as many years
Zählt mir das Leben heut,	Are counted in my life now,
Schon ist auf meine Haare	And already the first grey hairs
Der erste Reif gestreut.	Are beginning to show.
Doch der mich jung getrieben,	But the same good cheer
Derselbe frohe Muth,	That drove me on in my youth,
Ist mir bislang geblieben	Has remained this long with me
Und wärmt noch heut mein Blut,	And still warms my blood today,
Und der mich jung erfüllet,	And the same German spirit
Derselbe deutsche Sinn	that filled me in my youth
Ist heut noch unverhüllet	is now clearly my
Mein Werben und Gewinn.	Profession and my gain.
Viel Schlachten sind geschlagen;	Many battles have been fought;
Der Opfer waren viel,	The sacrifices were great,
Doch Deutschland ist getragen	But Germany has been carried
Zu einem sichren Ziel:	To a secure place:
Das Reich ist neu erstanden	The Empire is newly emerged
Nach langer Winternacht	After a long winter's night
Und aus des Schlummers Banden	And from slumber's bonds
Zu niegeahnter Pracht.	To unimagined splendour.
Soll nun kein Lied mehr klingen	Will no song ring out anymore
Im neuen deutschen Reich,	In the new German Empire,
Als wär' nun alles Singen	As if now all singing were
Unmännlich oder weich?	Unmanly or soft?
Das wolle Gott verhüten,	God forbid such a thing,
Daß man das Lied verstößt	That one should disown the Lied
Und seiner besten Blüthen	And deprive the German tree
Den deutschen Baum entblößt.	Of its finest blossom.
Laßt denn die Lieder tönen	Let the songs resound now
Heut wie zu aller Zeit,	And for all time,
Die hold in uns versöhnen	They sweetly reconcile in us
Des Lebens Widerstreit:	Life's conflicts:
Die Lieder deutscher Minne	The songs of courtly love
Und deutscher Männlichkeit	And German masculinity
Und die mit frommem Sinne	And those with pious spirit
Gott und Natur geweiht.	Consecrating God and Nature.

Und so sei heut gesungen,	And so let it be sung today,
Wie ich's vor Jahren sang,	As I sang it years ago,
Den Alten wie den Jungen	To the old, as to the young
Frischauf! mit frischem Klang,	Let us away! with a fresh sound,
Und treffen wir beim Wandern	And if we meet each other
Uns wo auf grünem Rain,	out walking somewhere on the green margins, Let us away,
Soll einem stets vom andern	
Frischauf! gesungen sein.	Shall always be sung by one to the other. (Translation by V Edge © 2019)

Mühlhausen in Thüringen, 1872
Wilhelm Osterwald

Towards the end of the lives of Robert Franz and Wilhelm Osterwald, in 1885, a new Franz album appeared which contained, in addition to opera 48, 50 and 51, Franz's only piece for solo piano, with no opus number, entitled *Albumblatt* (Leaf from an Album). Franz described it, according to Pfordten in 1923, in one word, *Entsagung* (Renunciation). Osterwald (13) says of it:

> *«Es ist ein kurzes Allegro im gebundenen Stile, das Trotz seiner strengen Haltung doch in jeder Note und ganz besonders in dem elegisch fragenden Schlusse den grossen Lyriker erkennen lässt. Es mutet an wie ein Rückblick, den der Tondichter auf sein eigenes Leben wirft, vor allem der Zeit gedenkend, in der er selbst noch ein Werdender war und wehmütig das Haupt schüttelnd bei den Fragen: Wo sind sie hin, die schönen Zeiten des ersten freudigen und begeisterten Schaffens und der hohen Hoffnungen und Erwartungen, die sich daran knüpften? Sind sie Wahrheit geworden oder blieben sie ein Traum?»*

> "It is a short allegro in legato style which despite his strict composure, in every note and quite especially in the mournful, questioning ending, reveals the great song-composer. It seems like a backward glance, which the composer is throwing on his own life, primarily with the time in mind when he himself was an emerging artist, melancholic and shaking his head, asking: where have they gone then, the happy days of the first, joyful and enthusiastic creativity, and the high hopes and expectations that went with them? Have they become the truth or remained a dream?"

Osterwald remarks on its questioning ending, but does not mention that the piece is redolent of *Verlass' mich nicht!* (Do not forsake me!), a song dedicated to the poet himself. Several embedded quotes from identifiable Osterwald songs are left there by Franz, waiting to be noticed.

Assuming their continued existence, concealed in readiness to be found are the following objects, tantalisingly mentioned in this account from *"Robert Franz*

Gedenkstätten" by Konstanza Musketa, *Zur Robert Franz-Rezeption in Halle in 1992*. (Musketa, 1993 (287).)

> «*Als die Stadt Halle im Jahre 1937 das Händel-Haus käuflich erworben hatte, beabsichtigte sie bereits damals, hier auch anderen hallischen Musikerpersönlichkeiten Gedenkräume einzurichten. Der Zweite Weltkrieg verzögerte die Realisierung dieses Vorhabens, doch hinderte er die Verantwortlichen nicht, sich um den Ankauf von Gegenständen aus dem Nachlaß von vershiedenen hallischen Komponisten wie Scheidt, Reichardt, Türk, Loewe und Franz zu bemühen. 1941 konnte mit der in Wiesbaden lebenden hochbetagten Schwiegertochter von Robert Franz, Margarethe Franz, einen Vertrag über den Ankauf von Dokumenten, Möbeln und anderen Erinnerungsstücken schließen.[...] Margarethe Franz starb im Dezember 1949, fast 96 jährig, und der Transport der Möbel erfolgte, bis auf einiges, was bei einem Bombenangriff zerstört worden war, erst im Sommer 1950.[22] Der Erbe von Margarethe Franz, ein «Herr Peter Weber [,] bot der Stadt Halle schriftlich noch weiteres vorhandenes Mobiliar aus dem Besitz von Robert Franz an und betonte dabei, daß auf dem Boden auch 2 alte, seit dem Jahre 1892 nicht wieder geöffnete Koffer gefunden seien, die vermutlich sehr viel handschriftliches Material oder andere persönliche Erinnerungsstücke von Robert Franz enthalten.» Was aus diesem geheimnisvollen Koffern geworden ist, darüber schweigen die Akten[23].*»

"When in 1937 the town of Halle purchased the Handel House, they had already intended to erect rooms in commemoration of other musical personalities from Halle. The Second World War postponed the realisation of this plan, but did not prevent those responsible from acquiring objects from the estates of different Halloren composers like Scheidt, Reichardt, Türk, Loewe and Franz. In 1941 a contract was agreed in Wiesbaden with the surviving, but aged, daughter-in-law of Robert Franz, Margarethe Franz, on the acquisition of documents, furniture and other memorabilia. [...] Margarethe Franz died in December 1949, at the extreme age of almost ninety-six, and the conveyance of items, apart from some destroyed in the bombing, was not completed before the summer of 1950. The beneficiary of Margarethe Franz, a "Mr Peter Weber, offered in writing to the town of Halle additional available property of Robert Franz and stressed that two old trunks, which had not been opened again since 1892, had been found in the attic. They were thought to contain a great deal of handwritten material or other personal memorabilia belonging to Robert Franz." What became of these mysterious trunks is not known, as on this, the files say nothing."

---

[22] Archiv des Händel-Hauses in Halle, Ankaufsakten, unpag.
[23] Ibid.

Quite apart from the missing document legitimizing Franz's surname, or any memorabilia from Franz's trip to Italy in 1843, with only seventeen autograph copies extant of two hundred and seventy-nine solo songs, and no more than six of these being dated (Sasse, 1986 (34-36)), there is evidently still much material waiting to be found.

The future will surely know when the truth has waited long enough.

© Victoria Edge 2019

BIBLIOGRAPHY

Apthorp, William Foster, 1902, Higham Massachusetts, USA. *Fifty Songs by Robert Franz,* (Preface). Oliver Ditson Co., New York 1903.

Bethge, Robert, 1908, *Robert Franz Ein Lebensbild,* Verlag von Max Niemeyer, Halle a.S.

Robert **Franz** und Arnold freiherr **Senfft von Pilsach**, *Ein Briefwechsel 1861-1888,* 1907 Berlin, Verlag von Alexander Duncker. Reprinted by the University of California, 2017.

Gorrell, Lorraine, 1993. *The Nineteenth-Century German Lied,* Amadeus Press, Oregon, USA.

Henning, Iris, 2006, *Karl Wilhelm Osterwald, (1820-1887)*
www.hainichland.de/2006/09/26/karl-wilhelm-osterwald-1820-1887

Johnson, Graham, 2014, Yale University Press, New Haven USA. *Franz Schubert: The Complete Songs,* Volume Two. ISBN: 9780300112672

Krehbiel, H.E., 1906, Blue Hill, Maine USA. *Robert Franz and his Songs,* Biographical and Critical Essay, Schirmer, Franz Vocal Album, Vol. 1572.

Liszt, Franz, *Robert Franz,* 1872, F E C Leuckart, Leipzig, expanded from Liszt's articles in *Neuen Zeitschrift für Musik,* Vol 43, Nos. 22 and 23.

Mann, Thomas, 1913, *Der Tod in Venedig.* Berlin, S. Fischer Verlag.

Musketa, Dr Konstanze unter mitarbeit von Götz Traxdorf, Halle an der Saale 1993. *Robert Franz (1815-1892) Bericht über die wissenshaftliche Konferenz anläßlich seines 100. Todestages am 12. Und 24. Oktober 1992 in Halle (Saale).* Schriften des Händel-Hauses in Halle • 9.

Osterwald, Wilhelm, 1886, Leipzig. *Robert Franz Ein Lebensbild,* Verlag von Gebrüder Hug.

Pfordten, Dr Hermann Frhr. v.d., 1923, *Robert Franz,* Verlag von Quelle & Meyer in Leipzig.

Procházka, Rudolph Freiherrn, 1894, *Musiker-Biographien sechzehnter Band Robert Franz,* Reclam, Leipzig.

Sasse, Konrad, Halle an der Saale, 1986, *Beiträge zur Forschung über Leben und Werk von Robert Franz 1815-1892,* bearbeitet und herausgegeben von Edwin Werner. Schriften des Händel-Hauses in Halle • 4.

Waldmann, Dr. Wilhelm, 1895, *Robert Franz Gespräche aus zehn Jahren,* Leipzig, Breitkopf und Härtel.

Notes

Tempos and durations

The duration of each song is that from the companion recording - *Robert Franz: Gesammelte Osterwald Lieder und Gesänge (MPR106)*. We have not suggested tempi. Franz did not add any metronome marks to any of his songs and performers should always settle on the tempo they feel is appropriate for the song. Franz himself noted:

> «Meine Lieder lehnen den schablonenartigen Vortrag entschieden ab. Sie wollen mit künstlerischer Freiheit, die der Unmittelbarkeit poetischen Empfindens keinen Zwang anlegt, gesungen sein. Die Persönlichkeit der Reproduzenten muß überall durchscheinen und darf nicht von traditionellen Ausdrucksmitteln beeinträchtigt werden: allerdings eine hochgestellte Forderung, die hier unerläßlich ist. Damit soll nicht etwa der dramatischen Willkür Thür und Thor geöffnet werden, denn die Ausführung hat sich stets den Gesetzen lyrischen Vortrags unterzuordnen. Die beste Schranke bietet der Text, dessen poetischer Gehalt ausnahmslos meiner Auffassung zu Grunde liegt.»

"My songs decisively reject stereotypical performance. They want to be sung with artistic freedom, which places no constraints on the immediacy of the poetic feeling. The personality of the artist must shine through everywhere and not be marred by traditional means of expression: certainly, this asks a great deal, which here though is essential. In this way the flood-gates to dramatic capriciousness shall not be flung wide open, because the performance has to be at all times subject to the rules of lyrical presentation. In my opinion, the fundamental poetic content of the text always offers the best restraint."

Robert Franz und Arnold freiherr Senfft von Pilsach, *Ein Briefwechsel 1861-1888* (282-3), 1907 Berlin, Verlag von Alexander Duncker. Translation by Victoria Edge.

Range and tessitura

The range of each song is given in Scientific Pitch Notation (SPN) assuming Franz's preferred Mezzo-Soprano voice. C4 is middle C on a piano and C5, the octave above middle C.

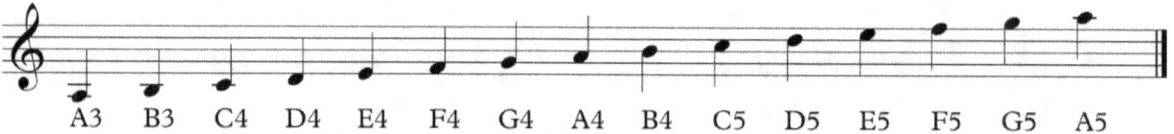

Tessitura is indicated by the 'median' (most common) note in the vocal line. A high median note indicates that the tessitura of the song lies high in the stated range.

Osterwald's Gedichte

Osterwald published the first edition of his *Gedichte* in 1848. This volume contained the poems for 39 of the 51 lieder set by Franz with the Lieder forming the second section after "Sagen und Sagenartiges" (Tales and Moralities). In this volume Osterwald extensively revised the 18 poems that had already between published as songs.

In the 'third' edition of Osterwald's *Gedichte* (1873), published by the song publisher; F E C Leuckart, the Lieder have pride of place as the 'Erstes Buch' and the poems for the remaining twelve songs appear for the first time as poems although all of them had already been published as songs. There does not seem to be an extant copy of a 'second' edition of Osterwald's *Gedichte.*

In the 1873 edition, Osterwald reversed many of the changes he made to the 18 poems published as songs prior to the 1848 edition of *Gedichte* to make the poems much closer to how they had first been published as songs. This may have been due to the popularity of the songs (some of which were published by F E C Leuckart) and the publisher wishing the poem versions to more closely match the songs. Alternatively, Osterwald may have felt that his first thoughts were indeed better.

What is of particular interest is where Osterwald assigned a different title to a poem from its song setting. The title and position as they appear in the 1873 edition of *Gedichte* is given, with the 1848 title also given where it differs.

Track Numbers

Disc and Track numbers refer to the companion MPR recording; *Robert Franz: Gesammelte Osterwald Lieder und Gesänge (MPR106),* where the songs have been arranged into four groups to correspond with the four seasons.

Ach wenn ich doch ein Immchen wär' - Op. 3 No. 6

Key:	F♯ major
Time signature:	3/8
Duration:	1'11"
Vocal range and median pitch:	E♯4-F♯5 (B4)
Title and Position in *Gedichte*:	Knabenwunsch (1848)
	Ach wenn ich doch ein Immchen wär (1873) (No. 2)
First edition publisher and year:	Breitkopf & Härtel, Liepzig, 1844
Track number on MPR CD:	Disc: 1, Track: 10

Ach wenn ich doch ein Immchen wär' | **Oh, were I but a little bee**

Ach wenn ich doch ein Immchen wär',
Frisch, flink und frei und klein und fein:
  An jedem süssen Blumenblatt,
  Tränk' ich im Frühlingsduft mich satt.

Wie wollt' ich saugen Tag und Nacht
An all der frischen Frühlingspracht.
  Husch! ging's zu allen Blumen hin,
  Sie wissen schon, dass ich es bin.

Die ganze, ganze Frühlingslust,
Sög' ich dann ein in meine Brust,
  Und hätt' ich ihn so ganz in mir,
  Den Frühling, Liebchen, brächt' ich dir.

Oh, were I but a little bee
bright, nimble and free and small and dainty.
  On every sweet petal
  in vernal fragrance I would drink my fill.

How I would wish to suckle day and night
on all the splendour of spring.
  Whoosh! I would go to all the flowers.
  They already know it is I.

The entire spring's joy
I would then draw into my breast,
  and were I to have it all within me,
  the spring, dearest, I would bring to you.

Kurzes Wiedersehen - Op. 4 No. 8

Key:	A minor
Time signature:	2/4
Duration:	2'28"
Vocal range and median pitch:	E4-F#5 (B4)
Title and Position in *Gedichte*:	Kurzes Wiedersehen (No. 93)
First edition publisher and year:	Kistner, Leipzig, 1845
Track number on MPR CD:	Disc: 2, Track: 10

Kurzes Wiedersehen

Ach! musstest du denn scheiden,
    Sobalde, so geschwind,
Und muss ich es denn leiden,
    Dass wir geschieden sind?
Da ich dich kaum empfangen
    Und drückte dir die Hand,
So warst du schon gegangen,
    Weit in ein fremdes Land.

Ach! ist solch' wiedersehen
    Ein Trost für langes Leid,
Wenn wir vonander gehen
    Nach also kurzer Zeit?

Nun fliegen mir und schweifen
    Die Augen auf und ab,
Ich kann es kaum begreifen,
    Dass ich Dich gesehen hab'.

Mir war es ob ich träume:
    Mai ward es noch einmal:
Es blühten noch einmal die Bäume,
    Es blühten die Rosen im Thal.

Und Du und ich wir stünden,
    Und freueten uns der Pracht,
Nun aber ist alles verschwunden
    Und Herbst da ich erwacht.

Brief Encounter

Oh, did you have to leave
so soon, so hastily?
And must I suffer
this separation?
No sooner had I greeted you
and taken your hand,
you were making your way
far off into a foreign land.

Ah! Is such a reunion
any recompense for this lengthy suffering,
if we simply part from one another
after such a short time?

Now your eyes avoid me and look elsewhere;
I can hardly grasp it,
that I have really seen you.

It was as if I were dreaming
that it was May once again,
the trees were in blossom and
the roses in the valley were blooming.

And you and I were standing
and delighting in such splendour –
but now I have awoken, everything has disappeared
and autumn is here.

Durch säuselnde Bäume - Op. 4 No. 9

Key:	E major
Time signature:	3/8
Duration:	1'13"
Vocal range and median pitch:	E4-F#5 (B4)
Title and Position in *Gedichte*:	Träume (No. 15)
First edition publisher and year:	Kistner, Leipzig, 1845
Track number on MPR CD:	Disc: 1, Track: 20

Durch säuselnde Bäume

Durch säuselnde Bäume
   Im Mondenschein,
Flattern die Träume
   Zum Fenster herein;
Regen der Schwingen
   Rauschend Gefieder,
Klingen und singen
   Die lieblichsten Lieder.

Ihr frohen Gesellen,
   Nur immer herein,
Schliesset den schnellen,
   Den luftigen Reihn:
Bis euch der Sonne
   Strahlen zerstreuen,
Soll selige Wonne
   Mein Herz erfreuen.

Aber den einen
   Von eurer Schaar,
Den schönsten der kleinen
   Mit lockigem Haar,
Lasset geschwinde
   Zurück sich schwingen,
Um meinem Kinde
   Viel Grüsse zu bringen.

Through murmuring trees

Through murmuring trees
in the moonlight,
dreams flutter
in through my window.
A stirring of the wings
of rustling plumage,
sounding and singing
the sweetest songs.

You cheerful companions
do enter in.
Close your rapid
airy ranks;
until the sun's rays
disperse you,
blessed joy
shall fill my heart.

But one of you
from this host,
the loveliest
with the curly hair,
have him fly back swiftly

to bring fond greetings to my sweet maid.

Herbstsorge - Op. 4 No. 10

Key:	C minor
Time signature:	2/4
Duration:	1'22"
Vocal range and median pitch:	C4-E♭5 (G4)
Title and Position in *Gedichte*:	Herbstsorge (No. 83)
First edition publisher and year:	Kistner, Leipzig, 1845
Track number on MPR CD:	Disc: 2, Track: 8

Herbstsorge

Gleich eines Herzens bangen Fieber-träumen,
   Langsam empor die schwarzen Nebel steigen:
   In Wald und Haide die Vöglein alle schweigen,
Das Laub fällt zitternd von den Bäumen.

Das schöne Licht des Sommers ist verglommen,
   Und durch die Luft zieht ein geheimes Schauern,
   Und alle schaun dem Flüchtling nach und trauern,
Als sollt' er nimmer wieder kommen.

Autumn Care

Like a heart's fearful feverish dream,
slowly the black clouds rise upwards.
In wood and moor the small birds are silent;
the autumn leaves fall trembling from the trees.

Summer's lovely light is dying
and through the air a secret shudder moves.
All watch the fugitive leave and they mourn,
as if he will never return.

Er kommt zurück, er bringt uns neue Lieder,	He does return, he brings us new songs.
Doch wird durch ihn die Angst auch fortbeschworen,	But does he assuage the fear that I have lost you – my only happiness?
Dass ich dich hab', mein einzig Glück verloren?	Alas, you have departed, never to return.
Denn ach! Du gingst und kehrst nicht wieder.	

Wanderlied - Op. 4 No. 11

Key:	B♭ major
Time signature:	6/8
Duration:	1'11"
Vocal range and median pitch:	F4-G5 (D5)
Title and Position in *Gedichte*:	Wanderlied (No. 25)
First edition publisher and year:	Kistner, Leipzig, 1845
Track number on MPR CD:	Disc: 1, Track: 16

Wanderlied

Und kommt der Frühling wieder her,
  Und wenn die Bäume treiben,
So kann ich nun und nimmermehr
  Nicht bleiben, nicht bleiben.

Ei komm du schöne Sommerzeit,
  Da sich die Vögel freien,
Und lustig sind, wenn's Blüthen schneit
  Im Maien, im Maien.

Dann schneid' ich mir vom grünsten Strauch
  Den Wanderstab im Hagen,
Und wand'r ich erst verlern' ich auch
  Das Klagen, das Klagen.

Und dass ich nie den Weg verlier',
  Und dass ich weiss zu reisen,
Das soll mein Kuss gar balde dir
  Beweisen, beweisen.

Song of the Wanderer

And when spring returns again,
and when the trees sprout,
then I can never ever remain.

Ha! Come you lovely summertime,
when birds mate
and are happy when the blossoms fall like snow
in May.

Then I will cut a walking staff from the greenest
shrub in the grove.
And once I'm hiking I shall forget all about
my complaining.

And very soon, my kiss shall prove to you that I
never lose the way, and know well the art of
travelling.

Ach dass du kamst - Op. 4 No. 12

Key:	G minor
Time signature:	2/4
Duration:	1'40"
Vocal range and median pitch:	D4-G5 (C5)
Title and Position in *Gedichte*:	Ach daß du kamst! (No. 82)
First edition publisher and year:	Kistner, Leipzig, 1845
Track number on MPR CD:	Disc: 2, Track: 13

Ach dass du kamst	**Oh that you came**

Ach dass du kamst, ach dass du kamst
   In Freuden einst gegangen,
Und mir mein arglos Herze nahmst
   Mit süssen Worten gefangen;

Und schmücktest mir das braune Haar
   Mit rothen Rosenkränzen,
Und liessest aus den Augen gar
   Viel tausend Lenze glänzen.

Der Lenz verblüht, der Lenz verblüht,
   Und nahm dich mit von hinnen,
Nun da die Sommersonne glüht,
   Ist mir todmüde zu sinnen.

O Liebe, morgenrother Strahl,
   Wie hast du mich betrogen
Und hast sobald mit schwarzer Qual
   Den Himmel mir bezogen!

Oh that you came, Oh that you once came
in joy
and captivated my innocent heart
with sweet words,

adorned my brown hair
with garlands of red roses
and bestowed upon me countless glances of
spring's radiance.

Spring has faded
and taken you with it.
Now the summer sun shines,
I am too weary even to think.

Oh love, rosy sunrise,
how you deceived me
and blackened my skies with dark torment!

Will über Nacht wohl durch das Thal - Op. 5 No. 4

Key:	C major
Time signature:	2/4
Duration:	1'41"
Vocal range and median pitch:	F♯4-G5 (C5)
Title and Position in *Gedichte*:	Kurzer Traum (No. 51)
First edition publisher and year:	Whistling, Leipzig, 1846
Track number on MPR CD:	Disc: 2, Track: 20

Will über Nacht wohl durch das Thal	**I so want to go overnight through the valley**

Will über Nacht wohl durch das Thal
   Von dannen gehn zur Liebsten schön,
Und nur ein einzig, einzig Mal
   Still unter ihrem Fester stehn....

Die schönsten Blumen pflanz' ich sacht,...
   Vergissnichtmein und Röselein,
Eh' noch die Sonn' und sie erwacht,...
   Dort unter ihrem Fenster ein.

Ach, armes Herz, was träumest du!
   Die Welt umher ist blüthenleer
Und Deine Liebe ging zur Ruh',
   Und keine Sonne weckt sie mehr.

I so want to go overnight through the valley
from here to my most beautiful beloved,
and just once
silently stand beneath her window.

The loveliest of flowers I will gently implant,
forget-me-nots and little roses,
before the sun rises and she awakes...
just underneath her window.

Ah, poor heart, what are you dreaming!
The world around us is empty of blossoms
and your love has gone to its rest,
and no sun awakens it anymore.

Ich lobe mir die Vögelein - Op. 5 No. 8

Key:	E-flat major
Time signature:	6/8
Duration:	1'24"
Vocal range and median pitch:	D4-G5 (B♭4)
Title and Position in *Gedichte*:	Der lustige Vogel (No. 1)
First edition publisher and year:	Whistling, Leipzig, 1846
Track number on MPR CD:	Disc: 1, Track: 18

Ich lobe mir die Vögelein

Ich lobe mir die Vögelein,
   Die auf den Zweigen springen,
Und um die Wett' Tag aus Tag ein
   Auf's allerschönste singen.

Sie fliegen hin, sie fliegen her,
   Als wären sie auf Reisen,
Und nimmer fällt es ihnen schwer,
   Ihr lustig Thun zu preisen.

Gott grüss' euch, traute Vögelein,
   Ich bin von eurer Sippe,
Und will ein lustiger Vogel sein,
   Wie ihr, mit Herz und Lippe.

Will singen frank und frei wie ihr,
   Und durch die Felder springen,
Behüt' uns Gott, dass nimmer wir
   Gerathen in arge Schlingen.

I cherish the little birds

I cherish the little birds,
hopping among the branches,
and in all weathers, day in, day out,
competing in song most beautifully.

Flying here and there
as if they were on a journey,
and they never find it hard
to praise their own jolly labours.

Greetings! Trusty little birds,
I am of your kind
and wish to be a happy bird
like you, with heart and voice.

I want to sing openly and freely like you
and hop through the fields.
God forbid that we ever get
caught in terrible snares.

Vergessen - Op. 5 No. 10

Key:	G♭ major
Time signature:	2/4
Duration:	1'28"
Vocal range and median pitch:	E♭4-E♭5 (G♭4)
Title and Position in *Gedichte*:	Vergessen (1848)
	Erinnerung (1873) (No. 54)
First edition publisher and year:	Whistling, Leipzig, 1846
Track number on MPR CD:	Disc: 2, Track: 21

Vergessen

O banger Traum, was flatterst du
   Mit schwarzem Flügel um mein Haupt?
Du hast mir, du, die ganze Ruh'
   Aus meinem Herzen wild geraubt.

Forgotten

Oh fearful dream, why are you fluttering around
in my head with black wings?
You have savagely robbed me of all my peace.

Ich träum': ich steh' am Baches Rand,
    Die Trauerweide hängt herein,
Die Quelle schwand, verdorrt – im Sand
    Sind all die blauen Vergissnicht-mein.

Vergessen, ach! vergessen sein
    Vom liebsten Herzen in der Welt,
Das ist allein die schwerste Pein,
    Die auf ein Menschenherze fällt.

I dream of standing at the edge of a stream,
the weeping willow hangs down,
but the well-spring has vanished, parched.
All the blue forget-me-nots are lying in the sand.

Forgotten, ah! To be forgotten
by the dearest heart in the entire world,
that alone is the worst pain
that can befall a human heart.

Die Liebe hat gelogen! - Op. 6 No. 4

Key:	B♭ minor
Time signature:	Common time
Duration:	1'40"
Vocal range and median pitch:	E♭4-G5 (B4)
Title and Position in *Gedichte*:	Wohin? (No. 75)
First edition publisher and year:	Whistling, Leipzig, 1846
Track number on MPR CD:	Disc: 2, Track: 14

Die Liebe hat gelogen!

Des Waldes Wipfel rauschen
    Unheimlich hin und her,
Die Vöglein schweigen und lauschen,
    Singt keines, keines mehr.

Was wölbst du noch die Bogen,
    Du stolzes Abendroth?
Die Liebe hat gelogen,
    Die Treu' ist todt, ist todt!

Die kleinen Blumen senken
    Wehmütiglich das Haupt,
Wenn sie des Tags gedenken,
    Der Alles mir geraubt.

Wie bleiche Blitze ziehen
    Mir Schmerzen durch den Sinn;
Ich möchte fliehen, fliehen,
    Und weiss doch nicht wohin?

Love has lied!

The tree-tops of the forest rustle
eerily to and fro.
The birds listen silently,
none sings anymore, none.

Proud sunset, why are your curves vaulting the
skies?

Love has lied,
fidelity is dead, is dead.

The small flowers
wistfully lower their heads,
when they think of the day
that robbed me of everything.

Like pallid lightning
pain is ripping through my senses,
I wish to flee
but do not know where.

Der Schnee ist zergangen - Op. 6 No. 5

Key:	E major
Time signature:	6/8
Duration:	1'10"
Vocal range and median pitch:	E4-G♯5 (B4)
Title and Position in *Gedichte*:	Im Frühling (No. 100)
First edition publisher and year:	Whistling, Leipzig, 1846
Track number on MPR CD:	Disc: 1, Track: 5

Der Schnee ist zergangen

Der Schnee ist zergangen,
   Der Winter ist fort, ist fort.
Nun Liebchen, nun lass dein Bangen,
   Ich halte mein Wort, mein Wort.

Der Lenz fliegt geschwinde,
   Ist da, wie zur Nacht ein Dieb,
Doch schneller als Frühlingswinde
   Fliegt Liebe zum Lieb.

Und eh' noch der Morgen
   Die Veilchen, die ersten, gegrüsst,
Sind all' deine bangen Sorgen,
   Hinweg schon geküsst, geküsst.

The snow has melted

The snow has melted,
winter has moved on.
Now dearest, stop your worrying,
I am keeping my word.

Spring flies quickly by,
is there like a thief in the night,
but quicker than the blusters of spring
love flies to love.

And even before the morning greets
the violets, the firstlings,
all your anxious cares
will already be kissed away.

Der junge Tag erwacht - Op. 7 No. 1

Key:	A♭ major
Time signature:	6/8
Duration:	2'07"
Vocal range and median pitch:	D4-F5 (C5)
Title and Position in *Gedichte*:	Frühe Klage (No. 22)
First edition publisher and year:	Whistling, Leipzig, 1846
Track number on MPR CD:	Disc: 2, Track: 5

Der junge Tag erwacht

Der junge Tag erwacht,
Der schöne Morgen lacht
   Und schüttelt sich die Locken,
   Wie Festgeläut der Glocken
Durch-bebt die Luft ein Klang
Mit lieblichem Gesang.

Durch meine Seele zieh'n
Die alten Melodien
   Aus meiner Kindheit Tagen,
   Wie wenn von ferne schlagen
Die Nachtigallen sacht
In einer Maiennacht.

Und in dem Herzen schwillt
Und aus dem Auge quillt
   Ein Bangen und Verlangen,
   Als wär' schon wieder gangen,
Nach dem sie kaum erwacht,
Der jungen Sonne Pracht.

The new day dawns

The new day dawns,
the lovely morning laughs,
and shakes its curly head
like ringing festival bells;
a sound penetrates the air
with its sweet song.

The old melodies from the days of my childhood
move through my soul.

As if from a distance,
the nightingales are softly singing
in a May night.

And my heart swells
and from my eyes well
fear and longing,
as if the young sun's splendour were already gone,
before it had hardly awoken.

Da die Stunde kam - Op. 7 No. 3

Key:	G minor
Time signature:	9/8
Duration:	1'53"
Vocal range and median pitch:	D4-F5 (C5)
Title and Position in *Gedichte*:	Wiederkehr (No. 99)
First edition publisher and year:	Whistling, Leipzig, 1846
Track number on MPR CD:	Disc: 2, Track: 4

Da die Stunde kam

Da die Stunde kam, dass ich Abschied nahm,
   Sah ich nicht den wunderschönen Mai,
Hab' nur eins gewusst, als ich wandern musst,
   Dass von dir ich ferne sei.

Sang und Blüthenduft schwebten durch die Luft,
   Doch an mir zog alle Lust vorbei:
Hab' nur eins gewusst, als ich wandern musst
   Dass von dir, ich ferne sei.

Nun ich widerkehr', fühl' ich nimmermehr
   Ob die Geißel schon der Winter schwingt...
Denn ich weiss es ja, dass die Stunde nah,
   Die zu dir mich wiederbringt.

When the time came

When the time came to take my leave,
I did not see wonderful May,
I knew only one thing; that I was compelled to wander,
to be far from you.

Song and floral fragrance were floating through the air,
but all pleasure passed me by.
All I knew was I had to move on
to be away from you.

Now upon my return, I don't even notice
if winter is already cracking its whip,
because I know it, yes, that the hour is nigh
which brings me to you again.

Treibt der Sommer seinen Rosen - Op. 8 No. 5

Key:	C major
Time signature:	2/4
Duration:	1'17"
Vocal range and median pitch:	G4-G6 (D6)
Title and Position in in *Gedichte*:	Im Sommer (No. 80)
First edition publisher and year:	Breitkopf & Härtel, Liepzig, 1846
Track number on MPR CD:	Disc: 2, Track: 17

Treibt der Sommer seinen Rosen

Treibt der Sommer seinen Rosen
   Gluth in's Angesicht hinauf,
Brechen auch in meinem Herzen
   Alle Wunden wieder auf.

Klagend irren meine Blicke
   Durch der Blumen bunte Schaar,
Ach, ich kann es nicht vergessen,
   Dass ich einst so glücklich war.

When summer makes the roses blush

When summer makes the roses
blush every wound in my heart opens once again.

Sorrowfully my glances
wander through the host of gay blossoms;
Oh, I cannot forget
that I was once so happy.

Gewitternacht - Op. 8 No. 6

Key:	E♭ minor
Time signature:	Common time
Duration:	3'56"
Vocal range and median pitch:	B♭3-G♭5 (B♭4)
Title and Position in *Gedichte*:	Gewitternacht (No. 33)
First edition publisher and year:	Breitkopf & Härtel, Liepzig, 1846
Track number on MPR CD:	Disc: 2, Track: 6

Gewitternacht

Grolle lauter, zürnend Gewitter,
   Sturmwind, rase, du wilder Geselle,
Öffne dem Blitz das Wolkengitter,
   Dass er die schwarze Nacht mir erhelle.
Tröstlich ist mir, O Himmel, dein Hadern:
Zweifel im Herzen, Zorn in den Adern,
   Bin ich von meinem Mädchen geschieden,
     Ohn' Kuss und Wort
     So ging ich fort
In die grollende Nacht und suche Frieden.

Weh! Auf ewig ist mir verloren
   Jenes selige Glück des Bundes,
Das ihr Auge mir zugeschworen
   Und der glühende Hauch des Mundes.
Träume der Jugend, wie seid ihr verflogen,
Falsch wie die Schwüre habt ihr gelogen!
   Schneidend fühl' ich durch's Herz mir beben
     Das Blitzeslicht:
       Sie liebt mich nicht!
Mein Herz ist gebrochen, was soll ich leben?

Grolle lauter, Gewitterstimme,
   Flammender Himmel, wild und vermessen
Lass mich eifern mit deinem Grimme,
   Lass die Kalte mich ewig vergessen!
Aber du schweigst, in säuselnden Regen
Wandelt dein Zorn sich Himmel in Segen.
   Thränen der Liebe, o rieselt nieder.
     Ach! ohne sie
       Genes' ich nie!
   Mädchen, Geliebte, liebe mich wieder!

Stormy Night

Rumble louder, wrathful, noisy, furious storm;
gale rage, you wild companion!
Open the barred clouds to lightning flashes that they
may light my way through the dark night.
To me, oh heaven, your quibbling
is comforting. Doubt in heart, rage in my veins,
I am parted from my girl –
with neither kiss nor word of farewell,

I went into the wrathful night in search of peace.

Alas! That blissful happiness of our bond is lost to me
forever,
which her eyes swore to me -
and the ardent breath of her mouth.
Dreams of youth, how you have faded away,
false like those vows have you lied!
I feel a lightning flash cut through my trembling heart.

She does not love me!
My heart is broken –why should I live?

Rumble louder, wrathful noisy voice of the storm,
flaming heaven! Wildly and boldly,
let me rail against your fury;
let me forget the Cold One forever!
But skies, you have fallen silent, in murmuring rain
your rage is transformed into a blessing.
Tears of love drizzle down.
Ah! Without her
I will never recover!
Maid, dearest, love me again!

Vom Berge - Op. 9 No. 5

Key:	G major
Time signature:	2/4
Duration:	1'34"
Vocal range and median pitch:	E4-G5 (B4)
Title and Position in *Gedichte*:	Vom Berge (No. 21)
First edition publisher and year:	F E C Leuckart, Leipzig, 1847
Track number on MPR CD:	Disc: 2, Track: 2

Vom Berge

Jetzt steh' ich auf der höchsten Höh',
    Und lug' in das Land hinein,
Ob ich nicht mein Herz allerliebste seh',
    Aber ach! Es kann nicht sein.

Wär's nicht zu weit, zu weit von hier
    Bis zu der Liebsten hin,
Wär' ich lange schon bei ihr,
    Der ich nun so ferne bin.

Sie sitzet wohl am Fernsterlein
    Und schauet hinaus in die Fern',
Und flüstert leis: „Vergiss nicht mein!"
    Lieber Schatz, ich käme gern.

Als die erste Frühlingssonne schien,
    Zog ich aus in den jungen März;
Wenn die Vögel in den Mittag zieh'n,
    Komm' ich an dein warmes Herz.

From the Mountain

Now I stand on the highest peak
and peer into the landscape;
might I not see my heart's desire –
but alas! It cannot be.

Were it not too far, too far from here
to my beloved,
I would have been with her long since
and not now so far away.

She is probably seated at her little window,
looking out into the distance
and whispering softly, "Forget me not!"
My treasure, I would gladly come.

When the first spring sun shone
I strode out into early March.
When the birds fly south,
I shall return to your warm heart.

Und die Rosen, die prangen - Op. 10 No. 5

Key:	C minor
Time signature:	3/8
Duration:	1'05"
Vocal range and median pitch:	C4-G5 (A4)
Title and Position in *Gedichte*:	Einsame Trauer (No. 57)
First edition publisher and year:	Whistling, Leipzig, 1850
Track number on MPR CD:	Disc: 2, Track: 18

Und die Rosen, die prangen

Und die Rosen, die prangen,
    Drüber hin fährt der Wind,
Und die Lust ist vergangen
    Fast eh' sie beginnt.

And the roses flourish resplendent

And the roses flourish resplendent,
the wind wafts over them;
and joy is a thing of the past,
before it even begins;

Und die Vöglein, die singen,	and the small birds sing,
Und die Luft, die verweht's,	and the breezes die down.
Durch die Welt geht ein Klingen,	Through the world sounds a ringing
Und Keiner versteht's.	that no one understands.
Und die Sterne, die scheinen	And the stars shine so brightly
So hell durch die Nacht,	through the night.
Ich aber muss weinen	Among all this splendour, I, however, must weep.
Inmitten der Pracht.	

Umsonst - Op. 10 No. 6

Key:	D major
Time signature:	2/4
Duration:	1'13"
Vocal range and median pitch:	F4-E5 (A4)
Title and Position in *Gedichte*:	Umsonst (No. 53)
First edition publisher and year:	Whistling, Leipzig, 1850
Track number on MPR CD:	Disc: 2, Track: 24

Umsonst — **In Vain**

Des Waldes Sänger singen,	The forest's minstrels sing,
Die rothe Rose blüht,	the red rose blooms.
Die Quellen rauschen und springen,	The springs gurgle and leap;
Es ist das alte Lied.	it is an ancient song.
Das klingt und singt so selig	It sounds, and sings so blissfully
Vom seligen, lieblichen Mai,	of blessed lovely May –
Und machet mich doch nicht fröhlich,	and yet it does not make me happy,
Die lustige Melodei.	this cheerful melody.

Im Mai (Nun grünt der Berg) - Op. 11 No. 3

Key:	D♭ major
Time signature:	2/4
Duration:	2'20"
Vocal range and median pitch:	D♭4-G♭5 (C5)
Title and Position in *Gedichte*:	Das schönste Lob (No. 89)
First edition publisher and year:	Stern & Co, Berlin, 1847
Track number on MPR CD:	Disc: 1, Track: 3

Im Mai — **In May**

Nun grünt der Berg, nun grünt das Thal	Now the hills and vales are verdant
In Maienlust und Duft,	in May's delight and fragrance;
Und Vogelsang und Sonnenstrahl	and bird-song and sun-beams
Wogt durch die linde Luft.	surge through the mild air.

Was Leben hat, das lobt den Mai,	All living things commend May
In Blühten und Gesang;	in blossom and song.
Komm' süsses Lieb, das nicht uns zwei	Come sweet lover, so spring does not find the two
Der Frühling finde krank.	of us out of sorts.
Die liebste Ehr', die ihm geschieht	The greatest honour paid to spring
Zu dieser schönen Zeit,	at this beautiful time of year
Ist doch wenn Aug' in Auge sieht	is, after all, when eyes meet
Voll stiller Seligkeit.	full of silent bliss.

Im Sommer - Op. 11 No. 4

Key:	A♭ major
Time signature:	2/4
Duration:	2'11"
Vocal range and median pitch:	E♭4-F5 (B♭4)
Title and Position in *Gedichte*:	Im Sommer (No. 107)
First edition publisher and year:	Stern & Co, Berlin, 1847
Track number on MPR CD:	Disc: 1, Track: 19

Im Sommer	**In the Summer**
Da der Sommer kommen ist,	Since summer has arrived
Blüthen auszustreuen,	to scatter its blossoms,
Will ich in der kurzen Frist	I will, in that brief time,
Deiner, die du schöner bist,	delight in you, who are even lovelier,
Mich von Herzen freuen.	with all my heart.
Mich erfüllt mit süsser Ruh'	Your blessed presence fills me with sweet peace;
Deine holde Nähe,	
Flüsterst du mir heimlich zu	if you but secretly whisper to me
Nur ein leises, liebes; Du ...	one soft, loving, "You...",
Schwindet jedes Wehe.	all my pain will vanish.
Wie ein Augenblick verrinnt,	As a moment passes,
Muss der Lenz verschweben,	so must spring.
Doch die Ewigkeit beginnt,	But eternity only begins,
Wo das Herz ein Herz gewinnt,	when one heart wins another,
Sterbend erst zu leben.	dying and becoming.
Wenn an deinem Angesicht	When my glance rests on your face,
Meine Blicke hängen,	
Weiss ich ob ich lebe, nicht	I know I am alive and not
Träum', ich wäre leicht und licht ...	dreaming; as if I have softly and gently
Schon von hinnen gangen.	vanished into the wide blue yonder.

Und welche Rose Blüthen treibt - Op. 12 No. 1

Key:	A major
Time signature:	2/4
Duration:	2'05"
Vocal range and median pitch:	E4-F#5 (B4)
Title and Position in *Gedichte*:	Und welche Rose Blüthen treibt (No. 81)
First edition publisher and year:	André, Offenbach am Main, 1851
Track number on MPR CD:	Disc: 1, Track: 17

Und welche Rose Blüthen treibt — **And whichever rose comes into bud**

Und welche Rose Blüthen treibt,
   Und welches Herze freit,
Die frei'n und blühen beide
   Zur rechten Sommerzeit.
O blühe Röslein, blühe,
O glühe Mägdlein, glühe,
   Dieweil es eben Zeit.

Und wer die Rose pflücken will,
   Pflückt sie zur rechten Stund',
Und wen's geliebt zu küssen,
   Der küsst auf rothen Mund.
O pflücke, Knabe, pflücke,
Und Lipp' an Lippe drücke,
   Es ist jetzt an der Stund'.

Es weht ein kalter Winterwind,
   Wohl über den Blüthenhag,
Die Rosen sind verblühet,
   Eh's Einer denken mag:
Drum herzt sein Lieb von Herzen,
Wer nicht will Zeit verscherzen
   Am schönen Sommertag.

And whichever rose comes into bud,
and whichever heart woos,
both bloom and court
best in the summertime.
Oh bloom little rose, bloom,
oh glow mistress, glow,
while the time is ripe.

And whoever wishes to pluck
the rose, pluck at the right moment,
and whoever loves to kiss,
kisses a red mouth.
Oh pluck lad, pluck
and press lip on lip,
now is the time.

A chill winter wind blows
hard over the flowery grove.
The roses are faded
before you know it.
Therefore, unless you wish to forfeit your chance,
embrace your love with all your heart
on a lovely summer's day.

Um Mitternacht - Op. 16 No. 6

Key:	D♭ major
Time signature:	2/4
Duration:	3'19"
Vocal range and median pitch:	D♭4-G5 (C5)
Title and Position in *Gedichte*:	Um Mitternacht (No. 24)
First edition publisher and year:	Whistling, Leipzig, 1852
Track number on MPR CD:	Disc: 1, Track: 7

Um Mitternacht

Um Mitternacht
Ruht die ganze Erde nun;
Doch heimliche, stille Liebe wacht –
Wann könnte die Liebe ruh'n?
Darf sie am liebsten Herzen nicht weilen,
Muss sie auf Sturmes Flügeln eilen,
Kann nicht rasten, muss jagen und wagen,
Jauchzen und klagen,
Und sie wandert verstohlen und sacht –
Um Mitternacht.

Um Mitternacht beim Sternenglanz
Schwingt vom Lager sich empor
Zu heimlicher Lust, zum Elfentanz
Der nächtliche Geisterchor.
Nicht der Gestorbenen Schatten und Schemen,
Die um verlorene Herzen sich grämen,
Nein, die lebendige, liebende Seele
Sucht, was ihr fehle,
Sucht und findet und jubelt und lacht
Um Mitternacht.

Um Mitternacht im heißen Traum
Kann nicht ruh'n die Seele mir,
Sie fliegt auf der Wolken gold'nem Saum,
Will fliegen, mein Kind, zu dir.
Oft schon sind sie, die neckischen Jungen,
Meine Gedanken zu dir gedrungen,
Um mir von deinem rosigen Munde
Himmlische Kunde
Küssend zu rauben verstohlen und sacht
Um Mitternacht.

At Midnight

At Midnight
now the whole earth rests.
But secret, silent love keeps watch.
When can love rest?
If it may not tarry with its dearest heart
then it must hurry away on the wings of a storm;
it cannot rest, it must hunt and venture,
exult and lament,
and it wanders furtively and softly
at midnight.

At starlit midnight,
soaring upwards from its resting place
to secret pleasure; to the elfin dance,
comes the nightly chorus of spirits.
Not the shades and spectres of the departed,
which grieve after lost loves;
no, the living, loving soul
seeks what it lacks,
seeks and finds and rejoices with laughter
at midnight.

At midnight in ardent dreams
my soul cannot rest.
It flies on the golden edge of clouds;
it means to fly to you my child.
How often have my thoughts, those cheeky boys,
intruded upon you,
that they may with a kiss, softly and furtively steal
divine words from your rosy lips

at midnight.

Ständchen - Op. 17 No. 2

Key:	B major
Time signature:	2/4
Duration:	1'29"
Vocal range and median pitch:	D♯4-F♯5 (B4)
Title and Position in *Gedichte*:	Heimlicher Gruß (No. 9)
First edition publisher and year:	Whistling, Leipzig, 1853
Track number on MPR CD:	Disc: 1, Track: 2

Ständchen

Der Mond ist schlafen gegangen,
Die Sterne blinzeln blind,
Als ob sie müde sind
Von allem Funkeln und Prangen.
Und vor dem Fenster leise
Säuselt so lieb und lind
Ein frischer Frühlingswind;
Ich wünsch' ihm gute Reise.

Serenade

The moon has gone to sleep,
the stars blink blindly.
As though they are weary
of all their sparkling resplendence.
And at my window
a fresh spring breeze gently murmurs so kindly and mildly;
I wish it a good journey.

Und hörst du's sachte pochen:
  „Gute Nacht, gute nacht, mein Kind!"
  Dich grüsst der Frühlingswind,
Er hat es mir versprochen.
	And if you hear it gently tapping,
	  "Good night, good night my child!"
	  It is the spring breeze greeting you,
	just as it promised me.

Im Frühling - Op. 17 No. 5

Key:	A minor
Time signature:	2/4
Duration:	1'46"
Vocal range and median pitch:	C4-G5 (A4)
Title and Position in *Gedichte*:	Frühlingsdämmerung (No. 7)
First edition publisher and year:	Whistling, Leipzig, 1853
Track number on MPR CD:	Disc: 1, Track: 6

Im Frühling

In Spring

Im Grase lieg' ich manche Stunde
  Und sonne mich im Frühlingslicht;
Die Augen schweifen in die Runde,
  Warum, wohin? ich weiss es nicht.
	For many an hour I've been lying in the grass
	  sunbathing in the bright spring;
	my gaze wanders all around me –
	  why, to where? I do not know.

Ein Blümchen pflück' ich hin und wieder
  Und steck' es träumend an die Brust;
Horch' auf der Vögel süsse Lieder,
  Doch fehlt zum singen mir die Lust.
	Now and again I pick a little flower
	  and place it dreamily on my breast.
	Hear the sweet birdsong!
	But I don't feel like singing.

Und wenn die Wolken blau und blauer
  In lichter Wonne sich verweh'n,
so überkommt's mir fast wie Trauer
  Und nimmer weiss ich's zu versteh'n.
	And as the clouds disperse with bright joy into the blue,
	I am overcome by a feeling almost like grief
	and cannot begin to understand it.

Ein Immchen summt in stetem Kreise
  Wie'n altes Lied in meiner Näh',
wenn es mich stäche leise, leise,
  Vielleicht! ich wüsste dann mein Weh!
	A little bee hums as it circles,
	like an old melody close by –
	if it stung me, ever so gently –
	perhaps! I'd know what ails me then!

Nun hat das Leid ein Ende - Op. 18 No. 3

Key:	B♭ major
Time signature:	2/4
Duration:	1'39"
Vocal range and median pitch:	D4-G5 (B♭4)
Title and Position in *Gedichte*:	Mit leiser Bitte (No. 31)
First edition publisher and year:	Whistling, Leipzig, 1853
Track number on MPR CD:	Disc: 1, Track: 9

Nun hat das Leid ein Ende

Nun hat das Leid ein Ende,
   Der Frühling kommt gezogen
Und mit ihm ist behende
   Die Lieb' herbei geflogen.

Sie wird sich bald, die lose,
   Im grünen Busch verstecken,
Und die verschlaf'ne Rose
   Zum Leben auferwecken.

Und blüht die Rose wieder,
   Dann hat sie leichtes Siegen,
Wenn lustig auf und nieder
   Die gold'nen Wünsche fliegen.

Doch wirst du meine Schritte,
   Du Liebesfrühling, segnen,
Wenn ich mit leiser Bitte
   Ihr suche zu begegnen.

Now Sorrow has an End

Now sorrow has an end,
Spring has arrived
and with it, love flies in and descends.

It will soon hide itself mischievously
in a green bush
and awaken the sleepy rose to life.

And when the rose blooms again,
it will have an easy victory,
when happily up and down
the golden wishes fly.

But will you bless my steps,
you blissful spring,
when I, with soft entreaty,
seek to encounter it?

Abends - Op. 20 No. 4

Key:	D♭ major
Time signature:	2/4
Duration:	2'04"
Vocal range and median pitch:	D♭4-G5 (A♭4)
Title and Position in *Gedichte*:	Nicht mehr allein (No. 32)
First edition publisher and year:	Whistling, Leipzig, 1854
Track number on MPR CD:	Disc: 2, Track: 26

Abends

Der Tag beginnt zu dunkeln,
   Die Sonne geht zur Ruh',
Die bleichen Sterne funkeln
   Den Scheidegruss ihr zu.

Der Mond wirft mir in's Zimmer
   Ein lächelnd Licht hinein,
Als früg' er: bist du immer,
   Geselle, so allein!

Und ein geheimes Klagen
   Mein Herz zur Ruh' beschwört,
Als hätte es zu schlagen
   Schon lange aufgehört.

Da klingen Frühlingslieder,
   Da, Mädchen, denk' ich dein,
Und lebe selig wieder,
   Und bin nicht mehr allein.

In the Evening

Darkness begins to descend on the day,
the sun goes to its rest,
and the pale stars flash
their parting shot to her.

The moon throws its smiling light into my room,

as if it were asking, are you always so alone my friend?

And a secret lament
charms my heart to sleep
as if it had long since given up beating.

But spring songs resound,
then Maiden, I think of you,
and blissfully live again,
and am no longer alone.

Verlass' mich nicht! - Op. 21 No. 6

Key:	E♭ major
Time signature:	Common time
Duration:	1'42"
Vocal range and median pitch:	C4-A♭5 (B4)
Title and Position in *Gedichte*:	Die Schwalbe zieht (1848)
	Verlass' mich nicht (1873) (No. 47)
First edition publisher and year:	Whistling, Leipzig, 1854
Track number on MPR CD:	Disc: 2, Track: 9

Verlass' mich nicht!

Die Schwalbe zieht, der Sommer flieht,
    Und Alles will sich trennen,
Ich weiss nicht mehr, wie mir geschieht,
    Und meine Sinne brennen.
Verlass' mich nicht, verlass' mich nicht,
    Wenn alle Freuden eilen,
Und lass' mein zagend Angesicht
    An deinem Herzen weilen.

O zieh' nicht in die kalte Welt,
    Nicht in die Welt der Schlangen,
So lang' ein warmer Arm dich hält
    Mit sanftem Druck umfangen:
Verlass' mich nicht, verlass' mich nicht,
    Und lass mich nicht verderben.
Dich sehen ist Leben, Lieb' und Licht,
    Und Dich verlieren Sterben.

Ach! Nimmer rufest Du zurück
    Was einmal Dir entschwunden,
Denn leichte Schwingen hat das Glück
    Und weilet kurze Stunden:
Verlass' mich nicht, verlass' mich nicht,
    O Gott! In diesen Tagen,
Da kalter Tod die Blumen bricht
    Im Herzen und im Hagen.

Do not forsake me!

The swallows fly away, summer
with them and everything is about to depart.
I no longer know how this has happened to me
and my senses are burning.
Do not forsake me; do not forsake me
when all joy hastens away;
but let my anxious face rest a moment
on your breast.

Oh do not go out into the cold world,
into the world of serpents,
whilst warm arms can gently hold you
in a firm embrace.
Do not forsake me, do not forsake me
and do not let me perish.
Seeing you is life, love and light,
and losing you is death.

Oh, you can never reclaim
what has once escaped you,
for happiness has light wings
and does not tarry long.
Do not forsake me; do not forsake me,
Oh God, at this time,
since cold death breaks the flowers
in my heart and in the groves.

Frühe Klage - Op. 22 No. 4

Key:	G♭ major
Time signature:	Common time
Duration:	2'22"
Vocal range and median pitch:	D4-F5 (B♭4)
Title and Position in *Gedichte*:	Vorbei! (No. 78)
First edition publisher and year:	Senff, Leipzig, 1855
Track number on MPR CD:	Disc: 2, Track: 23

Frühe Klage

Aus der Ferne schallen Gesänge,
Froh von zittern der Luft gewiegt;
Müsset verwehen, liebliche Klänge,
Luftig und leicht wie die Jugend verfliegt.

Kränze im frischen Frühling gewunden,
Welken, noch ehe der Mai verblüht;
Ach! Und ehe der Lenz geschwunden,
Schleichet die Sorge zum jungen Gemüth.

Zieht vorüber, frohe Lieder,
Macht mir das Herze nicht enge, nicht bang,
Alter Zeiten gemahnt ihr mich wieder –
Leise verhallend schwinde der Klang.

Early Lament

From a distance songs resound,
happily rocked by the trembling of the wind.
They must die down, lovely sounds,
airily and lightly as youth flies.

Garlands wound in early spring
wither, even before May is out.
Ah, and before spring has vanished,
cares creep into my youthful spirit.

Move on happy songs;
make my heart neither closed nor afraid.
You remind me again of old times -
may the resounding tune softly fade away.

Im Mai (Musst nicht allein im Freien) - Op. 22 No. 5

Key:	A♭ major
Time signature:	2/4
Duration:	1'28"
Vocal range and median pitch:	E♭4-G5 (B♭4)
Title and Position in *Gedichte*:	Im Mai (No. 102)
First edition publisher and year:	Senff, Leipzig, 1855
Track number on MPR CD:	Disc: 1, Track: 8

Im Mai

Musst nicht allein im Freien,
   Selbander musst du gehn,
Dann ist's im schönen Maien
   Noch eins, noch eins so schön.

Die Blumen, die du pflückest,
   Zerstreuet nicht der Wind,
Wenn du mit ihnen schmückest
   Ein liebes, liebes Kind.

Und wenn der Maie bliebe
   Die ganze Sommerzeit,
Bringt er dir nicht die Liebe,
   Wird er dir balde leid.

Doch hast du sie gefunden,
   Mag's blüh'n dann oder schnei'n,
Dann ist zu allen Stunden
   Ein ganzer Frühling dein.

In May

Do not venture out alone –
you must go in pairs,
because in May
it is twice as lovely.

The flowers that you pick
are not scattered by the wind
when you adorn
a lovely child with them.

And if May were to remain
all summer long
and not bring you love,
you would soon tire of it.

But if you have found it,
come blossoms or snow,
a perpetual spring will be forever yours.

Wenn ich's nur wüsste! - Op. 26 No. 1

Key:	D minor
Time signature:	2/4
Duration:	1'08"
Vocal range and median pitch:	D4-F5 (B4)
Title and Position in *Gedichte*:	Wenn ich's nur wüßte (No. 43)
First edition publisher and year:	Whistling, Leipzig, 1856
Track number on MPR CD:	Disc: 2, Track: 1

Wenn ich's nur wüsste!

Vor meinem Fenster regt
Die alte Linde
Das dunkle Haupt, bewegt
Vom Abendwinde.

O Linde, treuer Baum,
Was soll dein Schütteln?
Willst du aus süssem Traum
Mein Herze rütteln?

Ach hin ja hin und her!
Wenn ich's nur wüsste,
Ob er so immer wär'
Da er mich küsste!

If Only I Knew!

The old lime tree stirs outside my window,

its dark head moving
with the evening breeze.

Oh faithful lime tree,
why are you shaking?
Do you want to jolt my heart out of its sweet dream?

Oh, to and fro;
if only I knew
whether he has stayed constant –
since he kissed me!

Lieber Schatz, sei wieder gut mir - Op. 26 No. 2

Key:	B♭ major
Time signature:	3/4
Duration:	1'17"
Vocal range and median pitch:	D4-F5 (B♭4)
Title and Position in *Gedichte*:	In dem Dornbusch (No. 41)
First edition publisher and year:	Whistling, Leipzig, 1856
Track number on MPR CD:	Disc: 1, Track: 21

Lieber Schatz, sei wieder gut mir

In dem Dornbusch
Blüht ein Röslein,
Ist ein' Lust es anzuseh'n!
Wollt' es pflücken,
Mich zu schmücken,
Doch der Dorn lässt's nicht gescheh'n.

Sang ein Vöglein
In den Lüften,
Klang der Sang süss in's Gemüth:
„Willst du brechen, lass dich stechen,
Ohne Dorn kein Röslein blüht."

Dearest Sweetheart, be nice to me again

In the thorny bush
grows a little rose,
it's a delight to behold!
I wanted to pluck it
to adorn myself,
but its thorns won't let that happen.

A little bird sang
in the skies,
its song sounded so sweet-natured:
"if you want to break it, just let it prick you –
a rose cannot bloom without thorns!"

Lieber Schatz, sei	Dearest sweetheart,
Wieder gut mir,	be nice to me again,
Lieber Schatz, leg ab dein' Zorn:	my darling don't be cross,
Immer Schmollen,	always sulking,
Immer Grollen,	always moaning,
Für ein' Ros' wär's zu viel Dorn!	that would be far too many thorns for any rose!

Vergiss mein nicht! - Op. 26 No. 3

Key:	A major
Time signature:	2/4
Duration:	1'42"
Vocal range and median pitch:	E4-F♯5 (B4)
Title and Position in *Gedichte*:	Vergißmeinnicht (No. 84)
First edition publisher and year:	Whistling, Leipzig, 1856
Track number on MPR CD:	Disc: 2, Track: 3

Vergiss mein nicht! | **Forget me not!**

Den Strauss den sie gewunden
Zur schönsten aller Stunden
  Im schönen Mai zu mal,
  Küss ich viel tausend, mal.

The posy she tied
at the loveliest time
in that beautiful May,
I kiss many thousand times.

Ob Freud' ob Leid ihn feuchtet,
Wenn er von Thränen leuchtet
  An meinem Angesicht –
  Ich weiss es selber nicht.

If joy, if sorrow dampens it
when it lights up my face with tears,
I do not know myself.

Wohl nagt mit jedem Tage
Am Herzen mir die Klage
  Mit bösem Gift getränkt:
  Dass mein sie nicht gedenkt.

How, with each day,
the plaint gnaws at my heart,
soaked with the evil poison –
that she does not think of me.

Doch in der Thräne Schimmer
Der blüh'nde Strauss noch immer
  Wie sonst statt ihrer spricht:
  Vergiss, vergiss mein nicht!

But in the gleam of tears,
the blossoming posy still,
as if it were she, speaks:
forget – forget me not!

Schöner Mai, bist über Nacht - Op. 30 No. 4

Key:	C major
Time signature:	¾
Duration:	53"
Vocal range and median pitch:	F♯4-G5 (C5)
Title and Position in *Gedichte*:	Nachruf (No. 76)
First edition publisher and year:	Kistner, Leipzig, 1857
Track number on MPR CD:	Disc: 2, Track: 19

Schöner Mai, bist über Nacht

Schöner Mai, bist über Nacht
   Wie ein Traum davon geflogen
Und die Lust, die du gebracht,
   Ist an mir vorbei gezogen.

Alle Blumen sind verblüht,
   Die ich mir zum Kranz erkoren,
Und mein Herz, das heisser glüht,
   Sagt mir dass es mehr verloren.

Leise klagt mit süssem Klang,
   Nachtigall dein frühes Scheiden,
Und ich weiss nicht, bringt ihr Sang,
   Hoffnung oder tief'res Leiden.

Lovely May, overnight

Lovely May, overnight
you have flown away, like a dream,
and the joy that you brought
has now passed me by.

The flowers, which I chose for my garland, have all faded,
and my ardent heart
tells me that it has lost far more.

The nightingale's sad song softly mourns your early departure,
and I do not know if her song
brings hope or even deeper sorrow.

Dort unter'm Lindenbaume - Op. 31 No. 1

Key:	D major
Time signature:	Common time
Duration:	1'32"
Vocal range and median pitch:	A3-E5 (A4)
Title and Position in *Gedichte*:	Nachklingen (No. 103)
First edition publisher and year:	Senff, Leipzig, 1858
Track number on MPR CD:	Disc: 2, Track: 22

Dort unter'm Lindenbaume

Dort unter'm Lindenbaume
   In linder Sommernacht,
Hab' ich im süssen Traume,
   Süss Liebchen Dein gedacht.
Und als ich rief im Traume
   Den lieben Namen Dein,
Da rauschten im Lindenbaume
   Viel süsse Melodein.

Die goldnen Äste klangen
   Gar wundersamen Klang,
Die goldnen Vöglein sangen
   Gar wundersamen Sang.
Nun bin ich von dem Singen
   Erwacht im Morgenschein,
Und hör' ich immer klingen
   Den liebsten Namen Dein.

There under the lime tree

There under the lime tree
on a balmy summer's night,
in a sweet dream I thought of you dearest sweetheart.
And as I called out your dear name in my dream,

so murmured in the lime tree
many sweet melodies.

The golden branches made
such a wondrous sound,
the golden birds sang
quite wondrous songs.
Now I have awoken from that singing
in the morning light
and I hear, still resounding,
that dearest name – yours.

Ade denn, du stolze! - Op. 31 No. 2

Key:	E-flat major
Time signature:	2/4
Duration:	1'33"
Vocal range and median pitch:	D4-G5 (B♭4)
Title and Position in *Gedichte*:	Ade denn, du stolze (No. 60)
First edition publisher and year:	Senff, Leipzig, 1858
Track number on MPR CD:	Disc: 1, Track: 22

Ade denn, du stolze!

Ade denn, du stolze
  Blitzaugige Magd,
Du willst mich nicht haben,
  Du hast mir's gesagt -
Wär's gern noch geblieben,
  Im Land hier ist's schön –
Doch du willst mich nicht haben,
  So muss ich wohl gehn.

Doch sag' ich Ade nicht
  Auf Nimmermehr sehn,
Wer weiss, ei wer weiss, wie
  Die Wege noch gehn!
Dein Stolz kann sich legen,
  Du hörest mich an –
Doch du willst mich nicht haben,
  So geh' ich von dann.

Und ein Blitzmädel bist doch
  Und bleibst es fürwahr!
Werd' nimmer vergessen
  Dein schwarzbraunes Haar,
Dein' Wangen, dein Mündlein
  Zum küssen so schön –
Doch du willst mich nicht haben,
  So muss ich wohl gehn.

Farewell then, you haughty maid!

Farewell then,
you maid with flashing eyes,
you don't want me,
you've told me so;
I would gladly have stayed-
it's beautiful here in the countryside,
but you won't have me,
so I really must go.

But I don't say farewell
never to see you again,
for who knows, Oh who knows
what direction our paths will take!
Your pride can abate,
just hear me out,
but you won't have me,
so I take my leave.

Yet you are still a sparkling girl forsooth!

I shall never forget
your black-brown hair,
 your cheeks, your little mouth –
so lovely for kissing –
but you won't have me,
so I should probably go….

Die Harrende - Op. 35 No. 1

Key:	D major
Time signature:	2/4
Duration:	1'22"
Vocal range and median pitch:	D4-F♯5 (B4)
Title and Position in *Gedichte*:	Die Harrende (No. 27)
First edition publisher and year:	F E C Leuckart, Breslau, 1861
Track number on MPR CD:	Disc: 1, Track: 14

Die Harrende

Hör' ich ein Vöglein singen,
   So stimm' ich sacht mit ein,
Und hätte ich seine Schwingen,
   Ich bliebe nicht allein.

Er hat mir nicht versprochen
   Die frohe Wiederkehr,
Doch sagt mein Herzenspochen:
   Er bleibt nicht lange mehr.

Das ist ein Blüh'n und Prangen
   Da draussen in der Welt,
Als wäre nun alles Bangen
   Auf ewig eingestellt.

In's Herz wie Lenzgeläute
   Zieht lachend die Hoffnung ein:
Noch heute wird er, noch heute
   In meinen Armen sein.

She Awaits

If I hear a little bird sing,
   then I join in softly,
and if I had its wings,
   I would not remain alone.

He made no promises
   of a happy return,
but my beating heart tells me
   he won't stay away much longer.

What a splendid show of blossoms
   out there in the world,
as if all worry had been brought to an end.

Hope moves into my heart
with the laughing sound of chiming spring bells.
He'll be in my arms today for sure.

Aufbruch - Op. 35 No. 6

Key:	A♭ major
Time signature:	6/8
Duration:	1'27"
Vocal range and median pitch:	C4-A♭5 (C5)
Title and Position in *Gedichte*:	Aufbruch (No. 28)
First edition publisher and year:	F E C Leuckart, Breslau, 1861
Track number on MPR CD:	Disc: 1, Track: 1

Aufbruch

Die Lüfte werden heller,
   Die schwarzen Wolken flieh'n,
Mein Herz schlägt schneller und schneller,
   Möchte von hinnen zieh'n.

Hinaus in die weite, freie,
   In die freie, weite Welt,
Dort wo der grüne Maie
   Sein schönstes Lager hält.

Wer giebt mir das Geleite!
   Der linde West soll's sein,
Der weiss wohin ich schreite,
   Doch weiss er's nicht allein.

Noch Eine weiss es, noch Eine,
   O Frühlingslüfte weht,
Wandelt die Welt zum Raine,
   Auf dem's zu der Liebsten geht.

Departure

The skies become brighter,
the black clouds flee,
my heart beats faster and faster,
I would like to leave this place.

Out into the wide, free –
into the free, wide world.
There, where vernal May
keeps its most beautiful sleeping place.

Who will accompany me!
The balmy west wind it shall be.
It knows to where my steps will take me,
but it is not the only one who knows.

One other knows it, she,
Oh spring breezes waft,
travels the world to its margins,
to those which lead to my beloved.

Erster Verlust - Op. 36 No. 2

Key:	E minor
Time signature:	6/8
Duration:	1'52"
Vocal range and median pitch:	B♭3-F♯5 (B4)
Title and Position in *Gedichte*:	Des Mädchens Klage (No. 14)
First edition publisher and year:	F E C Leuckart, Breslau, 1862
Track number on MPR CD:	Disc: 2, Track: 15

Erster Verlust

Gestern hielt er mich im Arme
Und mit liebeglühendem Munde
Küsst er mir von Aug' und Wangen
Meine heissen Freudenthränen.

Und ein Lenz begann zu blühen,
Und es brachen auf die Veilchen,
Und wir wandelten auf Blumen,
Hand in Hand und Aug' in Auge.

Doch gelogen hat der Frühling,
Und kein Sonnenstrahl der Liebe
Küsst mir nun von Aug' und Wangen
Meine heissen Trauerzähren.

Denn es ist ein Schnee gefallen
Über Nacht auf alle Blumen,
Und die Veilchen sind gestorben,
Und mein Liebstes ist geschieden.

First Loss

Yesterday he held me in his arms
and, with his passionate mouth,
he kissed away my hot tears of joy from my eyes
and cheeks.

And spring began to blossom,
and violets were opening,
and we were strolling in the flowers
hand in hand, gazing into each other's eyes.

But spring had lied,
and no loving sunbeam kisses my hot, grieving
teardrops away from my eyes and cheeks now.

For snow has fallen
overnight on all the flowers,
and the violets are dead,
and my beloved has departed.

Bei der Linde - Op. 36 No. 4

Key:	A♭ major
Time signature:	Common time
Duration:	1'33"
Vocal range and median pitch:	E♭4-F5 (B♭4)
Title and Position in *Gedichte*:	Bei der Linde (No. 79)
First edition publisher and year:	F E C Leuckart, Breslau, 1862
Track number on MPR CD:	Disc: 2, Track: 7

Bei der Linde

Als die Linden trieben,
Weckte süsse Hoffnung
Neuer Lust entgegen
Meine schlummertrunkene Seele.

By the Lime Tree

When the lime tree sprouted,
sweet hope
for new pleasures
awakened my slumber-intoxicated soul.

Nun die Linden blühen,	Now the lime blossom is out,
Ist der Stern erloschen,	the star is extinguished
Und nach Ruhe zittern	and my daylight-weary eyes
Meine tagesmüde Augen.	tremble after peace.
In die weiche Rinde	In the soft bark
Schnitt ich ihren Namen,	I carved her name,
In ihr warmes Herze	into her warm heart
Senkt' ich meine junge Liebe.	I plunged my young love.
Rind ist hart geworden,	The bark has become hard
Und der Nam' verwachsen,	and the name overgrown.
Und ihr Herz erkaltet,	And her heart has cooled
Und die Hoffnung hat gelogen!	and hope has lied!

Nun hat mein Stecken gute Rast - Op. 36 No. 6

Key:	B♭ major
Time signature:	2/4
Duration:	1'27"
Vocal range and median pitch:	D4-G5 (B♭4)
Title and Position in *Gedichte*:	Warnung (No. 29)
First edition publisher and year:	F E C Leuckart, Breslau, 1862
Track number on MPR CD:	Disc: 1, Track: 25

Nun hat mein Stecken gute Rast

Now my staff rests easy

Nun hat mein Stecken gute Rast,	Now my staff rests easy,
Das Reisen hat ein Ende,	my travels have come to an end.
Seit du mein' Hand genommen hast	Since you took my hand in both of yours,
In deine beiden Hände.	
Du hast mir alle Wanderlust,	You have relieved me of all my wanderlust,
Du liebes Kind, genommen,	you dear child.
Hätt' ich zuvor darum gewusst,	If I had known of this before,
Wäre nie zu dir gekommen.	I would never have come to you.
Den Stab pflanz' ich im Garten ein,	I plant the staff in the garden,
Darin soll er verbleiben,	where it shall remain –
Vielleicht! Er kann im Sonnenschein	maybe! It can still once again sprout leaves in
Noch einmal Blätter treiben.	the sunshine.
Treibt er nur erst, nimm dich in Acht,	If it does sprout, be warned –
Er ist im Mai geschitten,	it was cut in May –
Dass ich nicht einmal über Nacht	that I don't just stride out in the night once more.
Bin wieder ausgeschritten.	

Zu Spät - Op. 37 No. 2

Key:	D♭ major
Time signature:	6/8
Duration:	50"
Vocal range and median pitch:	E♭4-G5 (C5)
Title and Position in *Gedichte*:	Zu spät (No. 4)
First edition publisher and year:	Kistner, Leipzig, 1866
Track number on MPR CD:	Disc: 1, Track: 12

Zu Spät   **Too Late**

Aus bangen Träumen
   Der Winternacht
   Die Ros' erwacht,
O Lenz, und kamst du noch säumen?

Und als die zage,
   Die Frühlingsbraut
   Ihn nimmer schaut,
„Vergessen!" so weint ihre Klage.

Und als den Stecken
   Der Frühling schwang
   Und lustig sang,
Sein trautes Liebchen zu wecken;

Da war die Süsse
   Vor Liebesnoth
   Schon lange todt,
Zu spät, ach! kamen die Grüsse.

From troubled dreams
at winter's close,
the rose awoke,
Oh spring, are you still tarrying?

And as the timid
spring bride
never saw it,
she whimpered, "Forgotten!"

And when spring
wielded its staff
and sang lustily
to wake its faithful sweetheart,

the dear little thing
was long since dead for want of love.

Too late, alas, came the greetings!

Sonnenwende - Op. 37 No. 5

Key:	E major
Time signature:	Common time
Duration:	1'32"
Vocal range and median pitch:	C♯4-E5 (G♯4)
Title and Position in *Gedichte*:	Sonnenwende (No. 16)
First edition publisher and year:	Kistner, Leipzig, 1866
Track number on MPR CD:	Disc: 2, Track: 12

Sonnenwende   **Summer Solstice**

Der Sommer ist zu Ende,
   Ach Liebchen gehst auch du,
   Und lässt mich ohne Ruh
Bei dieser Sonnenwende?

The summer is at a close,
ah dearest; do you go too
and leave me without peace
at this solstice?

Wenn alle Vöglein fliegen	When all the little birds fly off
Und keines bleiben will,	and none wishes to remain,
Dann wird's im Walde still,	then the woods become silent,
Bis sie zurücke ziehen.	until they return.

Doch wen verlässt die Liebe,
   Dem ist's im Herzen gar,
   Als ob viele tausend Jahr
Der eine Winter bliebe.

But he, whom love has abandoned,
feels deep inside his heart
as though one single winter is about to remain for
many thousand years.

Mein Schatz ist auf der Wanderschaft - Op. 40 No. 1

Key:	E♭ major
Time signature:	2/4
Duration:	1'22"
Vocal range and median pitch:	E♭4-G5 (B♭4)
Title and Position in *Gedichte*:	Mein Schatz ist auf der Wanderschaft (No. 61)
First edition publisher and year:	Kistner, Leipzig, 1867
Track number on MPR CD:	Disc: 1, Track: 15

Mein Schatz ist auf der Wanderschaft

Mein Schatz ist auf der Wanderschaft
   So lange,
Gott weiss, woher er nimmt die Kraft
   Zum Gange,
's wär' besser, wollt' er endlich nun
Sein allerletzte Reise thun
   Und kehren mir zum Glücke
     Zurücke.

Mein' Mutter hat den ganzen Tag
   Zu schelten,
Zu Dank mach' ich ihr meine Sach'
   Nur selten;
Ach Gott! Ich thät ja Alles gern,
Wär' nur mein Schatz nicht gar so fern,
   Dass ich an ihn ohn' Kränken
     Könnt' denken.

Ihr sprechet wohl, „Ich such' dir aus
   Ein'n andern" –
Frau Mutter, da wird nie was draus!
   Vom Wandern
Wird er zur rechten Stunde ruh'n
Und bald sein' letzte Reise thun,
   Und kehren mir – zum Glücke
     Zurücke!

My Sweetheart has been on his travels

My Sweetheart has been on his travels
so long now.
God knows where he gets the strength
to walk so far.
It would be much better if he were willing
to make this his last journey,
and return to me and make me happy.

My mother has to scold me all day long

and I pay her back by doing
as little as possible:
Oh God, I'd gladly do it all,
if only my dearest weren't so far away
that I could bear to think of him
without feeling angry.

You're probably saying, "I'll find you
another one"-
Mother, that can never be!
He'll be back in good time and soon be done with
travelling
and return to me
and make me happy!

Du grüne Rast im Haine - Op. 41 No. 6

Key:	B♭ major
Time signature:	2/4
Duration:	2'58"
Vocal range and median pitch:	D4-G5 (B♭4)
Title and Position in *Gedichte*:	Du grüne Rast im Haine (No. 52)
First edition publisher and year:	Breitkopf & Härtel, Liepzig, 1867
Track number on MPR CD:	Disc: 2, Track: 16

Du grüne Rast im Haine   **You verdant resting place in this grove**

Du grüne Rast im Haine,
    Lass mich in dir verweilen,
Du hast die Kraft alleine,
    Ein krankes Herz zu heilen.

You verdant resting place in this grove
let me linger here.
You alone have the power
to heal a sick heart.

Wo flüsternd sich die Bäume
    Ihr heimlich Glück erzählen,
Soll sich in meine Träume
    Kein bleicher Kummer stehlen.

Where the whispering trees
are sharing their tales of secret happiness,
no pallid sorrow shall stealthily intrude upon
my dreams.

Ihr blauen Himmelslüfte,
    Ihr süssen Waldeslieder,
Ihr frischen Waldesdüfte
    Gebt mir die Ruhe wieder.

You breezes from the blue sky,
you sweet songs of the forest,
you fresh forest fragrances;
restore my peace of mind.

Doch, wie erschreckt die Rehe
    Dort durch die Büsche beben,
So zuckt das alte Wehe
    Durch mein geheimstes Leben.

But, like the frightened fawn,
there trembling among the undergrowth,
so shoots that familiar pain
through my most secret life.

Verloren ach! verloren,
    Gestorben und verdorben!
Mein Lenz war kaum geboren,
    Und ist so früh gestorben!

Lost, ah, lost,
dead and ruined.
My spring had hardly begun,
and is now soon over.

Du grüne Rast im Haine,
    Lass mich in dir verweilen,
Du hast die Kraft alleine,
    Ein krankes Herz zu heilen.

You verdant resting place in this grove
let me linger here.
You alone have the power
to heal a sick heart.

Träume - Op. 43 No. 1

Key:	A♭ major
Time signature:	2/4
Duration:	2'07"
Vocal range and median pitch:	C4-F5 (C5)
Title and Position in *Gedichte*:	Kurze Hoffnung (No. 77)
First edition publisher and year:	Kistner, Leipzig, 1867
Track number on MPR CD:	Disc: 2, Track: 11

Träume	**Dreams**
Lieblich blüh'n die Bäume	The trees are blossoming beautifully,
Voller Schmelz und Duft,	full of lustre and fragrance.
Gold'ne Frühlingsträume	Golden spring-dreams
Schweben klingend durch die Luft.	float melodiously through the air.
Meine trunk'ne Seele	My intoxicated soul
Träumend vergisst,	dreamily forgets
Was ihr ewig fehle,	what it eternally lacks
Dass sie tief verwundet ist.	and how it is deeply wounded.
Was dahin gegangen,	What had once departed
Kehrt im Traum zurück,	reappears in my dream
Und mit scheum Bangen	and, with timid fear,
Hoff' ich wieder neues Glück.	I hope for the return of new happiness.
Aber durch die Blätter	But through the leaves
Zittert die Luft,	the air quivers
Und bald nimmt ein Wetter	and soon the weather takes away
Traum und Blüthen, Schmelz und Duft.	my dream, blossoms, lustre and fragrance.

Gleich wie der Mond so keusch und rein - Op. 43 No. 2

Key:	E major
Time signature:	Common time
Duration:	1'41"
Vocal range and median pitch:	E4-F#5 (A#4)
Title and Position in *Gedichte*:	Gleich wie der Mond so keusch und rein (No. 92)
First edition publisher and year:	Kistner, Leipzig, 1867
Track number on MPR CD:	Disc: 1, Track: 23

Gleich wie der Mond so keusch und rein	**Like the moon so chaste and pure**
Gleich wie der Mond so keusch und rein	Like the moon so chaste and pure
So bist du, holdes Mägdelein,	so are you blessed maid,
Mir in der Nacht des Herzens aufgegangen –	rising in the night of my heart,
O sanfter Schein, o mildes Licht,	soft gleam, gentle light,
Das mir aus deinem Angesicht	that towards me from your heavenly face
Entgegen nun mit süssem Zauber strahlet!	now radiates sweet enchantment.
Mein Herz war wie die wilde See,	My heart was like the wild ocean,
Wenn sie der Sturm treibt in die Höh,	when the storm rises in the heights,
Doch nun hat es dein sanfter Strahl gestillet.	but now your gentle radiance has silenced it.
Und ob es wallet oder ruht:	And if it surges or calms,
Du lenkest seine Ebb' und Fluth,	you guide its ebb and flow,
Du holde Maid, mit deinem sanften Scheine.	you blessed maiden, with your soft gleam.

Entschluss - Op. 43 No. 3

Key:	A minor
Time signature:	2/4
Duration:	1'50"
Vocal range and median pitch:	A3-G5 (B4)
Title and Position in *Gedichte*:	Entschluss (No. 59)
First edition publisher and year:	Kistner, Leipzig, 1867
Track number on MPR CD:	Disc: 1, Track: 13

Entschluss

Scheust dich noch immer, seliges Leben,
   Meiner Seele heissem Verlangen
Liebe um Liebe wieder zu geben,
   Soll ich dich nimmer umfangen?
Wie die schüchterne Jungfrau flieht,
Wenn sie den Suchenden sieht,
   Fliehend sucht und begehrt im Versagen,
   Zagend, hofft und wünscht zu verzagen:
Liebliches Leben, so fliehst du behende,
   Wenn ich zu dir mich wende.

Aber nicht länger will ich ertragen
   Dieses harrende Hoffen und Bangen,
Fort ihr Wünsche, lasset mich wagen,
   Ehe die Stunde vergangen,
Kühnen Muth in der Brust,
In den Adern Jugendlust,
   Keine Fragen im zögernden Munde,
   Halt' ich den Augenblick, halt' ich die Stunde,
Halt' ich das Leben, das selige, warme,
   Liebend und glücklich im Arme.

Resolve

Still shying away blessed life?
Shall I never embrace you again to imbue my soul's
hot desire with love and requited love?

As the shy virgin flees,
when she sees her suitor, fleeing seeks and desires
in refusal, timidly hoping and wishing to become
disheartened.
Dearest life, thus you swiftly flee
when I turn myself to you.

But no longer will I bear
this abiding hope and yearning.
Go forth you desires; let me dare,
ere time is up.
With bold courage in my breast,
youth's desire in my veins,
and no questions in my hesitating mouth,
I shall hold the moment; I shall hold the day,
and warmly hold life's bliss
lovingly and happily in my arms.

In Blüthen - Op. 43 No. 6

Key:	G major
Time signature:	2/4
Duration:	1'51"
Vocal range and median pitch:	B3-G5 (A♯4)
Title and Position in *Gedichte*:	In Blüthen (No. 86)
First edition publisher and year:	Kistner, Leipzig, 1867
Track number on MPR CD:	Disc: 1, Track: 4

In Blüthen

   Nun da die Bäum' in Blüthen steh'n,
     Seh' ich sie wohl allein,
   Sie Blume selbst nach Blüthen geh'n,
  Ahi, du Wunderschöne, ich wollt' du wärest mein!

In Blossom

Now the trees bear their blossoms,
I see her quite alone.
She, a flower herself, goes after blossoms,
heigh-ho you beauty, I wish you were mine!

Dein Haar ist braun, dein Auge rein	Your hair is brown, your eyes are pure
Und all dein Angesicht,	and your entire visage
Wie Apfelblüth' im Morgenschein,	is like apple-blossom in the morning light.
Doch wärst du stolz von Herzen, wär' all' mein Freud' zu nicht.	But were you haughty at heart, then all my joys would come to naught.
O schau die volle Blüthenpracht	Oh, see the splendour of the blossoms
Rings in dem grünen Thal:	around the green valley,
Der Wind verweht sie über Nacht,	the wind blows them away overnight.
Der Jugend schöne Blume, sie welkt auch dir einmal!	The beautiful flower of youth, this too will wither in you one day.
	Oh, if only I could be alone with you
O könnt' ich nur mit dir allein	in this lovely time,
Zu dieser schönen Frist	just once, you beauty.
Einmal, du Wunderschöne, sein,	Heigh-ho, you would see what true love is!
Ahi, du solltest sehen, was treue Liebe ist.	

Aprillaunen - Op. 44 No. 2

Key:	G major
Time signature:	Common time
Duration:	1'59"
Vocal range and median pitch:	D4-G5 (B4)
Title and Position in *Gedichte*:	Aprillaunen (No. 42)
First edition publisher and year:	Kistner, Leipzig, 1870
Track number on MPR CD:	Disc: 1, Track: 11

Aprillaunen

April Moods

Liebchen, was willst du?	Dearest, what is it you want?
Komm ich oft, so schiltst du,	If I visit often, you scold;
Komm ich nicht, so bin ich schlecht,	if I don't come, then I am bad.
Sage selbst: was ist dir recht?	Just say, what is right by you?
Küss' ich dich heute,	If I kiss you today,
Fürchtest du die Leute,	you're worried about other people,
Ja und morgen, spröde Maid,	yes, and tomorrow, stuck-up wench,
Willst du nichts von Heimlichkeit.	you want nothing to do with secrecy.
Seufz' ich, so lachst du,	If I sigh, you laugh;
Lach' ich, ach! So machst du	if I laugh – ah, you make
Mir ein bitterbös' Gesicht:	me a horrible face;
Was ich thu' behagt dir nicht.	whatever I do brings you no comfort.
Man lebt euch allen Nimmer zu Gefallen,	One lives never to please any of you at all.
Alle seid ihr, schweig' nur still!	You are all - but hush!-
Wie das Wetter im April:	like the weather in April.
Scheint's recht gelinde,	If it seems quite mild,
Werfen tolle Winde	crazy gales throw
Mitten in dem Sonnenschein	a handful of snow amidst the sunshine.
Eine Hand voll Schnee hinein.	

Ich bei dem Schneien	In this snow
Tröste mich des Maien.	I comfort myself with thoughts of May.
Willst du, Lieb? Ein Blick von dir	What do you want, love? A single glance from you
Bringt den Mai schon heute mir.	could well bring May to me today.

Dornröschen - Op. 51 No. 3

Key:	F major
Time signature:	3/4
Duration:	2'01"
Vocal range and median pitch:	D4-F5 (A4)
Title and Position in *Gedichte*:	Dornröschen (No. 5)
First edition publisher and year:	F E C Leuckart, Leipzig, 1879
Track number on MPR CD:	Disc: 1, Track: 24

Dornröschen — **Sleeping Beauty**

Dornröschen schlägt zum erstenmal
  Die Augen auf nach langer Ruh'
Und schauet bräutlich um im Thal,
  Doch fallen bald der Kleinen
        Im Weinen
Die müden Augen wieder zu.

Sleeping Beauty opens her eyes for the very first
time after her long rest
and gazes around the valley like a bride.
But soon the little one bursts
into tears,
closing her weary eyes once more.

Und als sie weint im schweren Traum,
  Kommt ihr Lieb', der Maie traut,
Und küsst sie wach, sie weiss es kaum:
  Von seinem Kuss erglühet,
        Erblühet
Zu holder Pracht die junge Braut.

And as she is crying in her deep sleep, her faithful
lover, May, comes
and kisses her awake – she hardly notices it.
Glowing from his kiss the young bride blooms to
blissful magnificence.

Nun freue dich der kurzen Lust,
  Und sei dem schönen Buhlen hold:
An seinem Kuss du sterben musst!
  Wie leide dir geschehe,
        Wie wehe,
Du selbst hast Leid und Weh' gewollt.

Now delight in brief happiness
and be well disposed towards your paramour. You
must die from his kiss!
Whatever suffering you feel,
whatever pain,
you yourself desired that suffering and that pain.

Erinnerung - Op. 51 No. 10

Key:	G minor
Time signature:	Common time
Duration:	1'52"
Vocal range and median pitch:	D4-G5 (B♭4)
Title and Position in *Gedichte*:	Erinnerung (1848)
	Die Sterne flimmern und prangen (1873) (No. 74)
First edition publisher and year:	F E C Leuckart, Leipzig, 1879
Track number on MPR CD:	Disc: 2, Track: 25

Erinnerung

Die Sterne flimmern und prangen
　Selig in stiller Nacht,
In Schmerzen aber und Bangen
　Mein klopfend Herze wacht.

Am Monde vorüber gleiten
　Die Wolken im luftigen Lauf,
Die alten, die seligen Zeiten
　Steigen wie Geister herauf.

Sie ziehen vorüber und neigen
　Wehmüthig das Haupt mir zu,
Schweig' stille mein Herz, o schweige,
　Lasse die Todten in Ruh!

Ein Stern fällt zitternd und schnelle
　Hinab in das dunkle Moor,
Die Nacht aber bleibet helle
　Und pranget so schön wie zuvor.

Remembrance

The stars flicker and shine
blessedly in the silent night;
in pain though and fear
my pounding heart awakes.

The clouds glide across the moon in their airy train;

the old, blissful times
rise up like spirits.

They pass by and incline their
melancholy heads towards me.
Be silent my heart, be silent;
let the dead rest in peace!

A trembling star falls swiftly
earthwards into the dark fen.
The night though remains bright,
as beautifully resplendent as before.

Translations copyright © Victoria Edge 2019

Discography

Despite the quality of Franz's Osterwald settings and their popularity when they were first published, until the recent complete recording, the songs were only occasionally recorded. The general preference has been to record the settings of the poets well known through settings by Schubert, Schumann and Wolf, particularly the early Heine poems, and not in the original keys.

Robert Franz: Gesammelte Osterwald Lieder und Gesänge (CD 2019) – Harriet Burns (soprano), William Searle (tenor), Marc Verter (piano) and Sebastian Wybrew (piano) – **Label:** MPR - **Catalogue No:** MPR106.

> The complete 51 settings by Robert Franz of original poems by Wilhelm Osterwald in their original keys.

Robert Franz Lieder (CD 2017) – Robin Tritschler (tenor) Graham Johnson (piano) **Label**: Hyperion - **Catalogue No:** CDA68128

> Track 45 - Ach wenn ich doch ein Immchen wär (Op. 3 No. 6)
> Track 46 - Um Mitternacht (Op. 16 No. 6)

Robert Franz Lieder (CD 1995) - Mitsuko Shirai (mezzo-soprano) and Hartmut Höll (piano) - **Label**: Capriccio - **Catalogue No:** C10515

> Track 26 - Umsonst (Op. 10 No. 6)
> Track 39 – Ständchen (Op. 17 No. 2)

Robert Franz Lieder (CD 2013) Yves Saelens (tenor) and Jan Vermeulen (piano) – **Label:** Etcetera - **Catalogue No:** KTC 1260

> Track 10 – Ständchen (Op. 17 No. 2)
> Track 15 - Gewitternacht (Op. 8: No. 6)
> Track 24 - Lieber Schatz, sei wieder gut mir (Op 26: No. 2)

Robert Franz Lieder Opp. 1-4 (CD 2003) Hans Jörg Mammel (tenor) and Ludwig Holtmeier (piano) - **Label:** Ars Musici - **Catalogue No:** AM13122

> Track 13 - Kurzes Wiedersehen (Op. 4 No. 8)
> Track 14 - Durch sauselnde Baume (Op. 4 No. 9)
> Track 15 - Herbstsorge (Op. 4 No. 10)
> Track 16 - Wanderlied (Op. 4 No. 11)
> Track 17 - Ach, dass du kamst (Op. 4 No. 12)
> Track 35 - Ach wenn ich doch ein Immchen wär (Op. 3 No. 6)

Stilwandlungen des Klavierliedes (1850-1950) (CD 2005)- Dietrich Fischer-Dieskau (baritone) and Aribert Reimann (piano) **Label:** Warner Classics - Parlophone **Catalogue No:** 0724356734951

> Disc 1, Track 3 - Gewitternacht (Op. 8 No. 6)

Robert Franz: Ordinary Man, Extraordinary Songs - Album One (CD and digital album 2017) Tim Krol (baritone) with Michael T C Hey, Rita Greenstein, Colin Fowler and Mark Janas (piano). Includes five songs by Robert Franz's wife; Marie Hinrichs.

>Track 6 – Sonnenwende (Op. 37 No. 4)
>Track 7 – Herbstsorge (Op. 4 No. 10)
>Track 12 – Umsonst (Op. 10 No. 6)
>Track 17 - Der junge Tag erwacht (Op. 7 No. 1)
>Track 25 - Im Frühling (Op. 17 No. 5)
>Track 36 - Ach, wenn ich doch ein Immchen Wär' (Op. 3 No. 6)
>Track 37 - Ich Lobe mir Die Vögelein (Op. 5 No. 8)
>Track 41 - Lieber Schatz, sei wieder gut mir (Op. 26 No. 2)

Lorri Lail Song Recital (1947-1948) (CD 2014) - Lorri Lail (soprano) and Gerald Moore (piano) - **Label:** Jube Classic - **Catalogue No:** Jube-NML1328

>Track 17 – Ständchen (Op. 17 No. 2)

Live from the New Opening of Semperoper Dresden (CD 1989) Theo Adam (bass-baritone) Rudolf Dunckel (piano) – **Label:** Ars Vivendi / Deutsche Schallplatten Berlin - **Catalogue No:** 2100115

>Track 15 - Gewitternacht (Op. 8 No. 6)

Lieder de Franz Joseph Haydn et Robert Franz (Undated LP c. mid 1950s) – Jérôme Piersault (tenor) Denyse Rivière (piano) - **Label:** Disques BAM - LD 090

>Side B, Track 7 - Umsonst (Op. 10 No. 6)
>Side B, Track 13 – Ständchen (Op. 17 No. 2)

Robert Franz Lieder (Undated LP c. mid-1950s) – Hilde Roessel-Majdan (contralto) Viktor Graef (piano) - **Label:** Westminster Hi-fi - **Catalogue No:** WLE 104

>Side A, Track 1 - Lieber Schatz, sei wieder gut (Op. 26 No. 2)
>Side B, Track 4 – Vergessen (Op. 5 No. 10)
>Side B, Track 5 – Ständchen (Op. 17 No. 2)
>Side B, Track 6 – Abends (Op. 20 No. 4)
>Side B, Track 11 - Da die Stunde kam (Op. 11 No. 3)
>Side B, Track 12 - Um Mitternacht (Op. 16 No. 6)

Herrn General-Musikdirektor Dr Felix Mendelssohn Bartholdy zugeeignet

Ach, wenn ich doch ein Immchen wär'

Wilhelm Osterwald
Robert Franz, Op. 3 No. 6

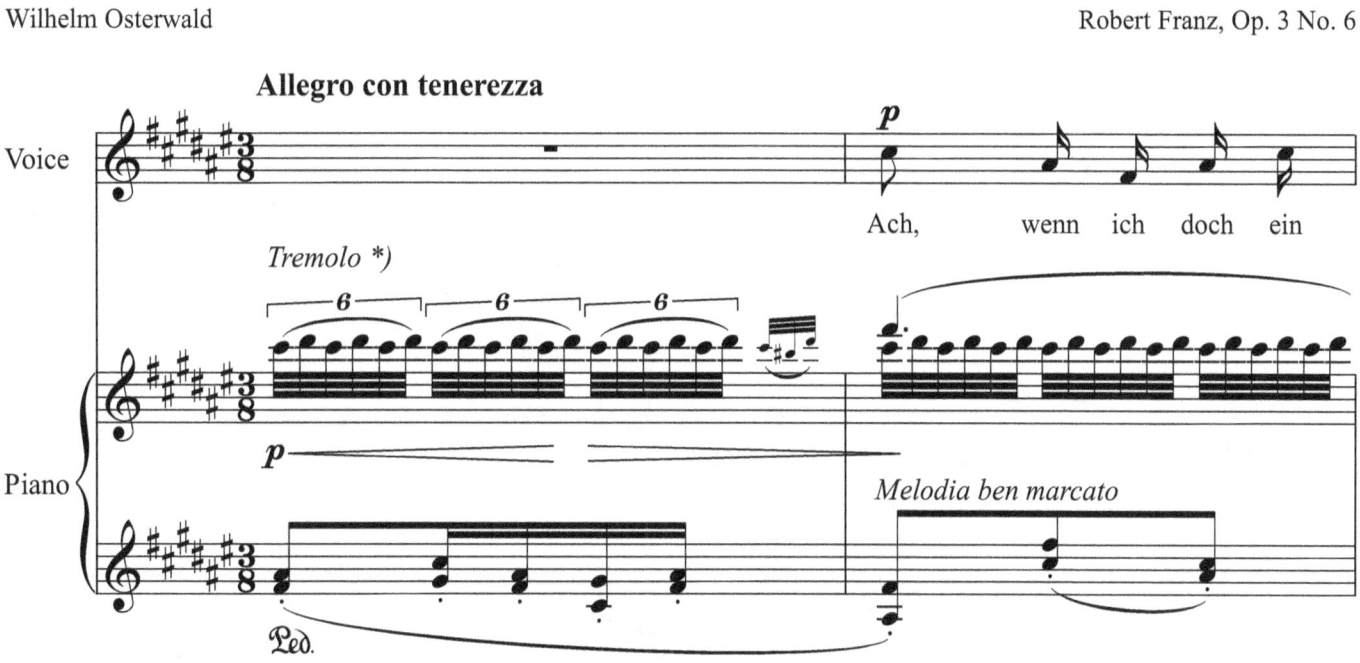

*) Das Tremolo muss frei und rund in der Trillerbewegung ausgeführt werden.

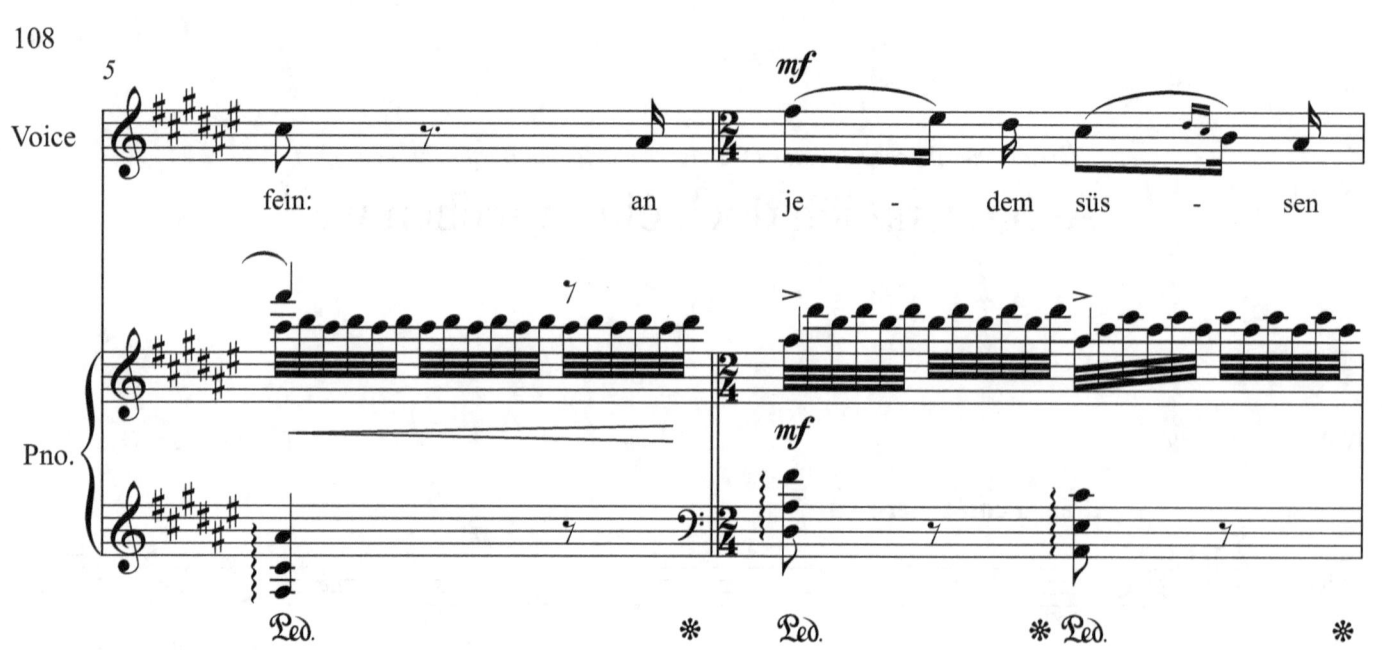
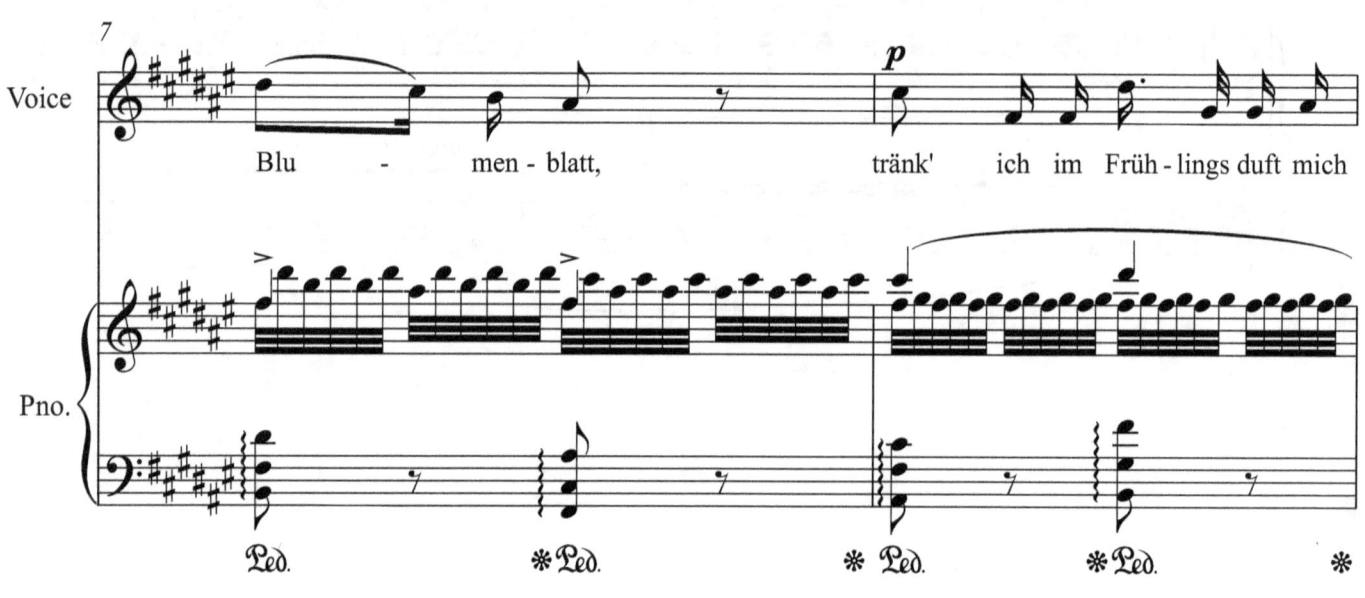

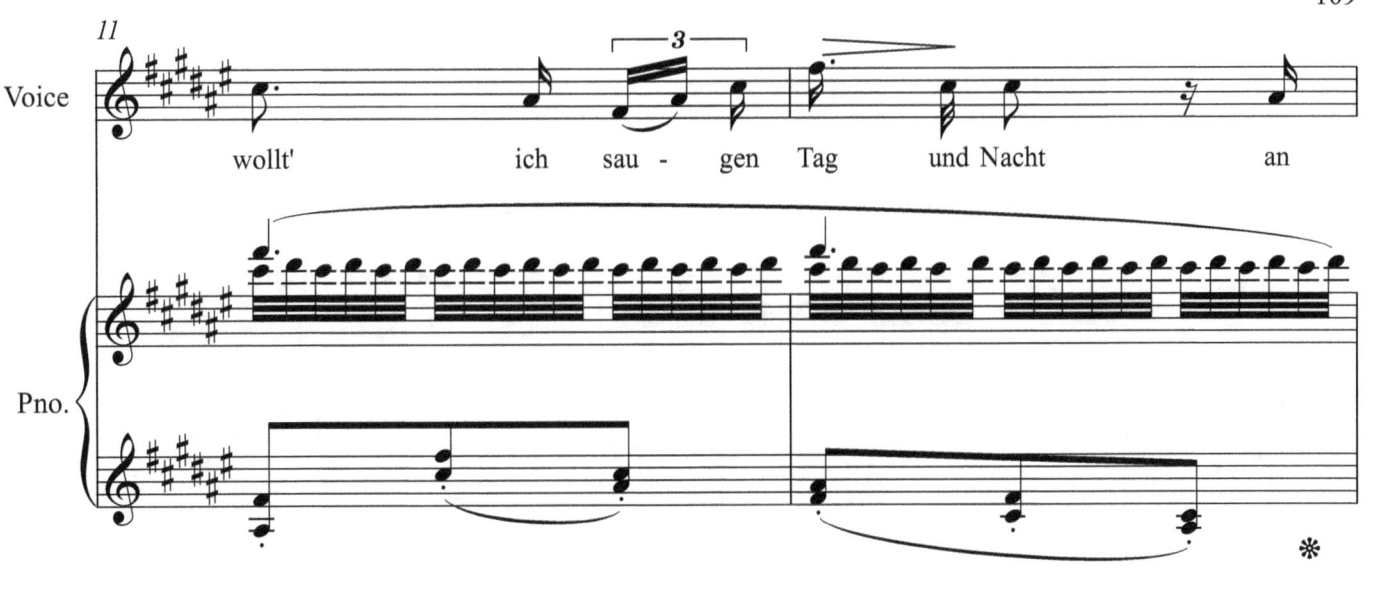
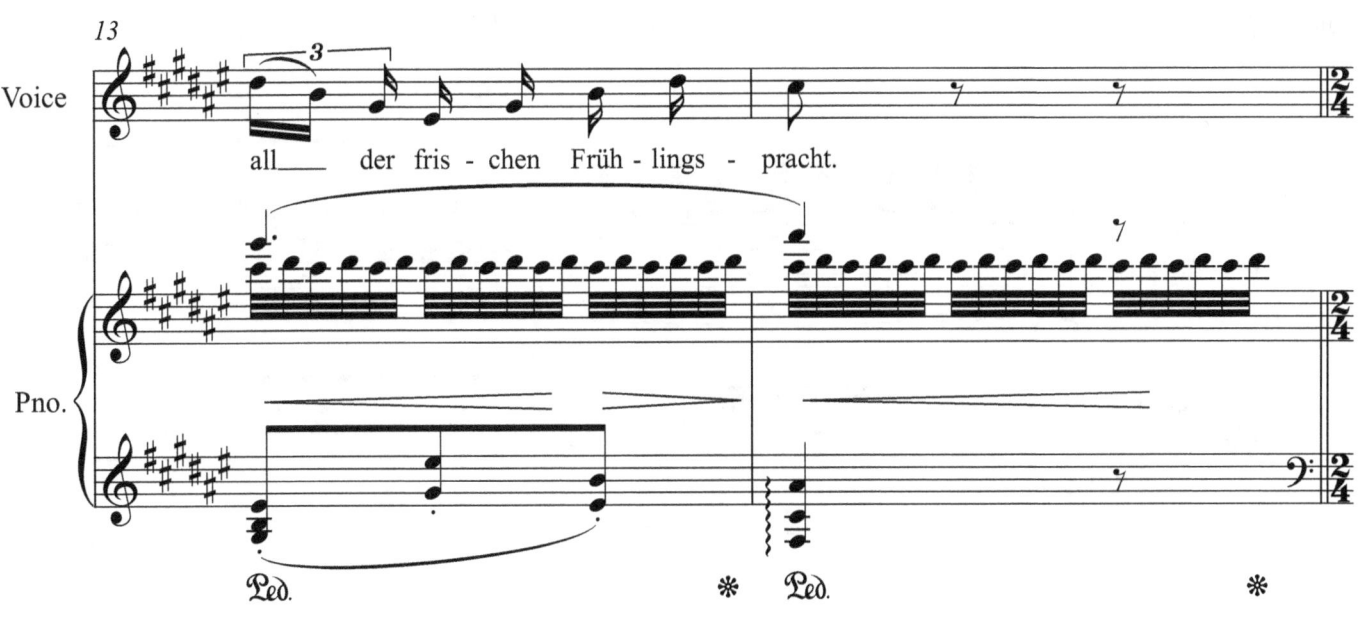
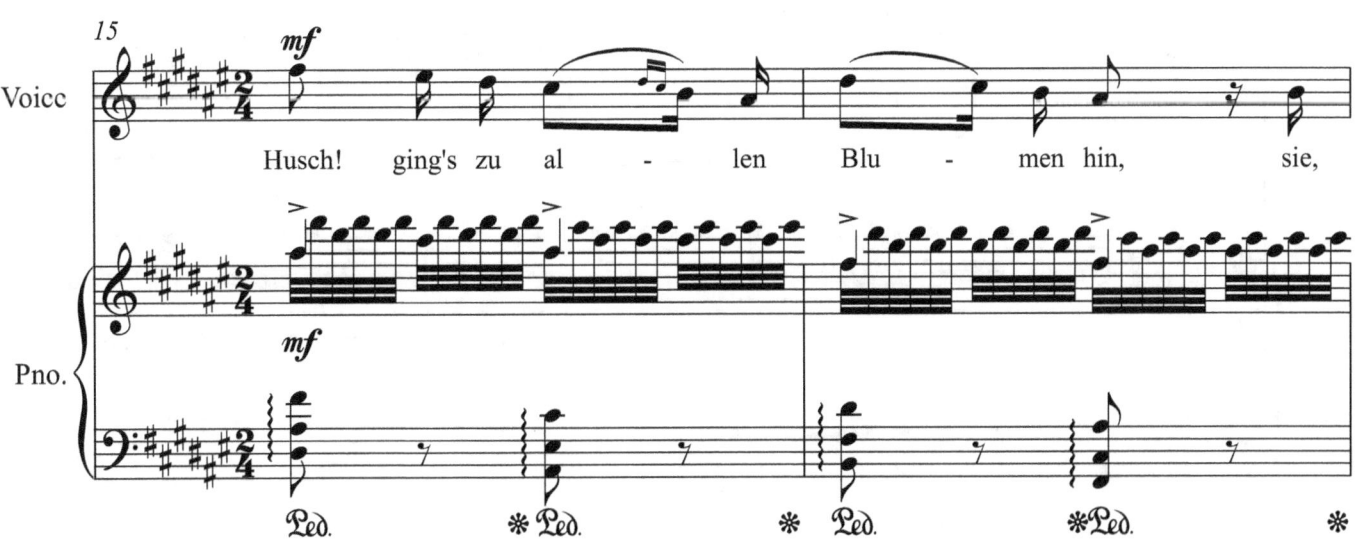

110

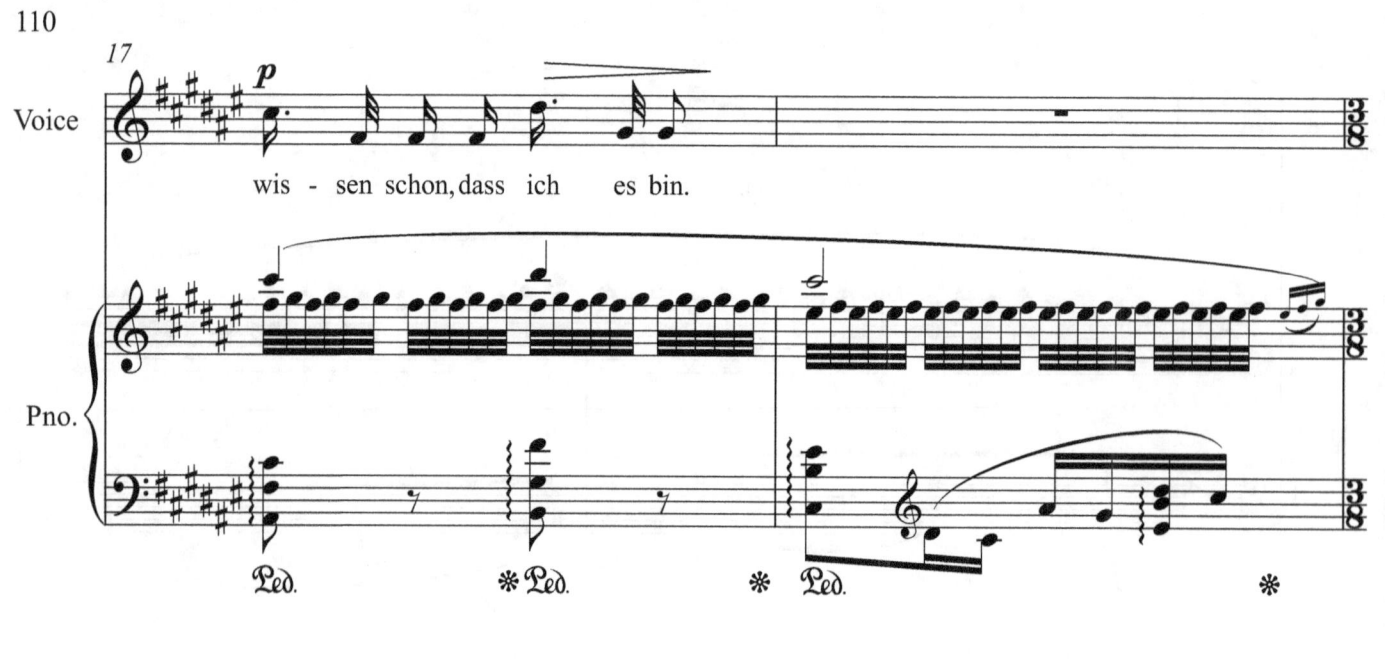

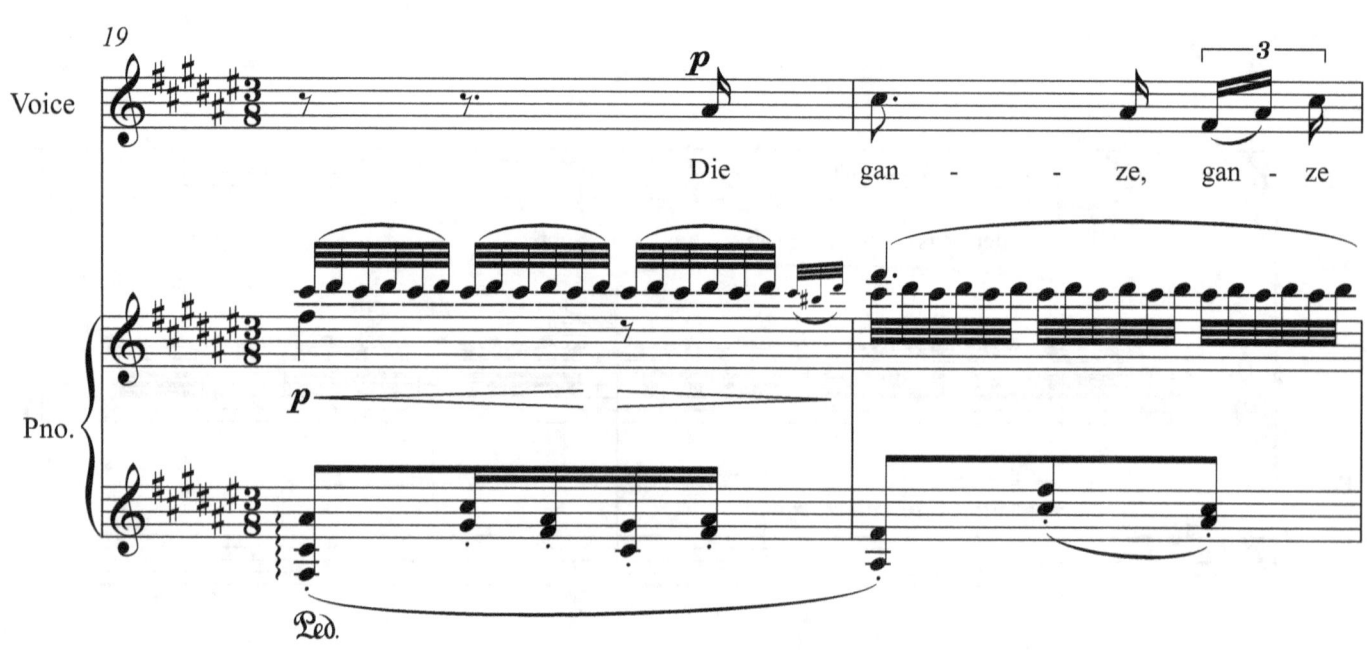

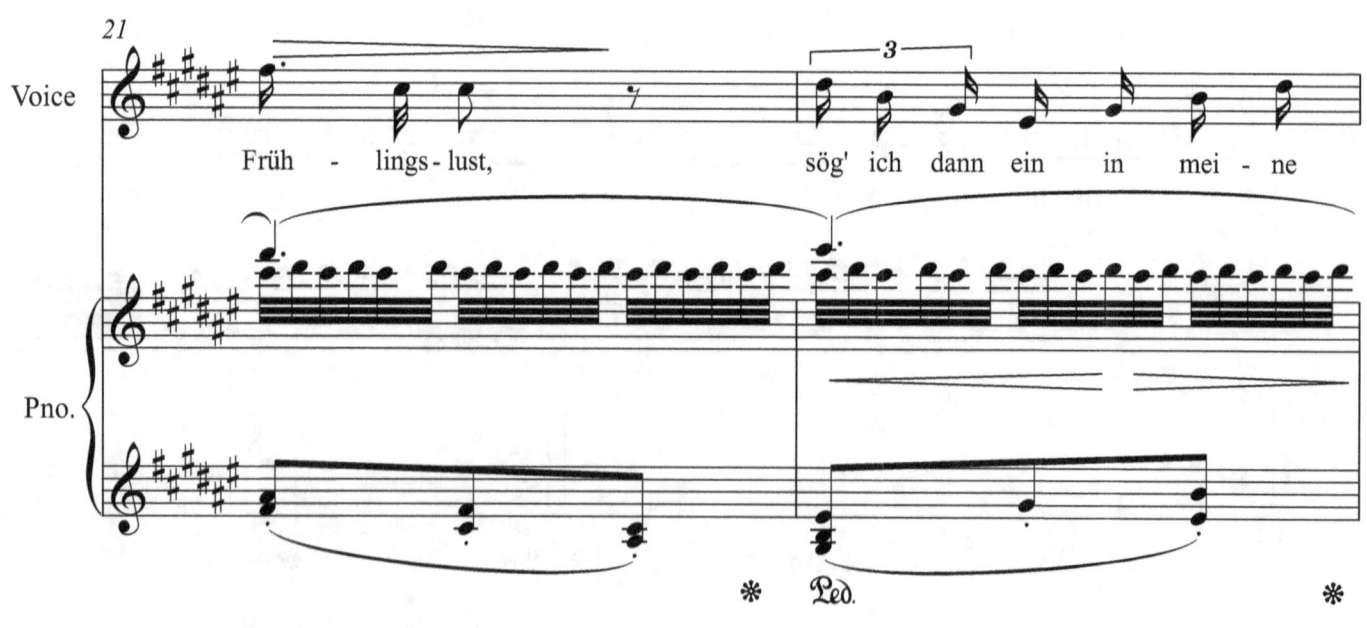

Durch säuselnde Bäume

Wilhelm Osterwald
Robert Franz, Op. 4 No. 9

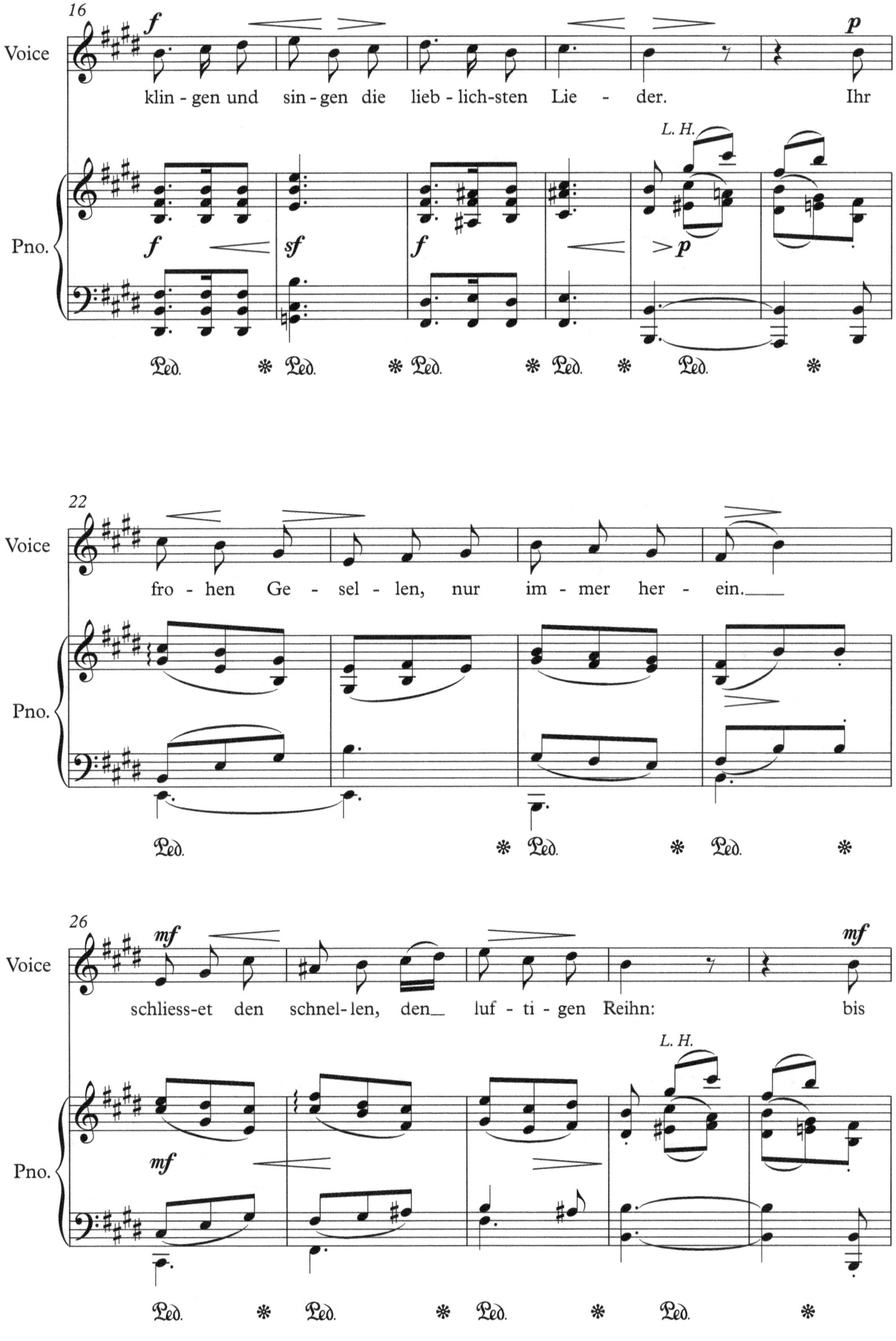
16
Voice
klin - gen und sin - gen die lieb - lich-sten Lie - der. Ihr
L. H.
Pno.
22
Voice
fro - hen Ge - sel - len, nur im - mer her - ein.
Pno.
26
Voice
schliess-et den schnel- len, den luf - ti - gen Reihn: bis
L. H.
Pno.

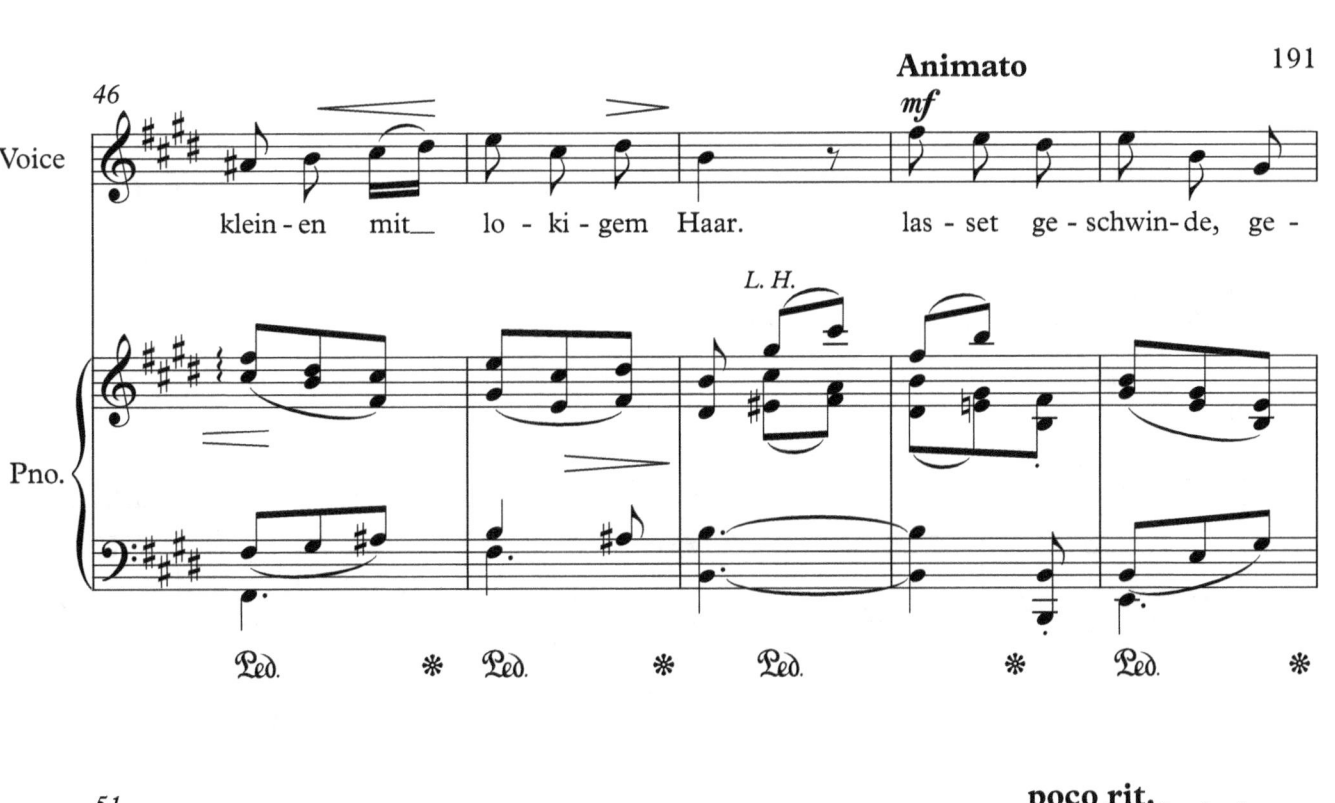

Herbstsorge

Wilhelm Osterwald
Robert Franz, Op. 4 No. 10

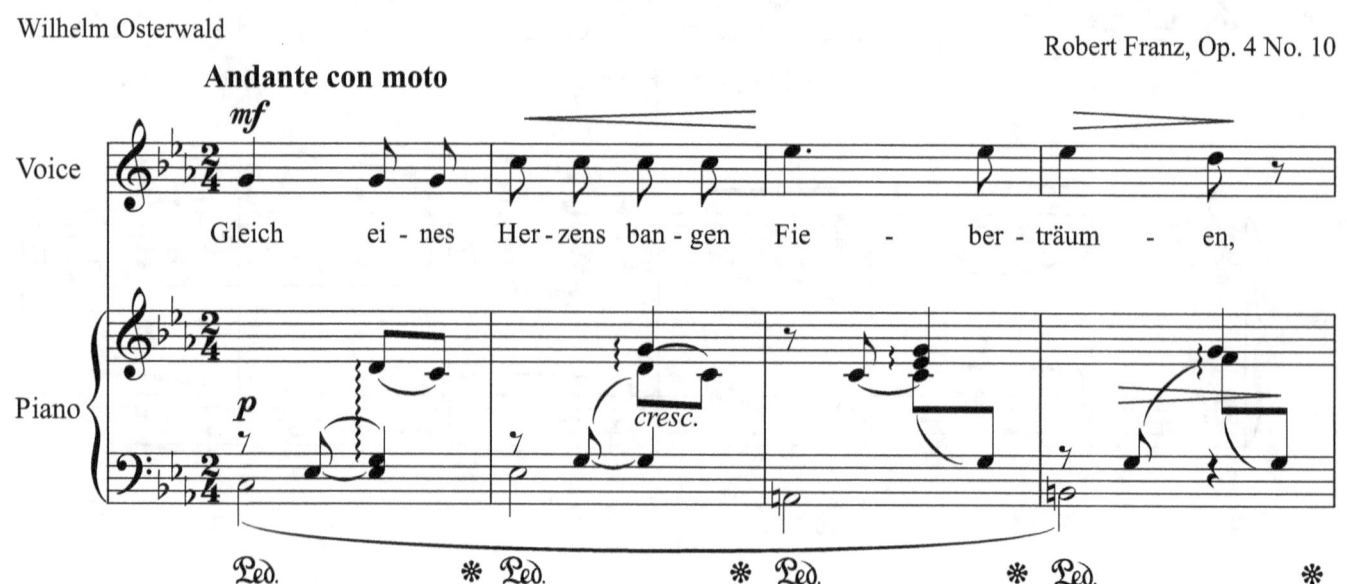
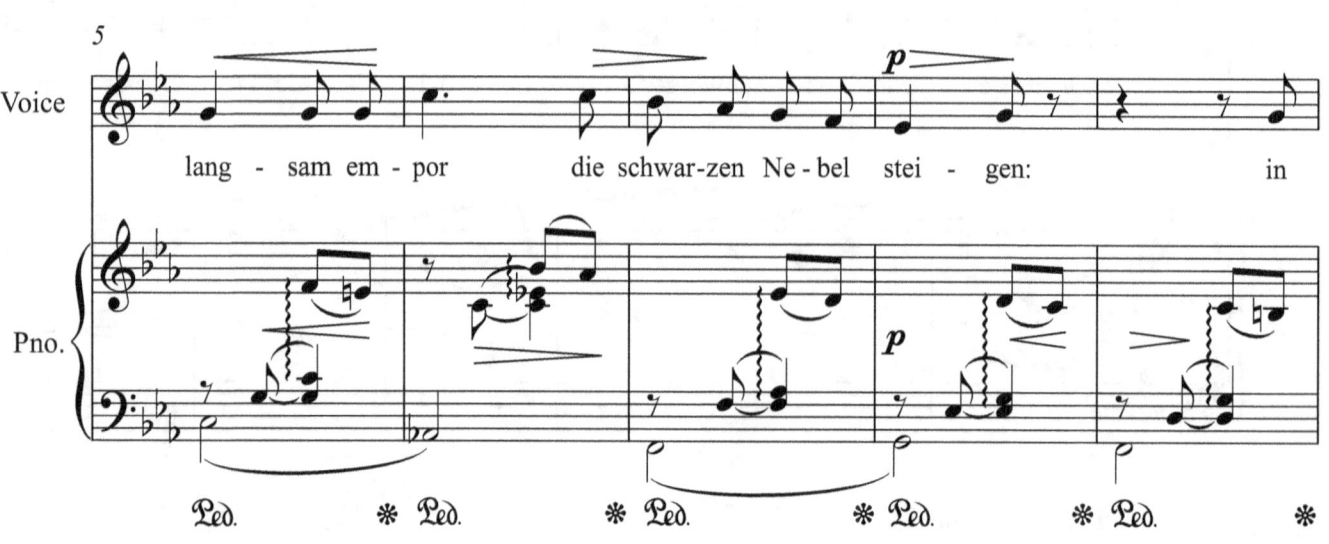

Copyright © Iain Sneddon 2019

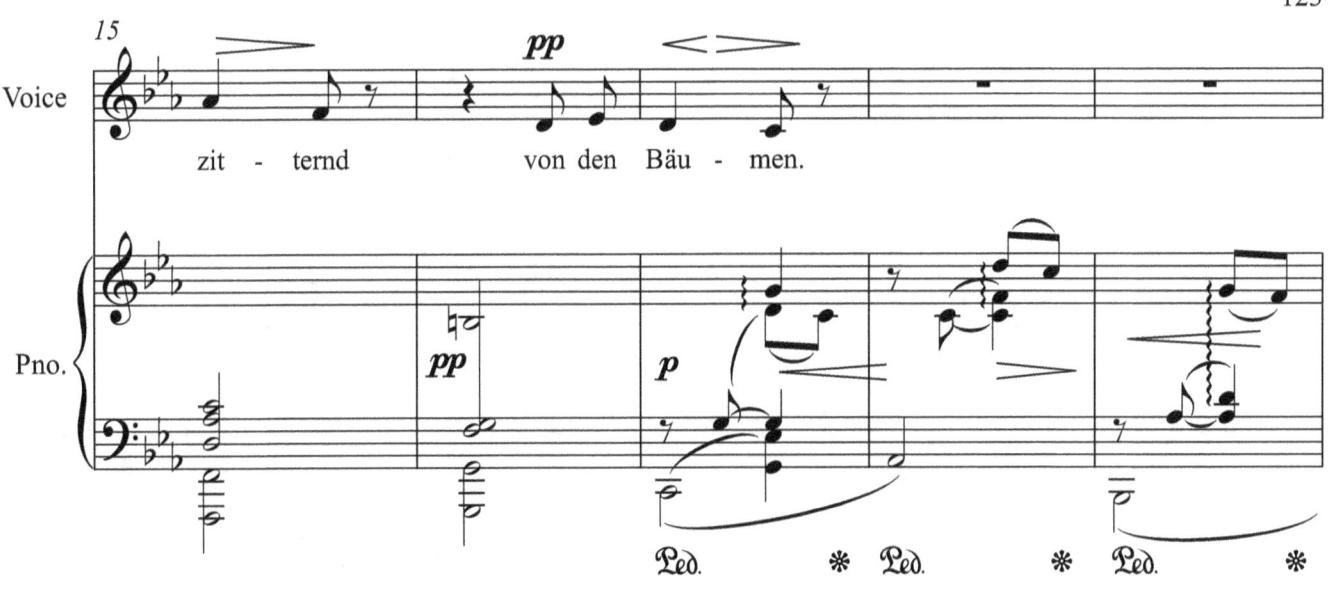

124

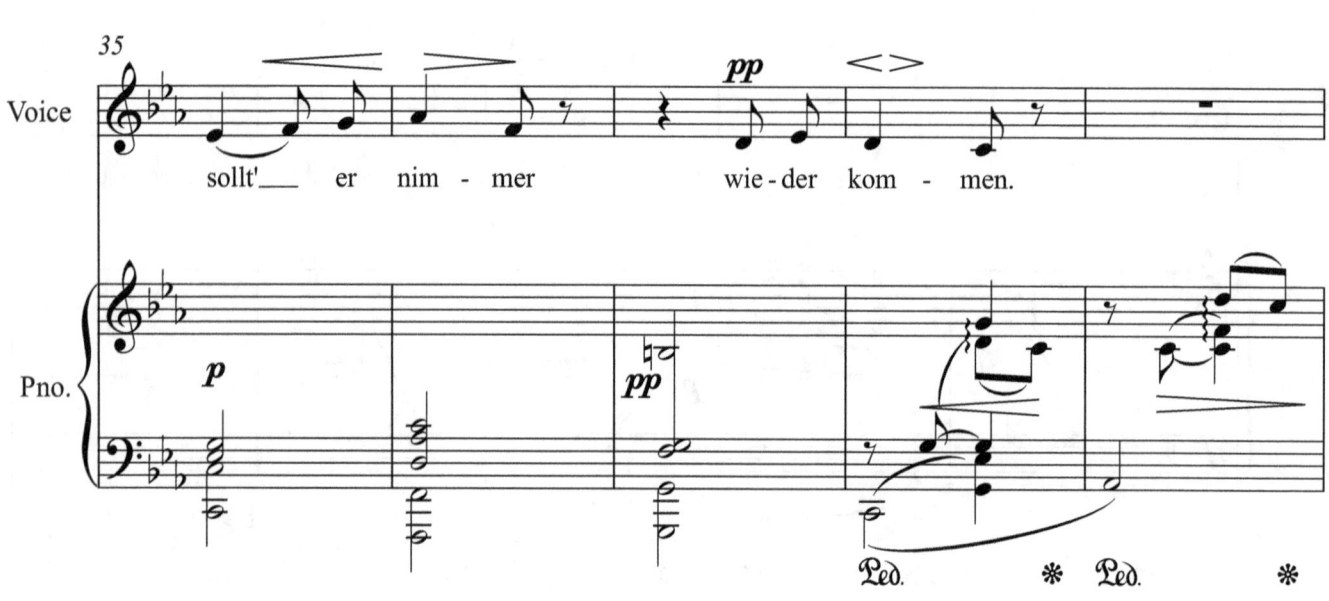

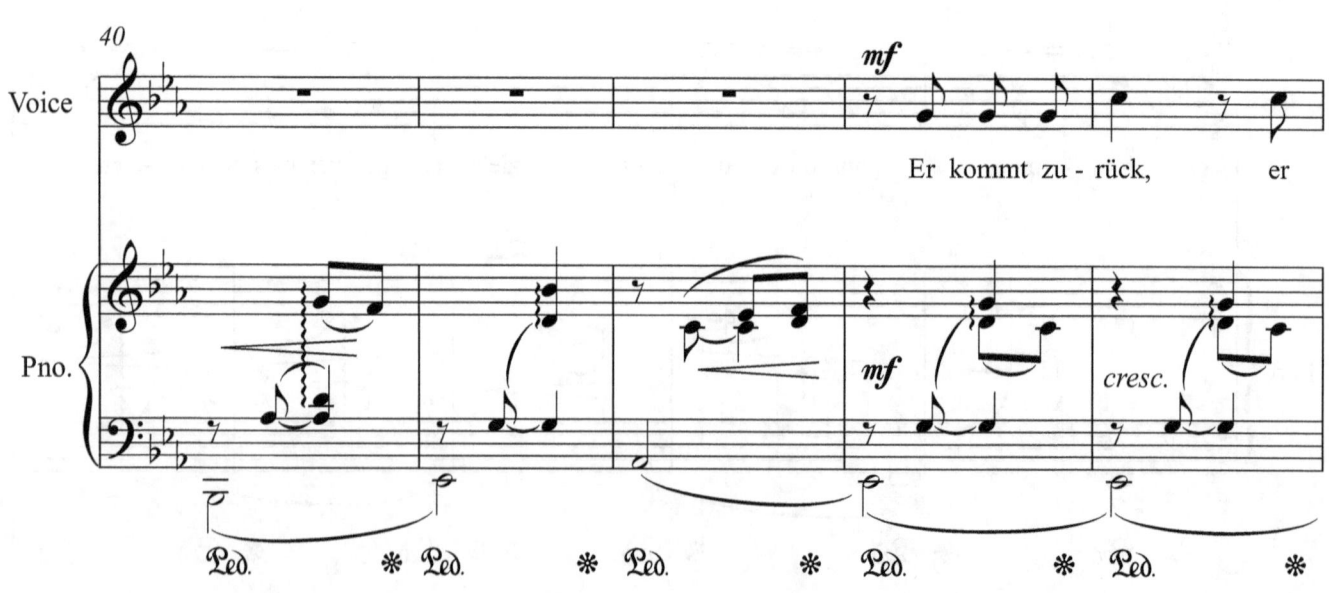

Wanderlied

Wlihelm Osterwald

Robert Franz, Op. 4 No. 11

Copyright © Iain Sneddon 2019

Ach dass du kamst

Wilhelm Osterwald

Robert Franz, Op. 4 No. 12

Agitato molto

Ach dass du kamst, ach dass du kamst in Freuden einst ge-gan-gen, und mir mein arg-los Her-ze nahmst mit sü-ssen Wor-ten ge-fan-gen;

Copyright © Iain Sneddon 2019

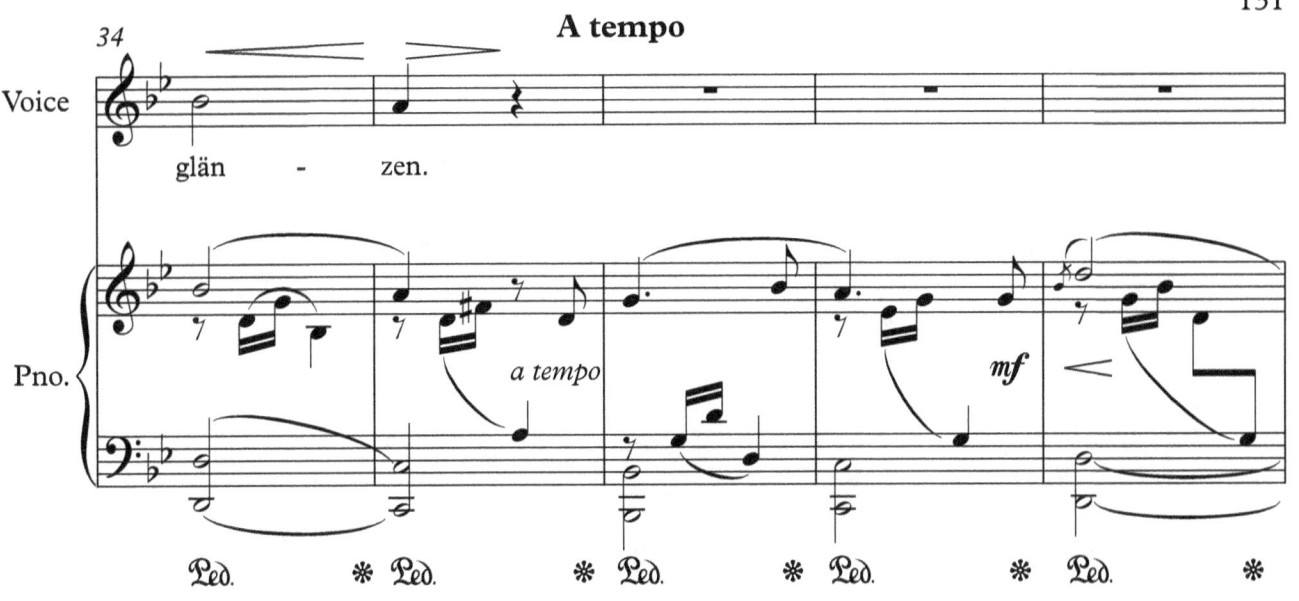
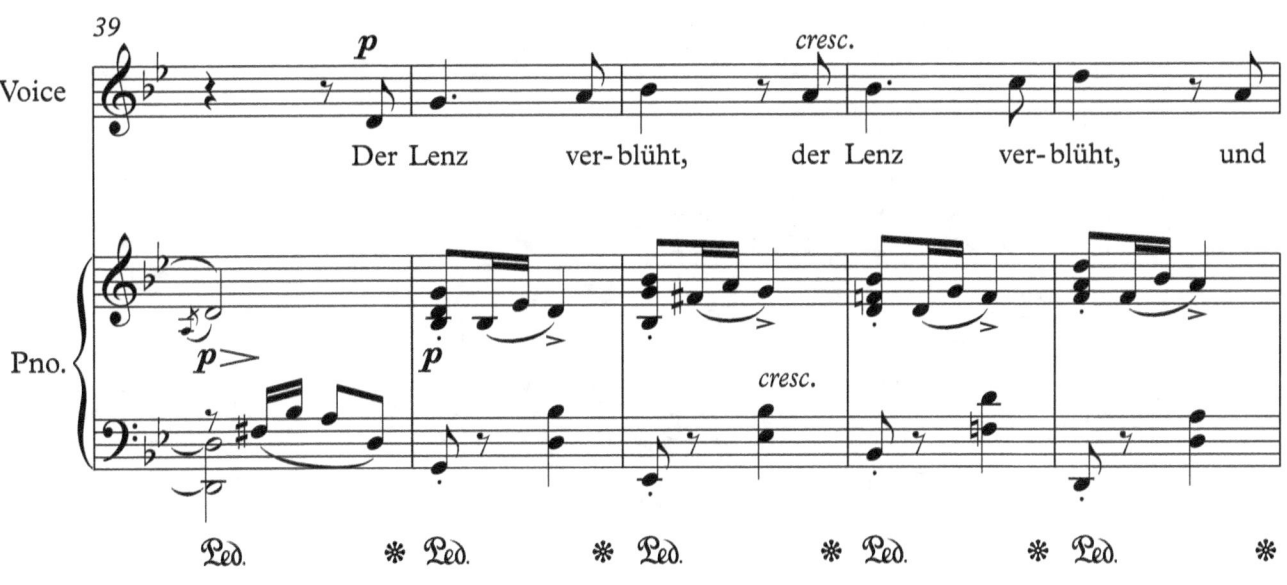

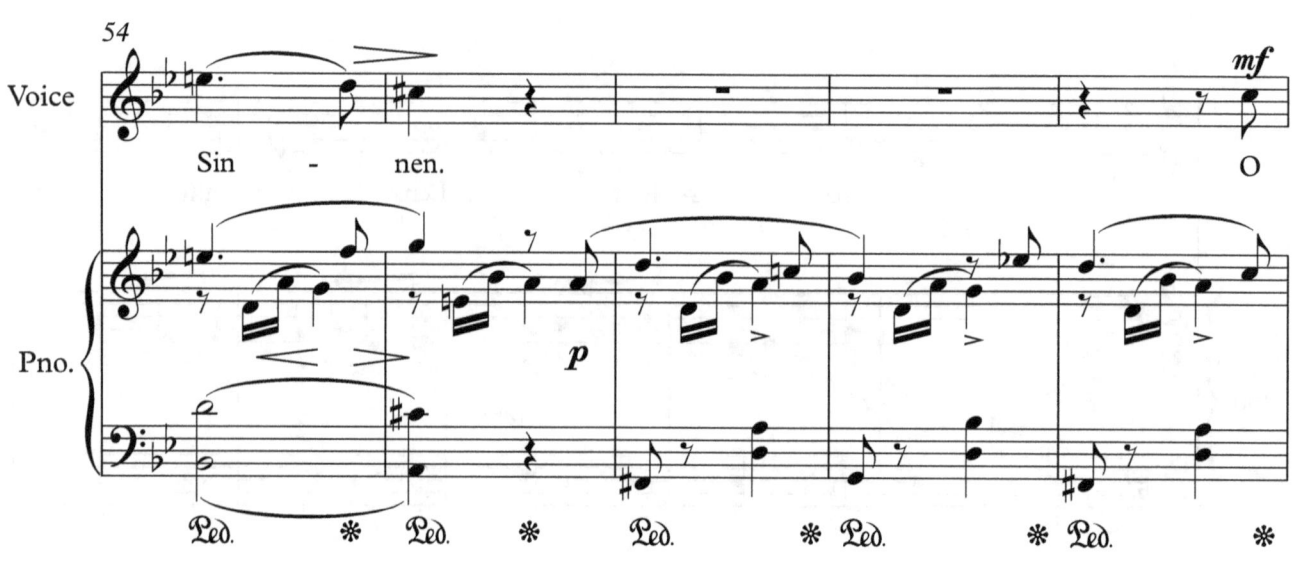

Will über Nacht wohl durch das Thal

Frau Dr Livia Frege zugeeignet

Wilhelm Osterwald
Robert Franz, Op. 5 No. 4

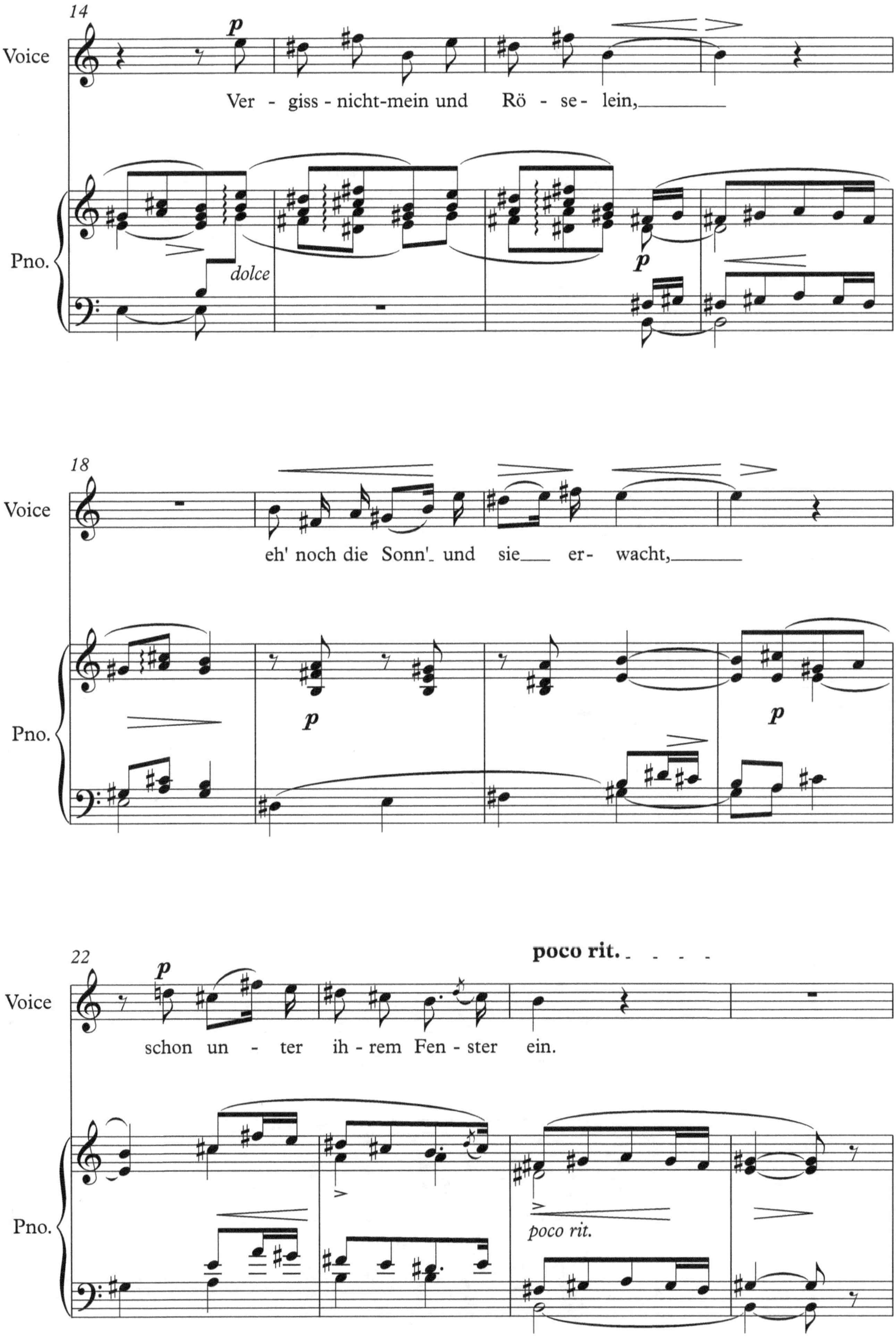
14
Voice
p
Ver - giss - nicht-mein und Rö - se - lein,
Pno.
dolce
p
18
Voice
eh' noch die Sonn' und sie er- wacht,
Pno.
p
p
22
poco rit.
Voice
p
schon un - ter ih - rem Fen - ster ein.
Pno.
poco rit.

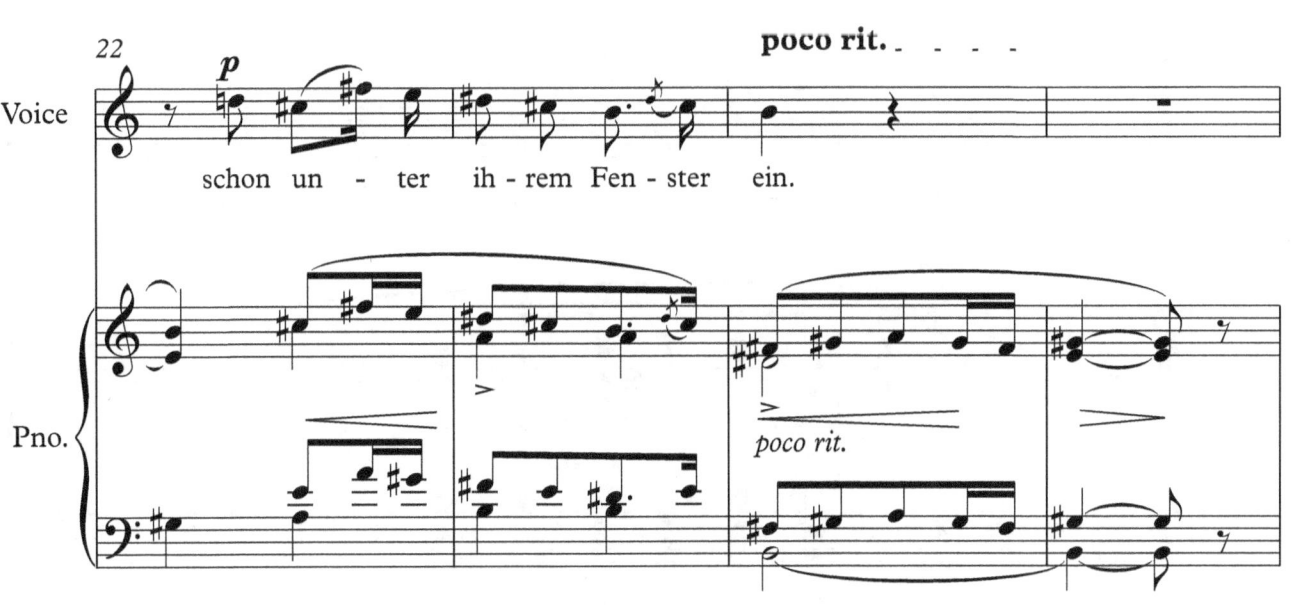

Ich lobe mir die Vögelein

Wilhelm Osterwald Robert Franz, Op. 5 No. 8

Copyright © Iain Sneddon 2019

Vergessen

Wilhelm Osterwald
Robert Franz, Op. 5 No. 10

Erschien früher unter der Überschrift 'Erinnerung'

Copyright © Iain Sneddon 2019

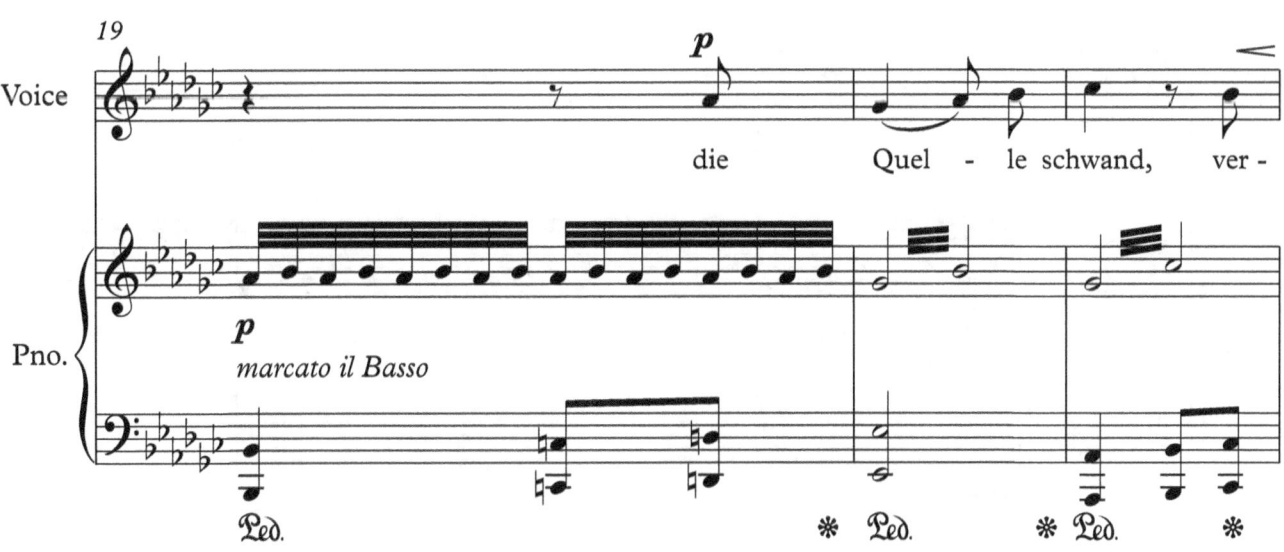

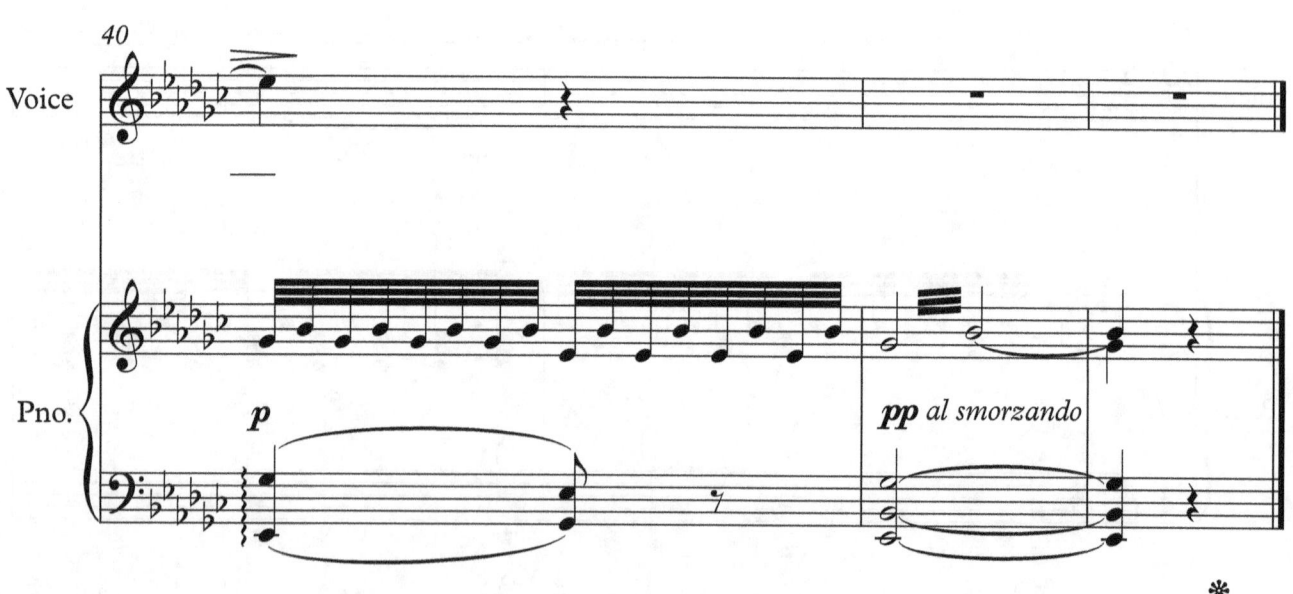

Seinem Freunde Friedrich Hinrichs zugeeignet

Die Liebe hat gelogen!

Wilhelm Osterwald
Robert Franz, Op. 6 No. 4

148

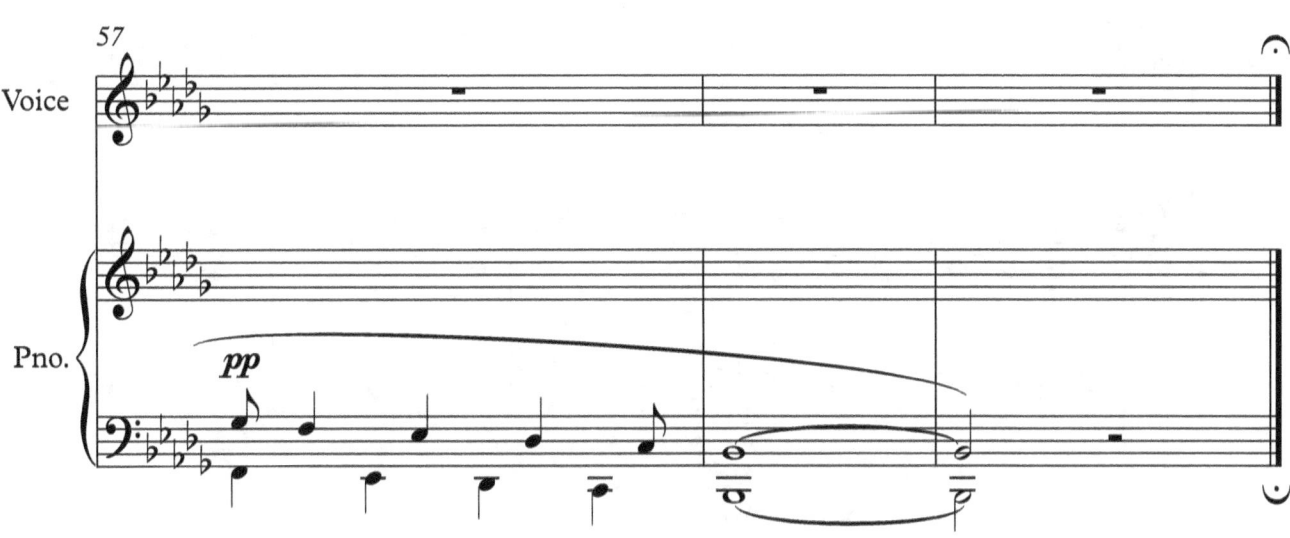

Der Schnee ist zergangen

Wilhelm Osterwald

Robert Franz, Op. 6 No. 5

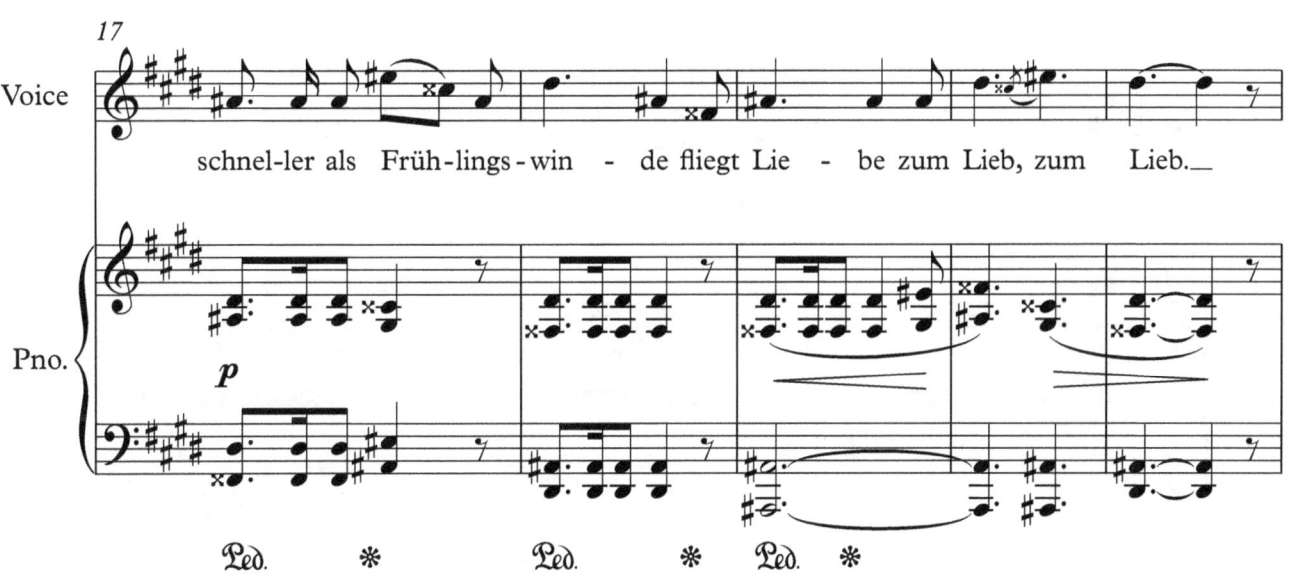
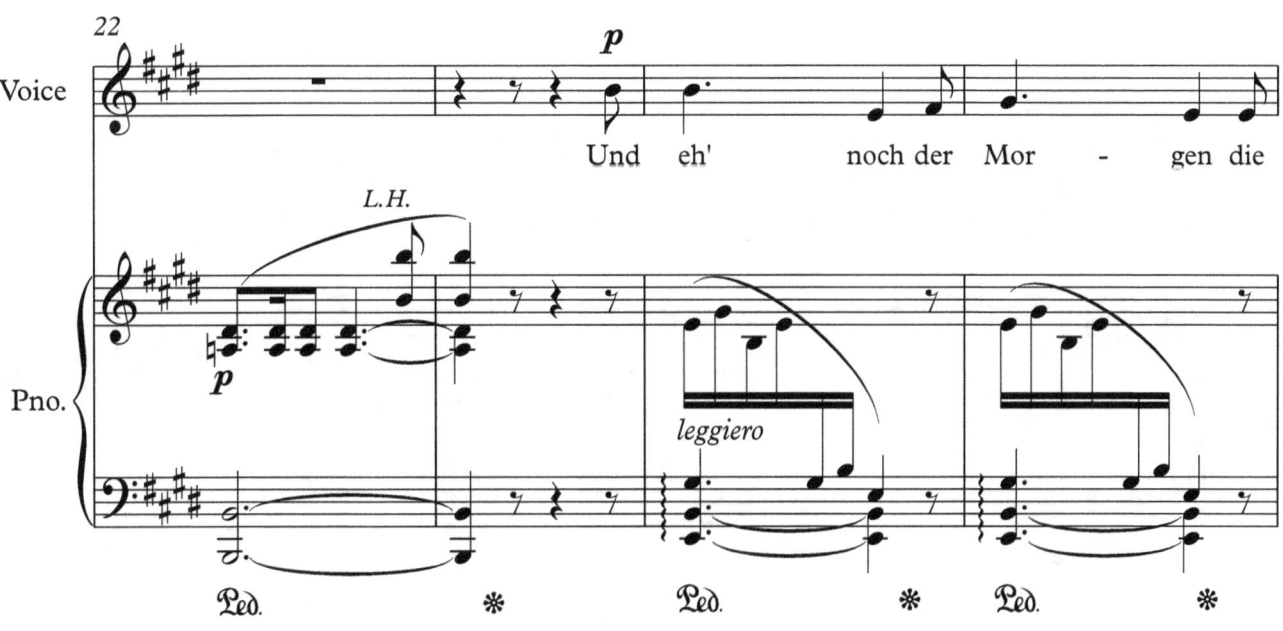

Franz Liszt zugeeignet
Der junge Tag erwacht

Wilhelm Osterwald

Robert Franz, Op. 7 No. 1

Copyright © Iain Sneddon 2019

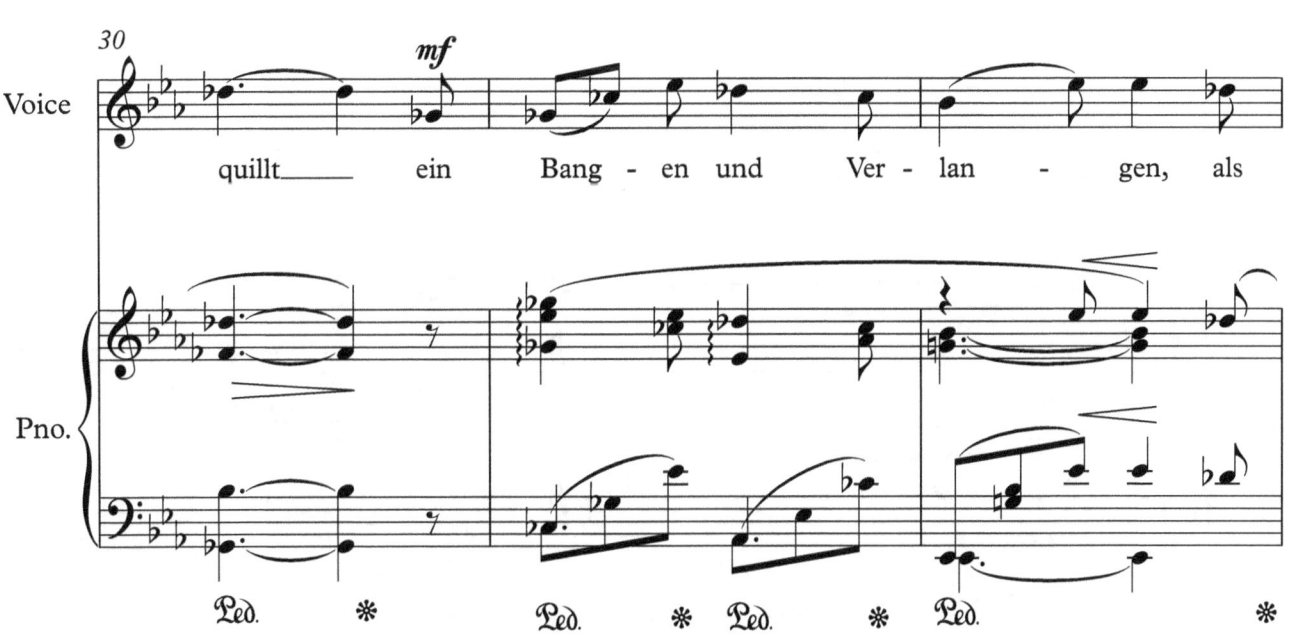

158

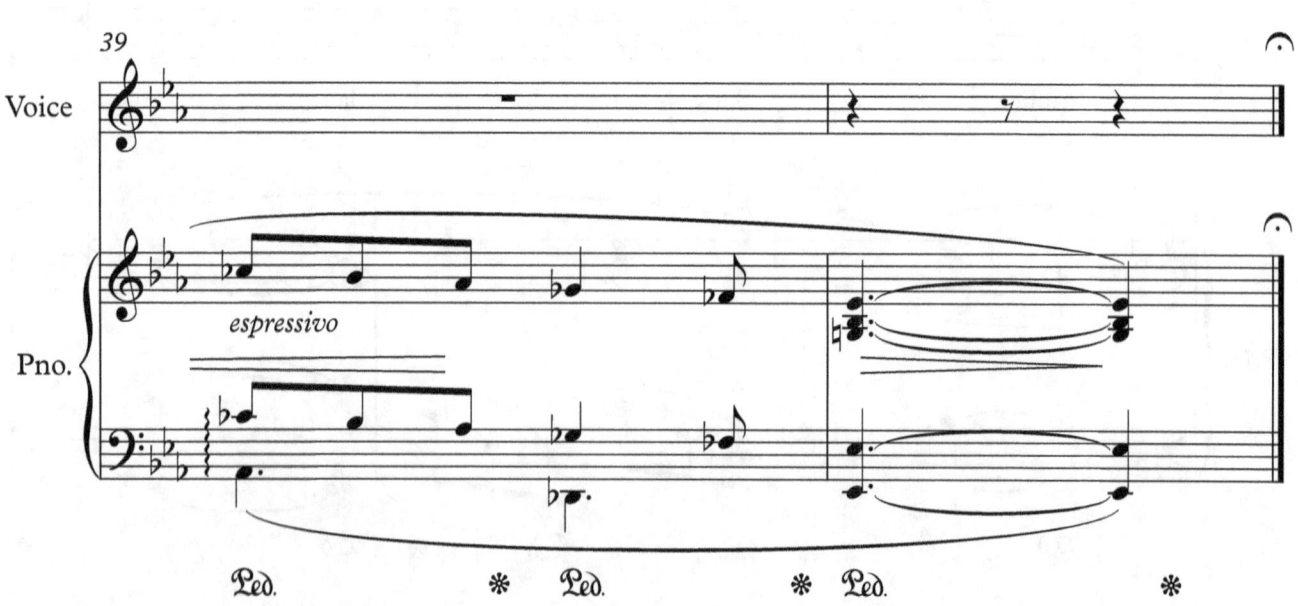

Da die Stunde kam

Wilhelm Osterwald
Robert Franz, Op. 7 No. 3

Treibt der Sommer seinen Rosen

Seinem Freunde Otto Dresel zugeeignet

Wilhelm Osterwald

Robert Franz, Op. 8 No. 5

Copyright © Iain Sneddon 2019

Gewitternacht

Wilhelm Osterwald
Robert Franz, Op. 8 No. 6

Copyright © Iain Sneddon 2019

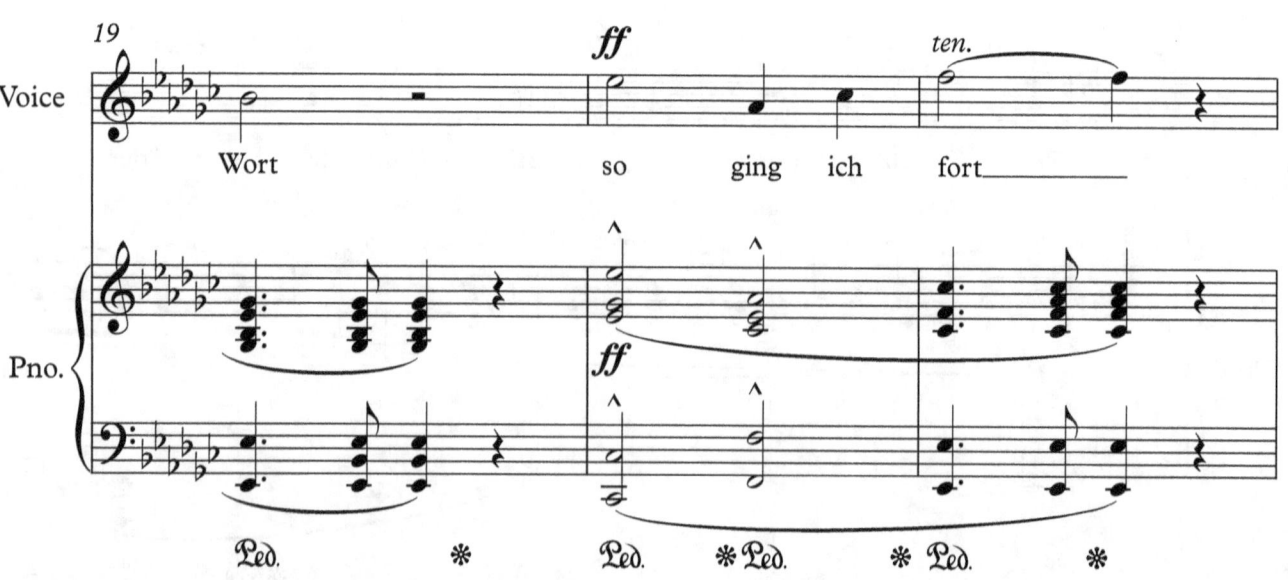

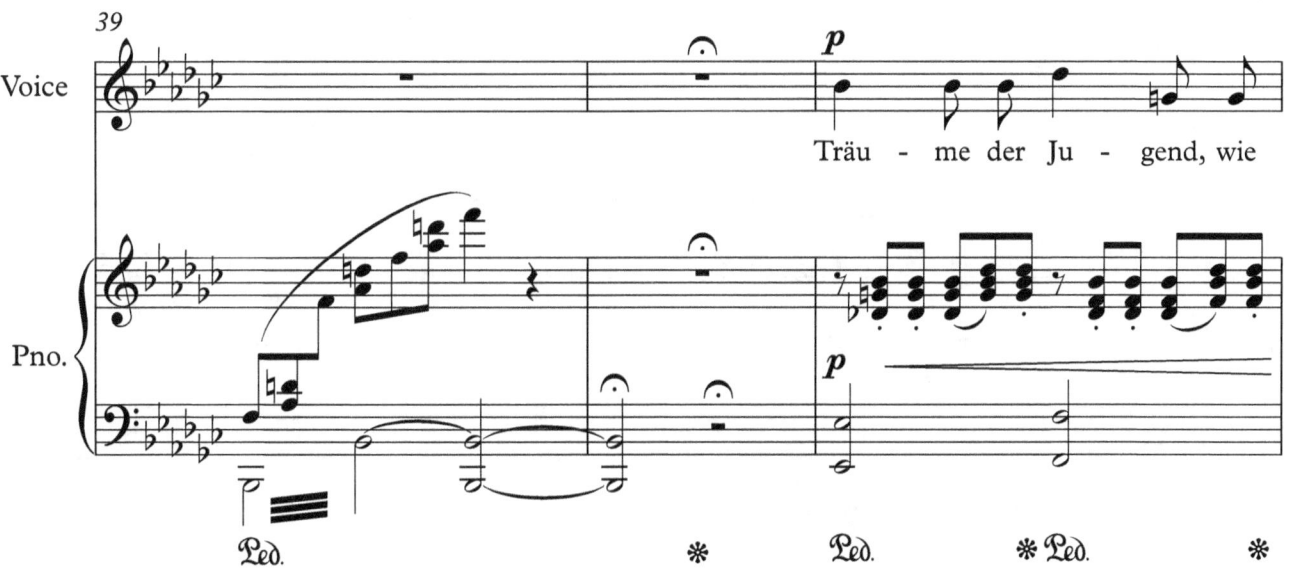

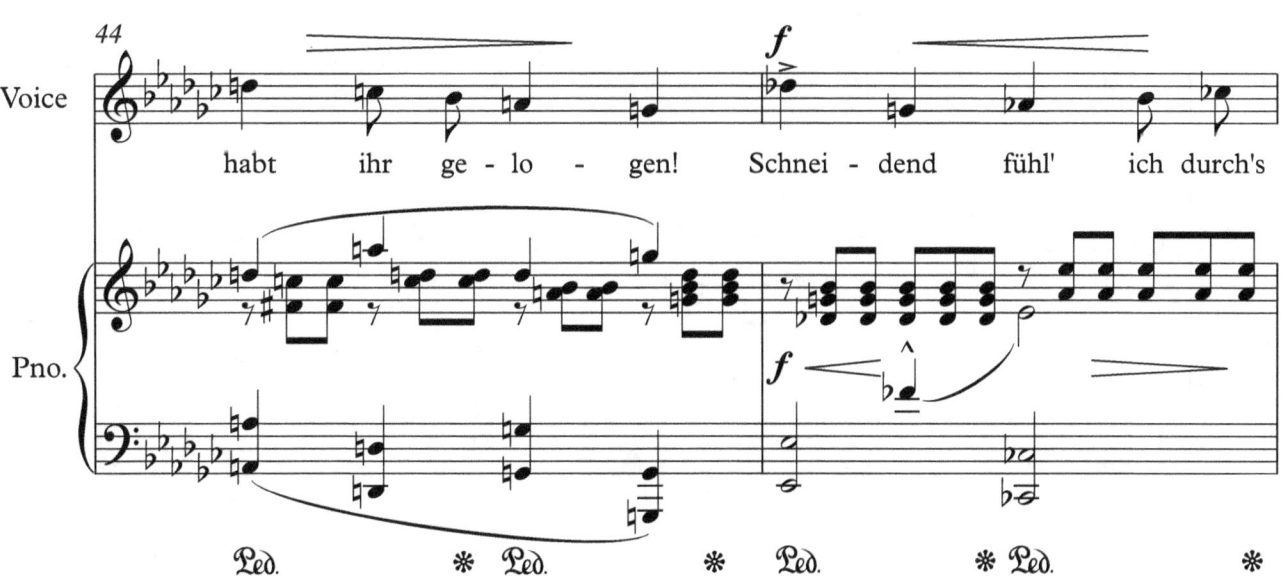

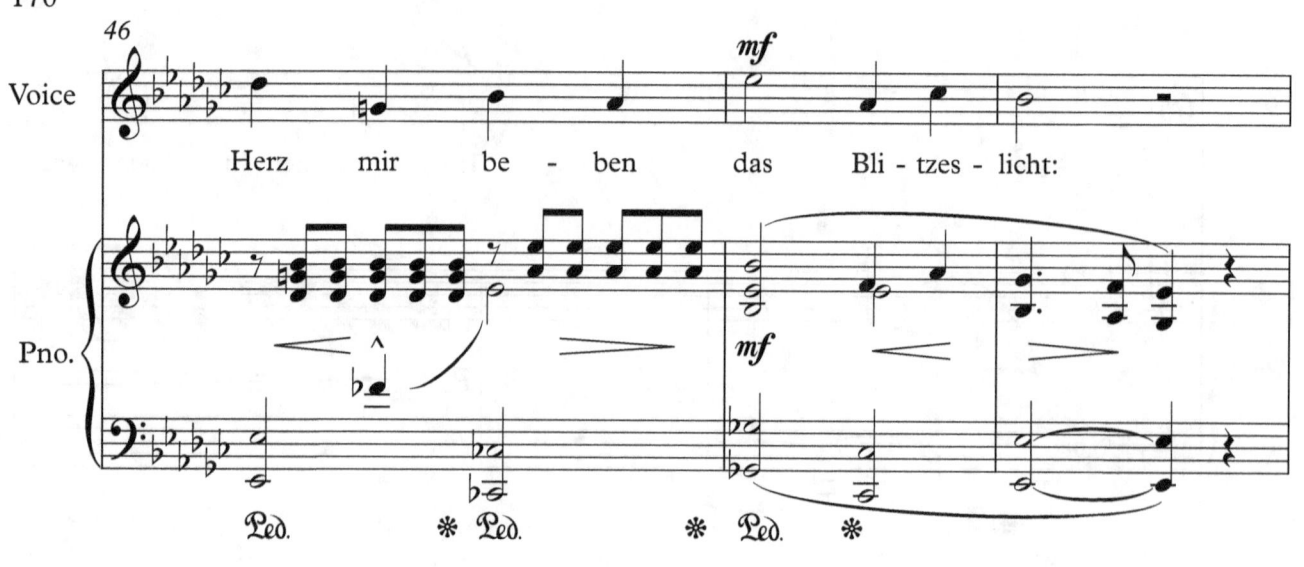

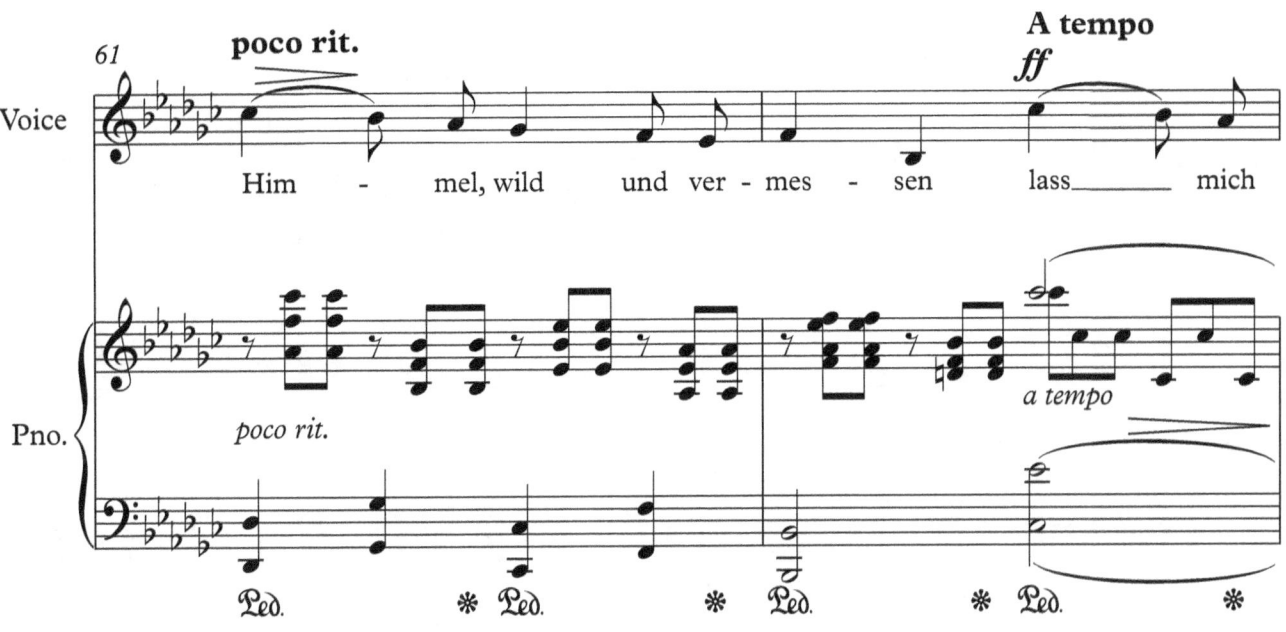
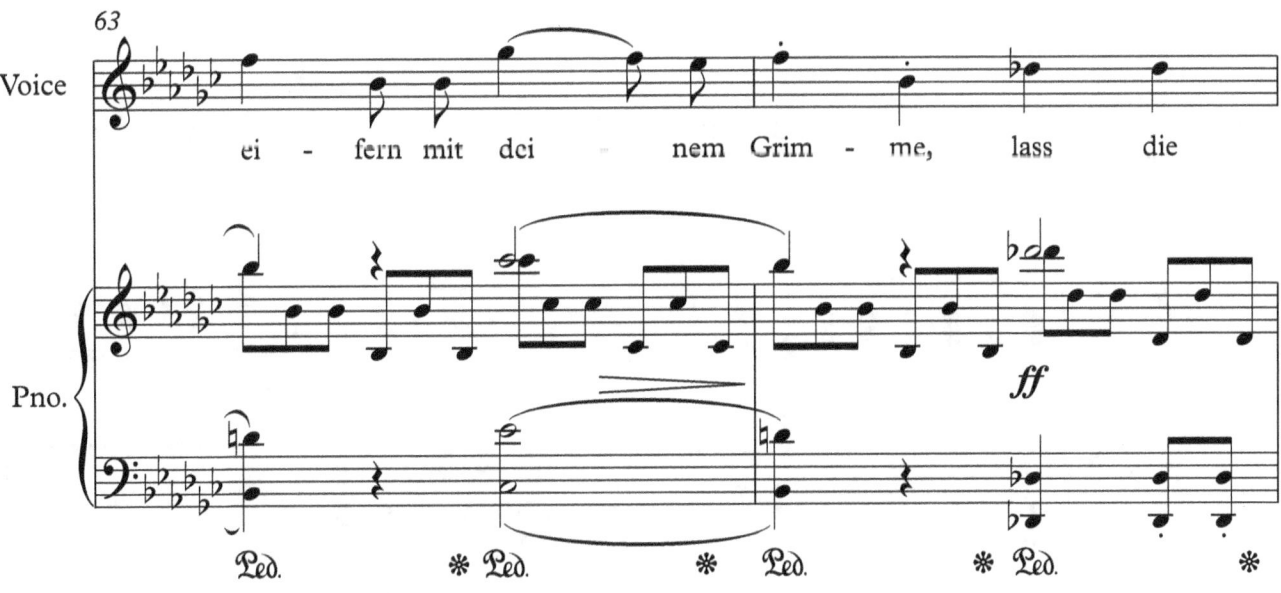

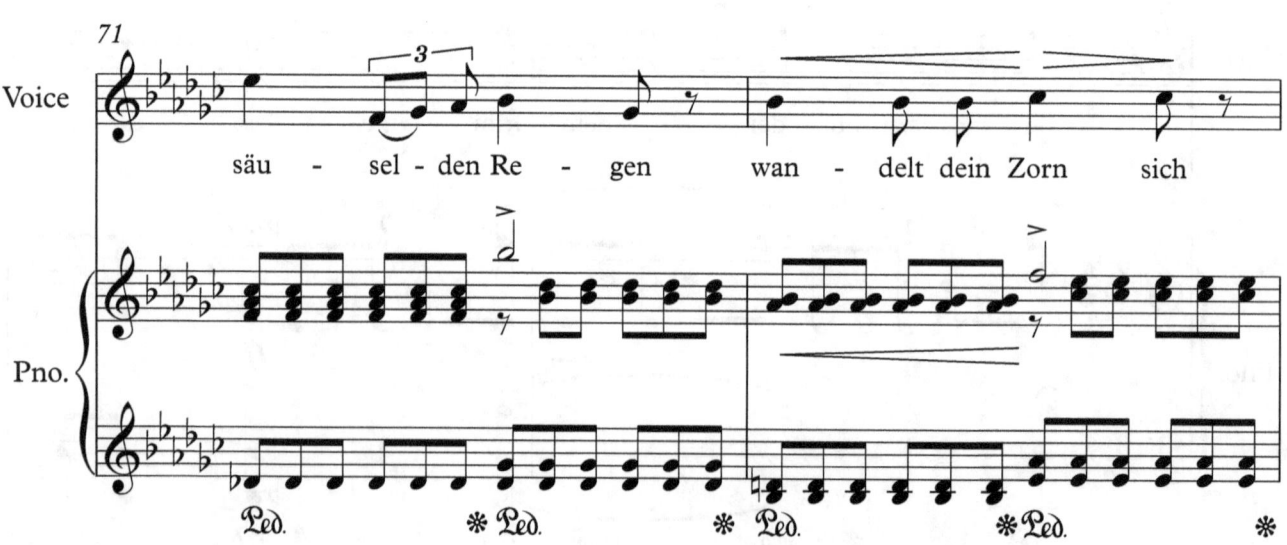

Vom Berge

Wilhelm Osterwald

Robert Franz, Op. 9 No. 5

Allegretto grazioso
Frisch, gut zu deklamiren

Jetzt steh' ich auf der höch-sten Höh', und lug' in das Land hin-ein, ob ich nicht mein Herz al-ler-lieb-ster seh', a-ber ach!

Copyright © Iain Sneddon 2019

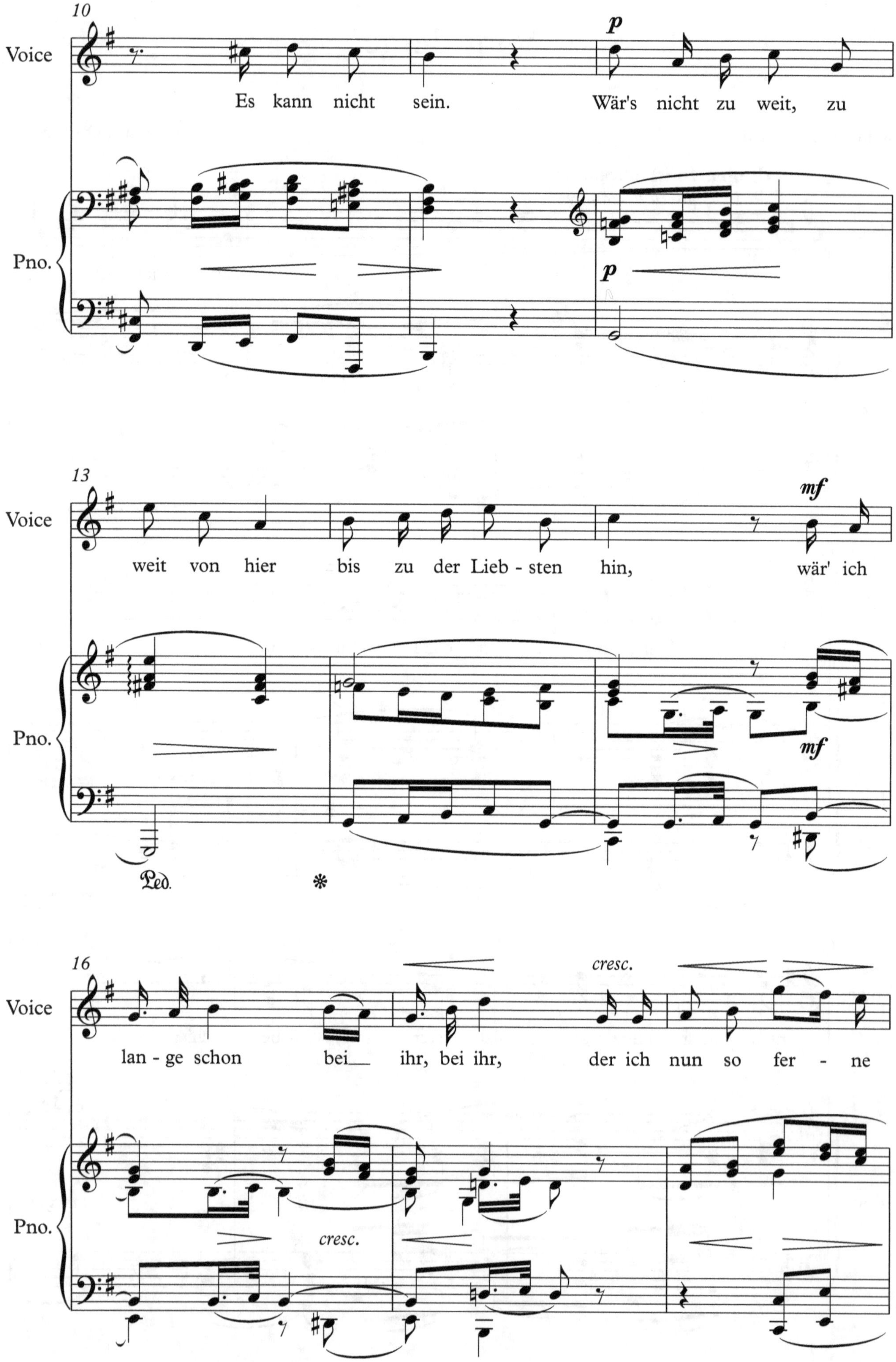
10
Voice
Es kann nicht sein. Wär's nicht zu weit, zu
Pno.
p
13
Voice
weit von hier bis zu der Lieb - sten hin, wär' ich
mf
Pno.
Ped.
16
Voice
lan - ge schon bei ihr, bei ihr, der ich nun so fer - ne
cresc.
Pno.
cresc.

Fräulein Louise von Platen zugeeignet

Und die Rosen, die prangen

Wilhelm Osterwald

Robert Franz, Op. 10 No. 5

Copyright © Iain Sneddon 2019

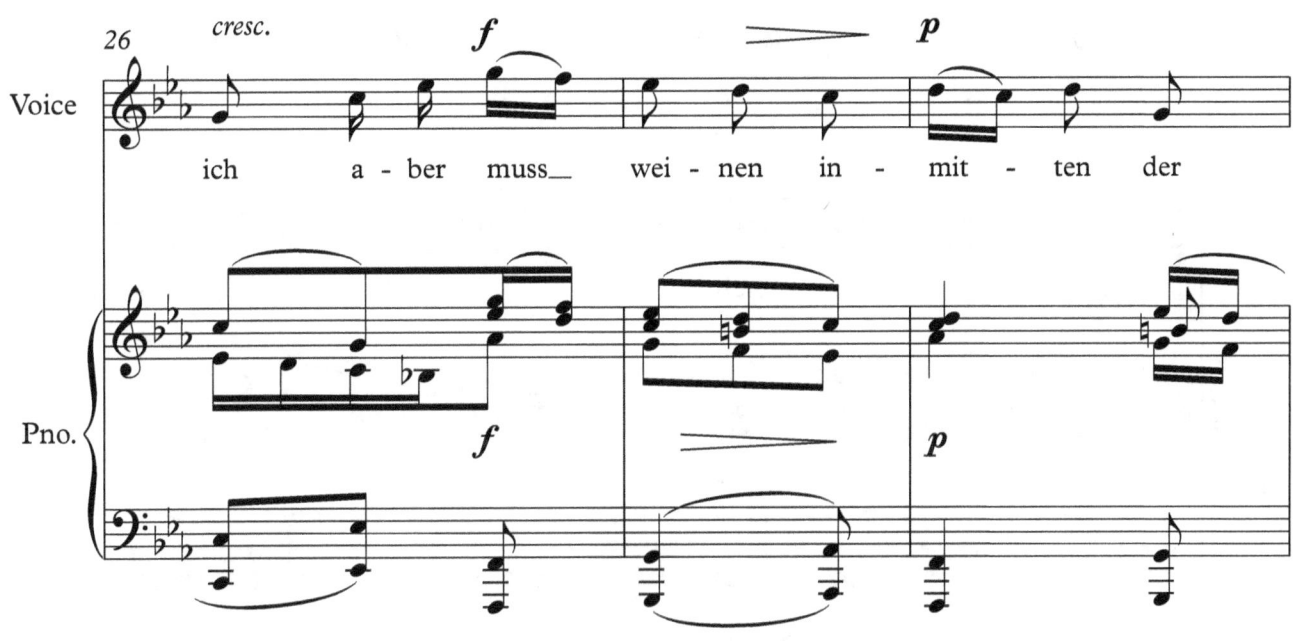

Umsonst

Wilhelm Osterwald
Robert Franz, Op. 10 No. 6

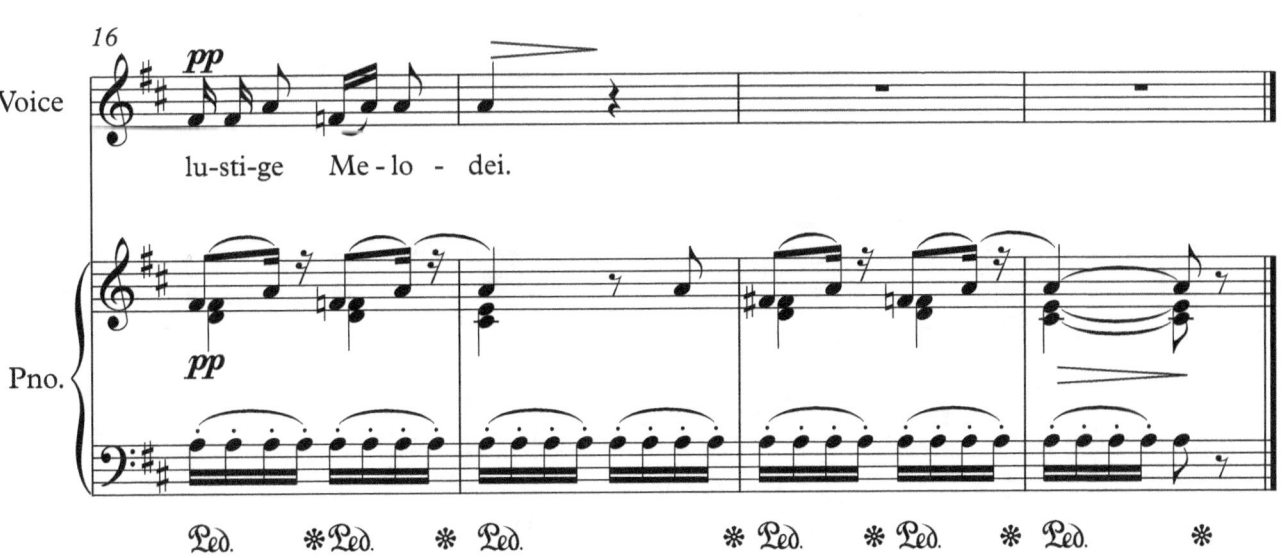

Im Mai

Fräulein Helen Göschel zugeeignet

Wilhelm Osterwald
Robert Franz, Op. 11 No. 3

Copyright © Iain Sneddon 2019

187

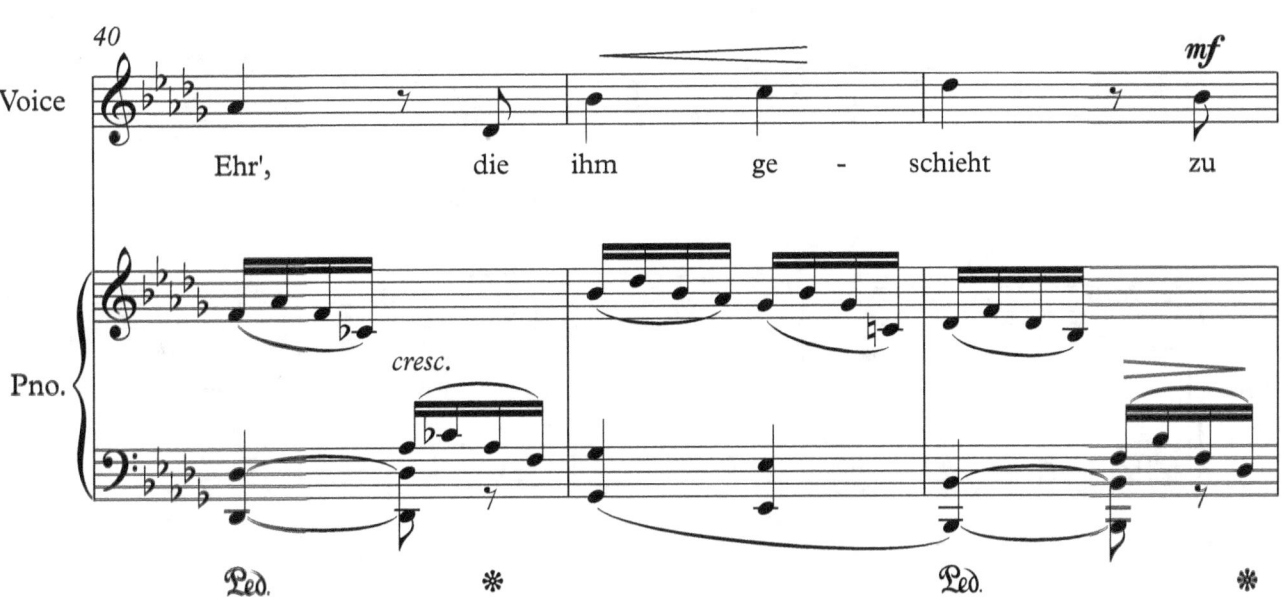

Im Sommer

Wilhelm Osterwald
Robert Franz, Op. 11 No. 4

Copyright © Iain Sneddon 2019

Und welche Rose Blüthen treibt

Wilhelm Osterwald

Andantino con moto
Mit innigem Ausdruck

Robert Franz, Op. 12 No. 1

198

*Ihrer Königlichen Hoheit der Durchlauchtigsten Fürstin und Frau Sophie Erb-Großherzogin
zu Sachsen geborne Prinzessin der Niederlande ehrfurchtsvoll zugeeignet*

Um Mitternacht

Wilhelm Osterwald

Robert Franz, Op. 16 No. 6

Copyright © Iain Sneddon 2019

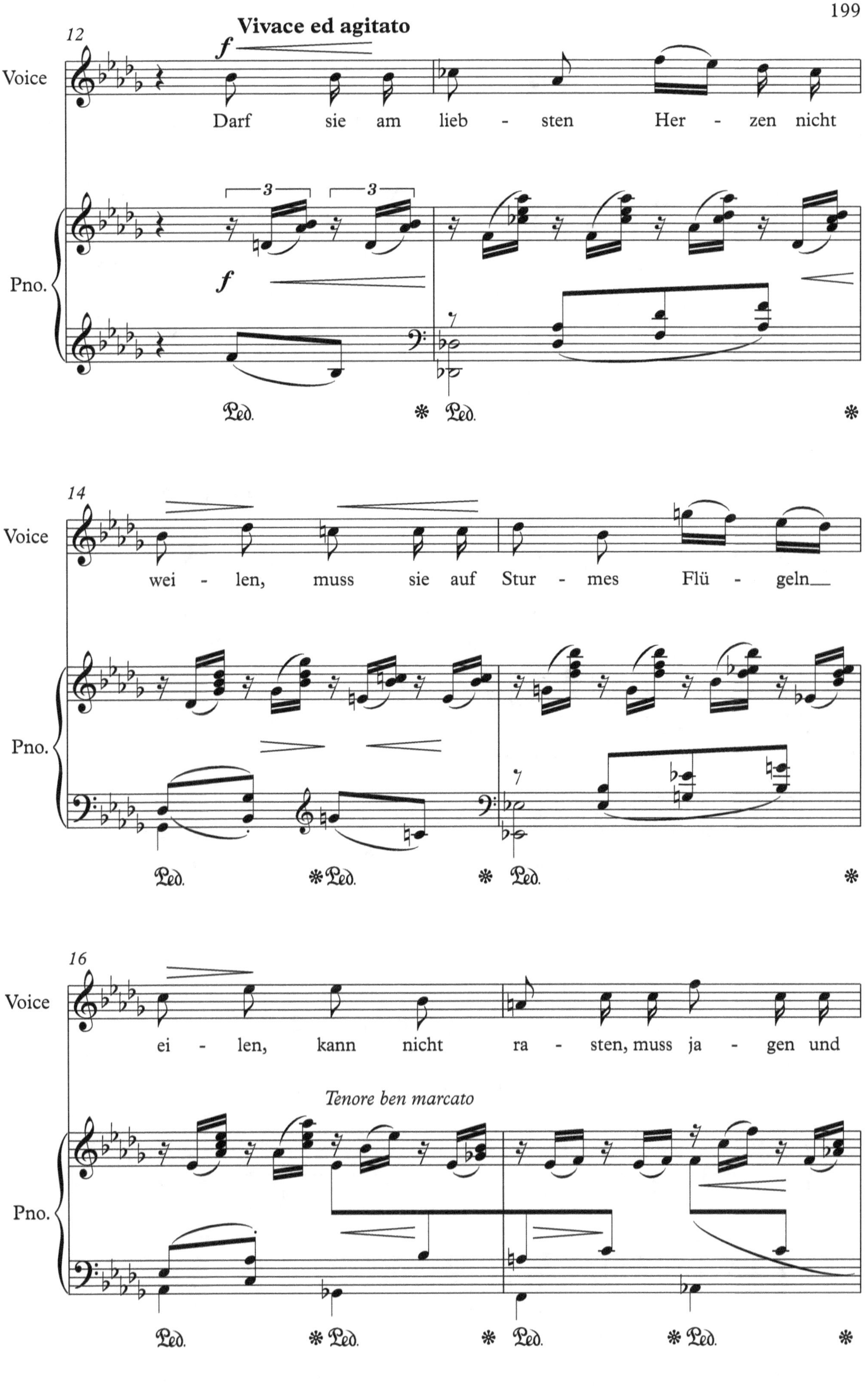
Vivace ed agitato
Voice
Pno.
Darf sie am lieb - sten Her - zen nicht
Ped.
wei - len, muss sie auf Stur - mes Flü - geln
ei - len, kann nicht ra - sten, muss ja - gen und
Tenore ben marcato

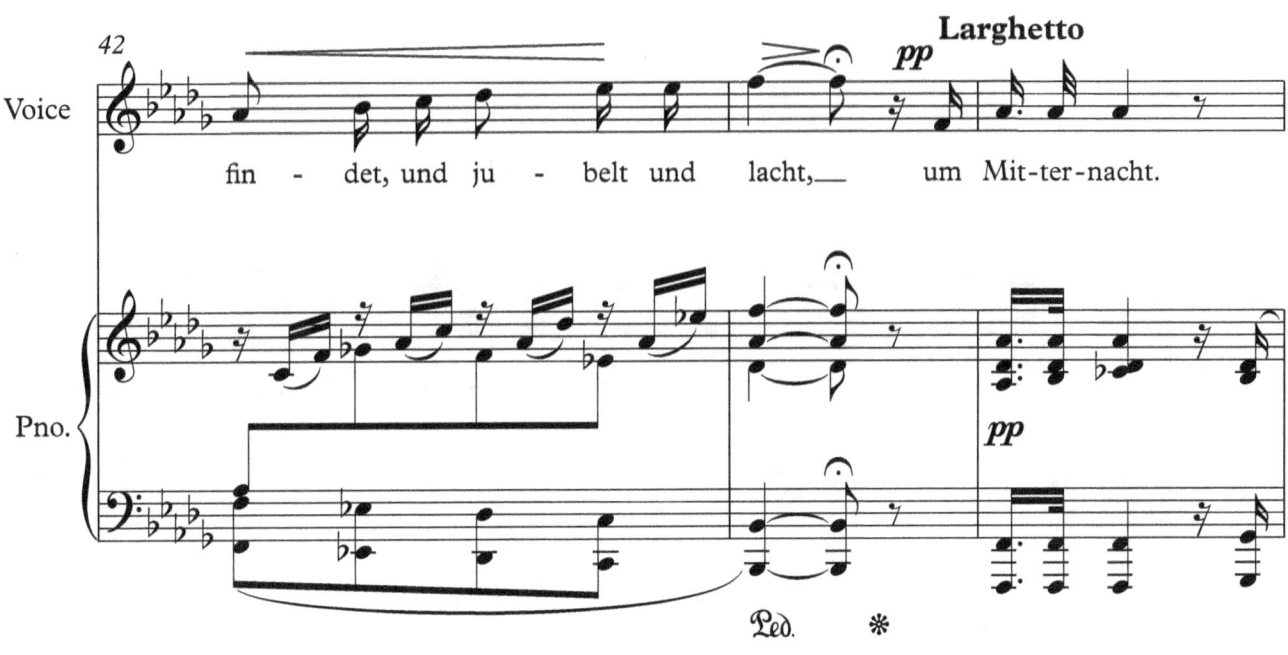
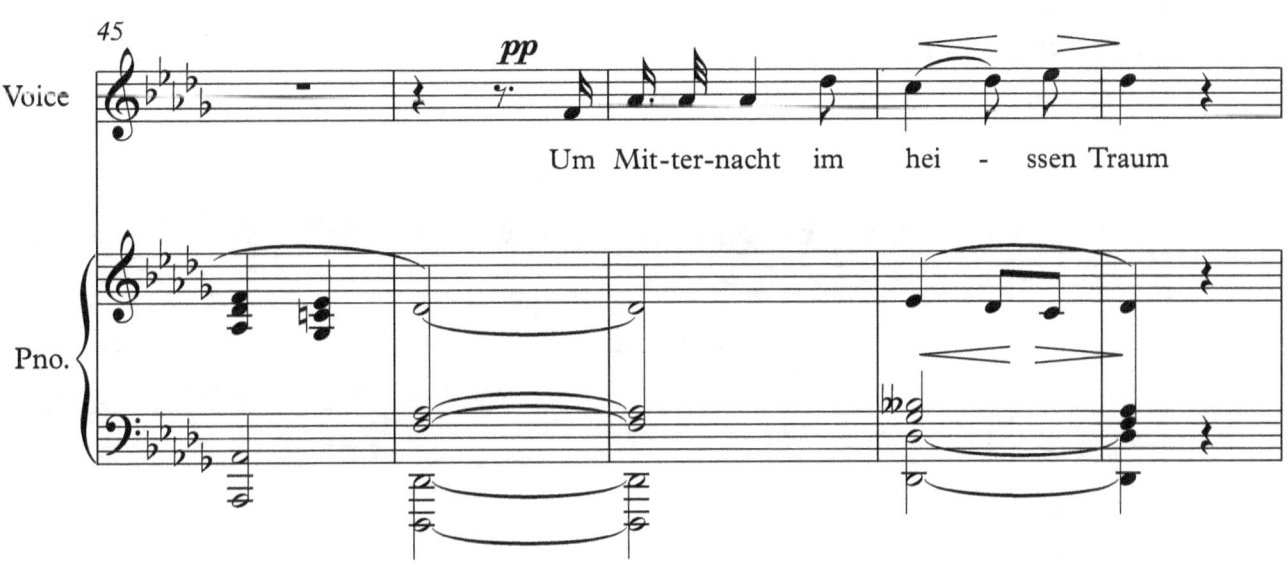

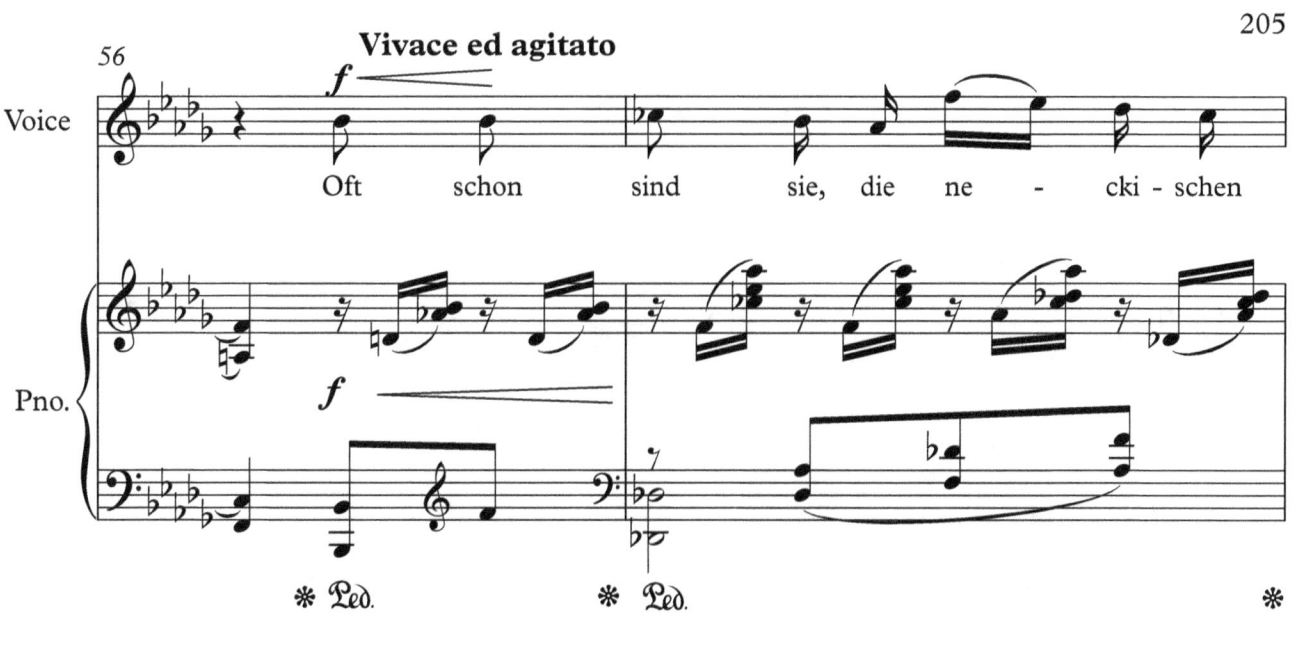

206

Joseph Tichatschek gewidmet
Ständchen

Wilhelm Osterwald
Robert Franz, Op.17 No. 2

208

Im Frühling

Wilhelm Osterwald
Robert Franz, Op. 17 No. 5

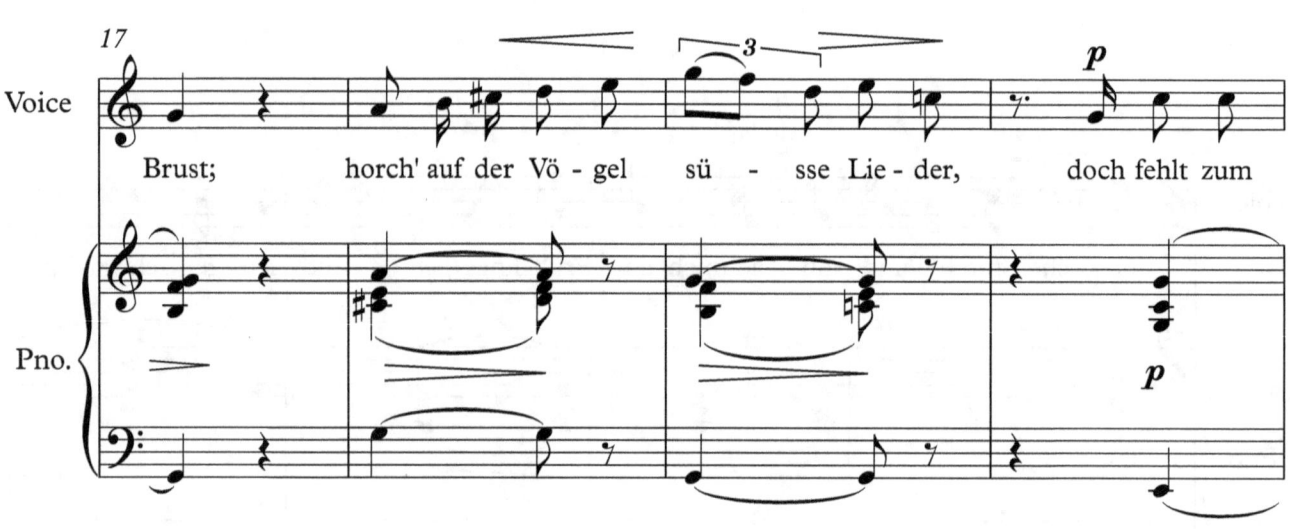

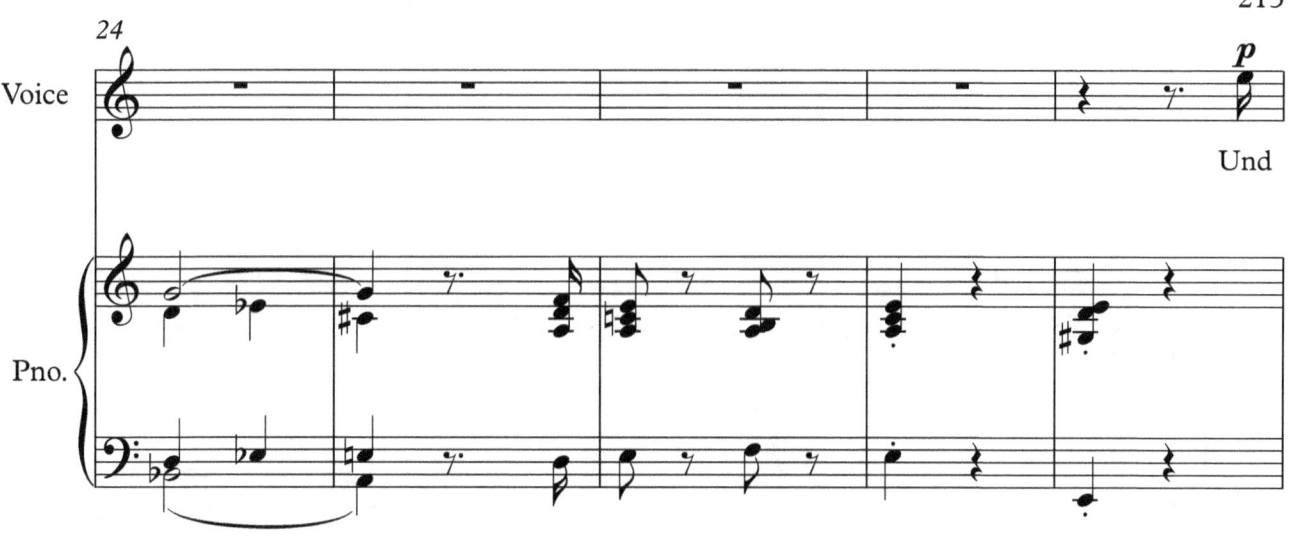

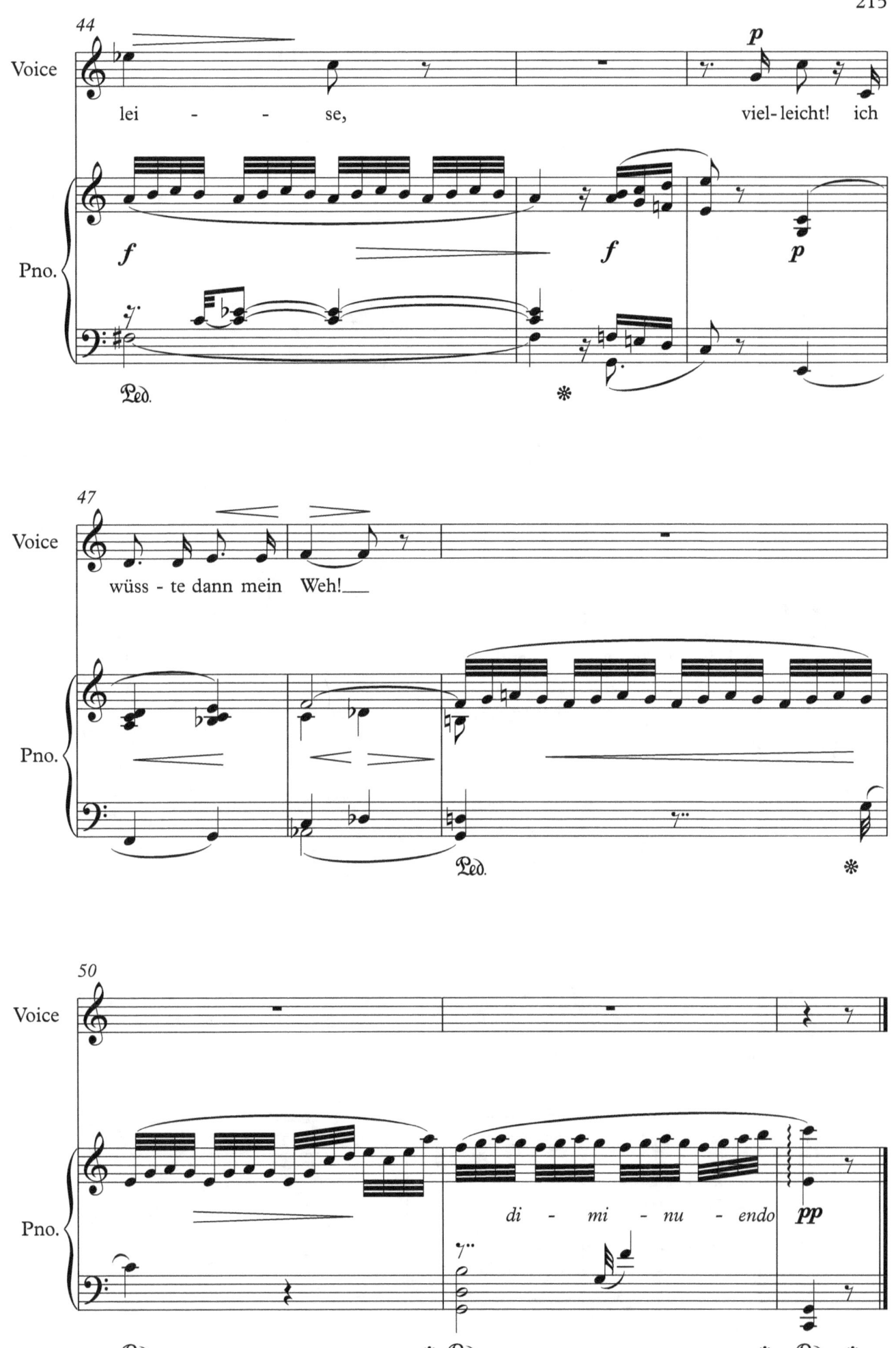

Herrn und Frau von Milde zugeeignet

Nun hat das Leid ein Ende

Wilhelm Osterwald

Robert Franz, Op. 18 No. 3

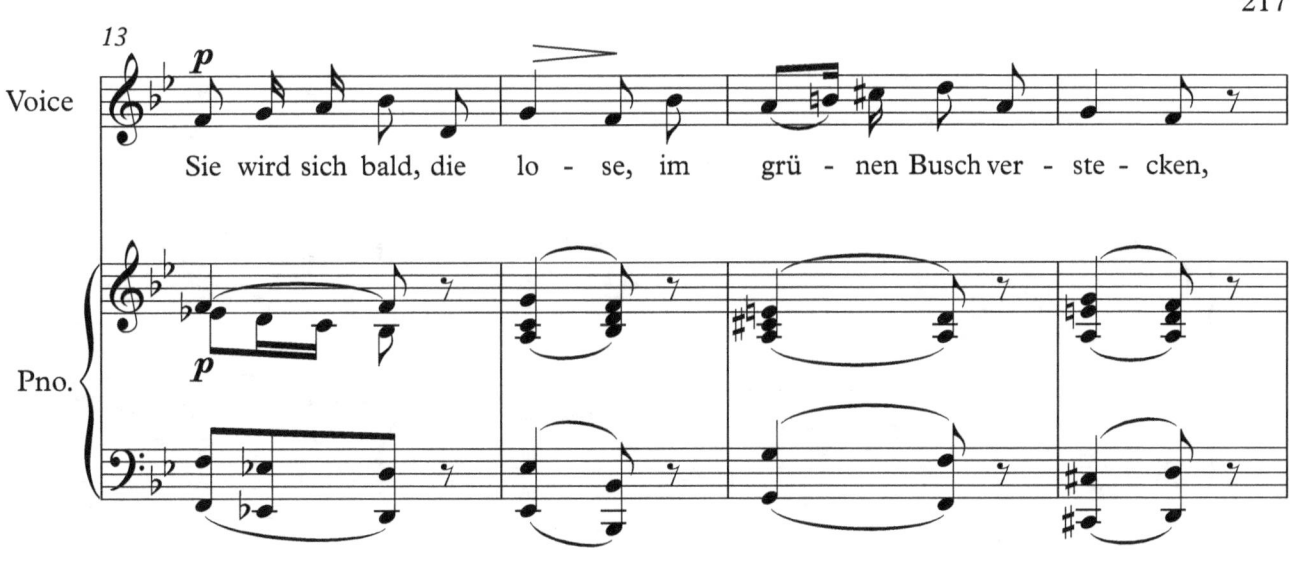

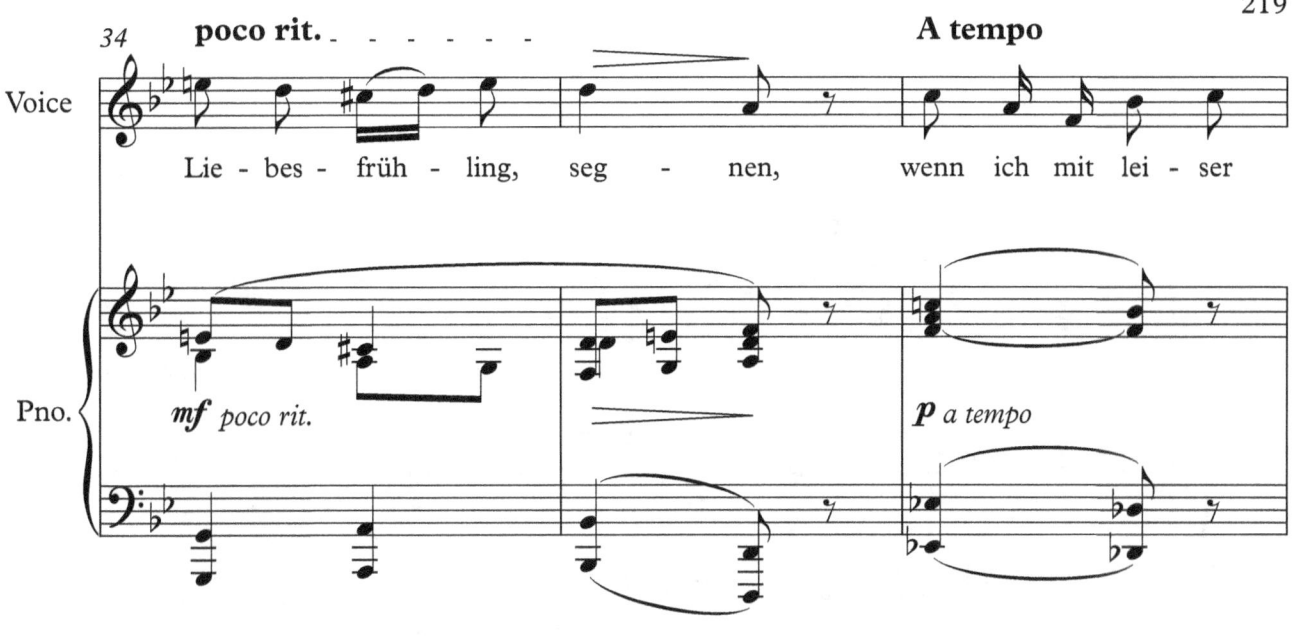

Dem Dichter und Componisten des Lohengrin Richard Wagner gewidmet

Abends

Wilhelm Osterwald
Robert Franz, Op. 20 No. 4

Copyright © Iain Sneddon 2019

222

Verlass' mich nicht!

Seinem Freunde Wilhelm Osterwald zugeeignet vom Componisten

Wilhelm Osterwald
Robert Franz, Op. 21 No. 6

Copyright © Iain Sneddon 2019

227

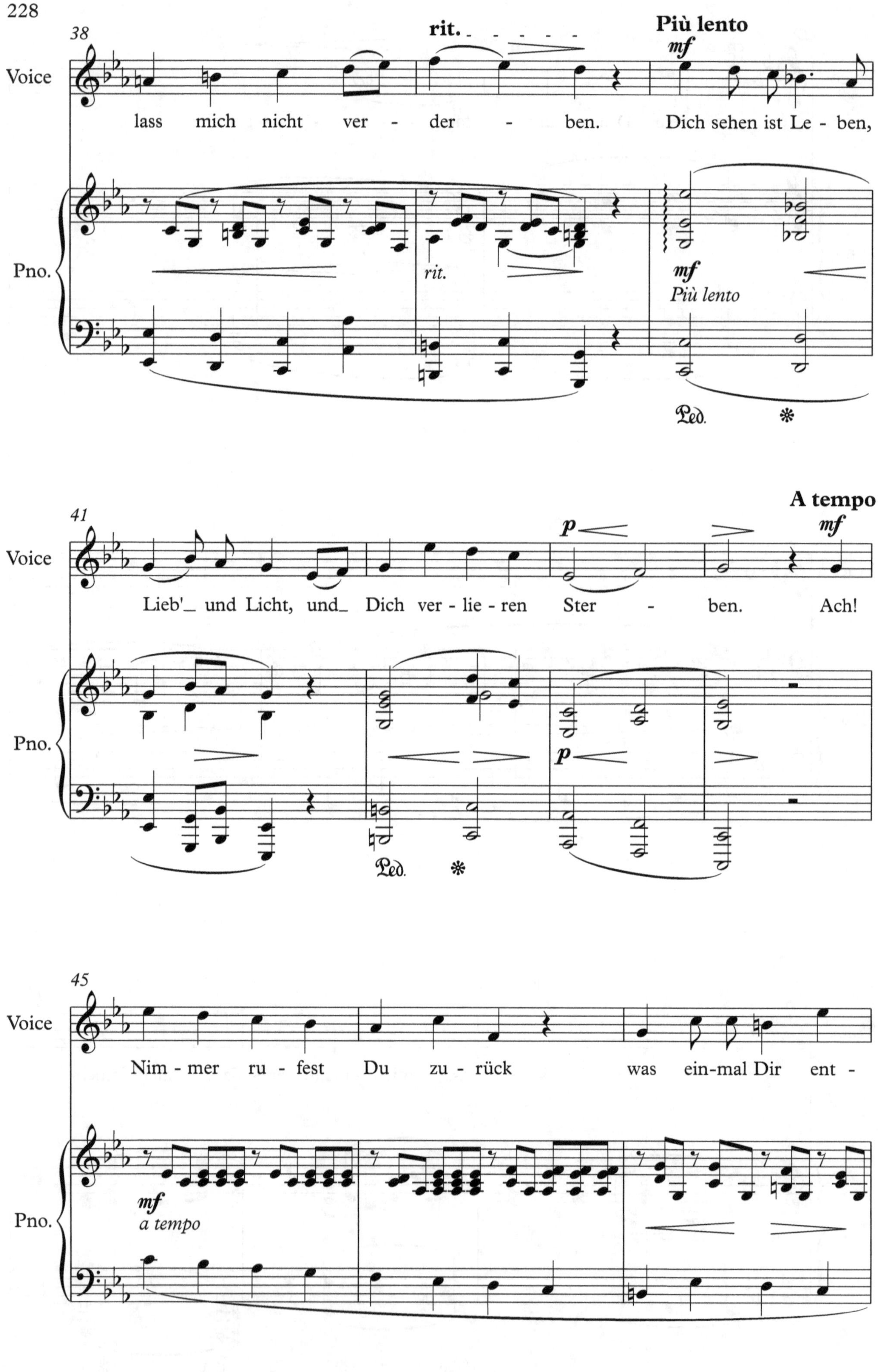
38
rit.
Più lento
mf
Voice
lass mich nicht ver - der - ben. Dich sehen ist Le - ben,
Pno.
rit.
mf
Più lento
Ped. *
41
A tempo
p
mf
Voice
Lieb'_ und Licht, und_ Dich ver - lie - ren Ster - ben. Ach!
Pno.
p
Ped. *
45
Voice
Nim - mer ru - fest Du zu - rück was ein-mal Dir ent -
Pno.
mf
a tempo

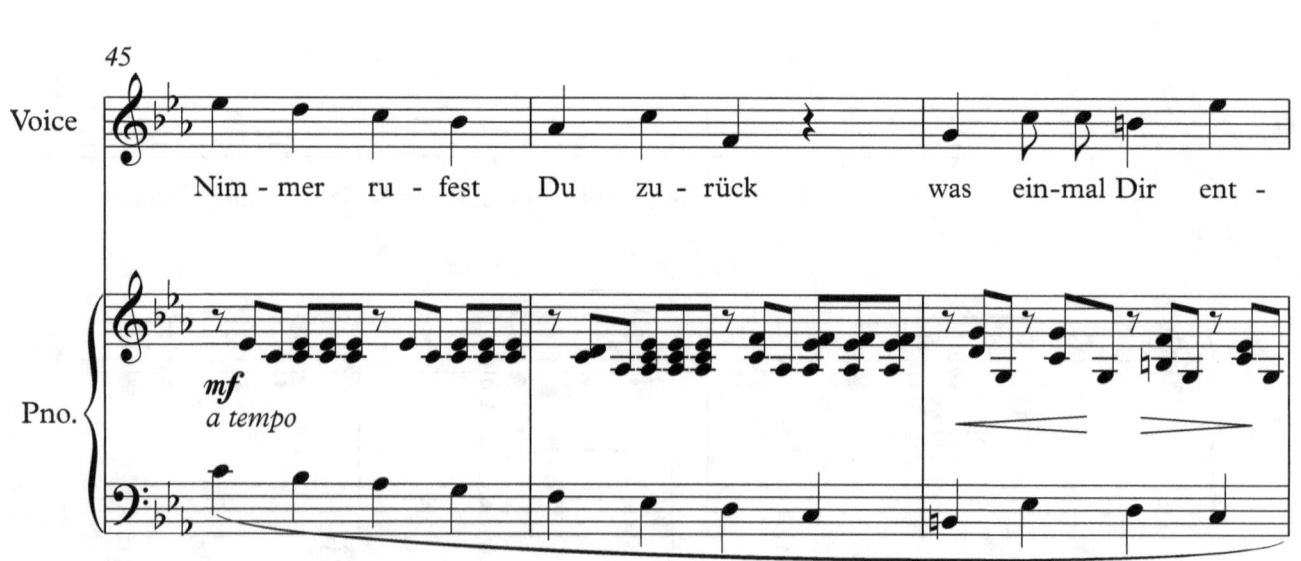

230

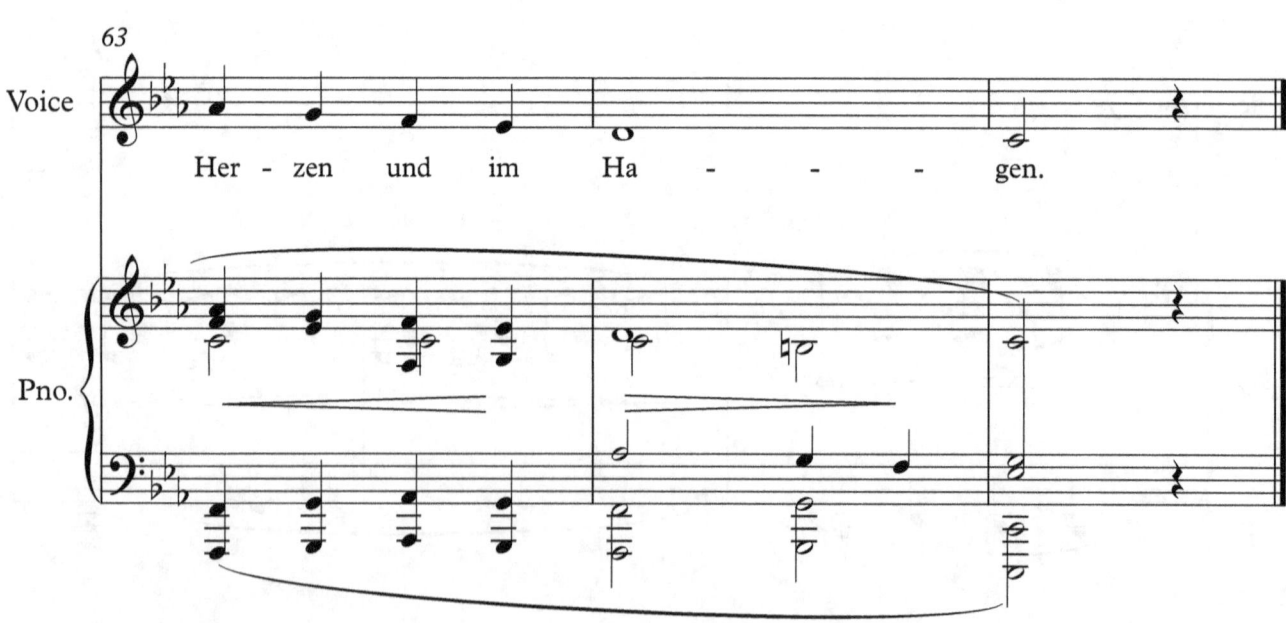

Frau Elizabeth Benzon gewidmet
Frühe Klage

Wlihelm Osterwald

Robert Franz, Op. 22 No. 4

Andante maestoso
p Nicht schleppend

Aus der Fer - ne schal - len Ge-sän - ge, froh von zit - tern der Luft___ ge wiegt;___ müs - set ver-we - hen, lieb - li - che Klän - ge, luf - tig und leicht wie die Ju - gend ver - fliegt.___

Copyright © Iain Sneddon 2019

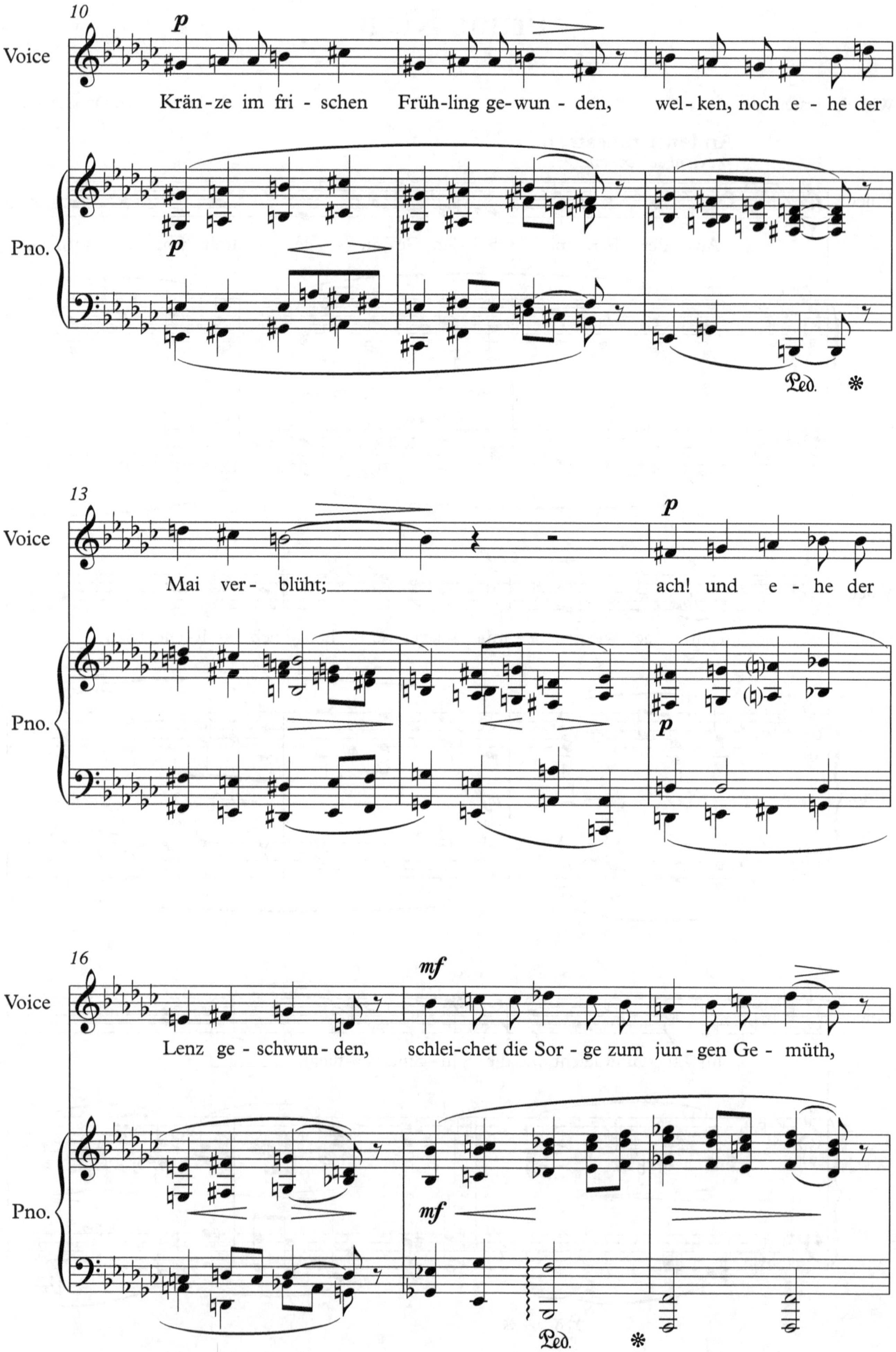
10
Voice
Pno.
Krän-ze im fri - schen Früh-ling ge-wun - den, wel-ken, noch e - he der
13
Mai ver - blüht; ach! und e - he der
16
Lenz ge - schwun - den, schlei-chet die Sor - ge zum jun - gen Ge - müth,

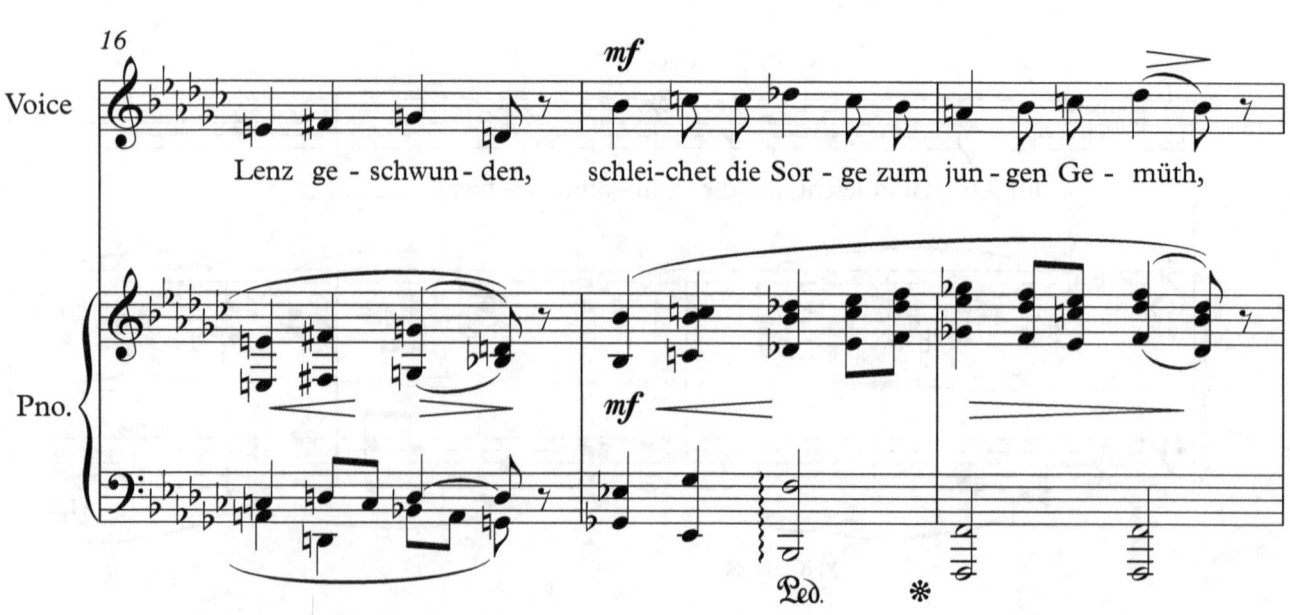

Im Mai

Wilhelm Osterwald

Robert Franz, Op 22 No. 5

Copyright © Iain Sneddon 2019

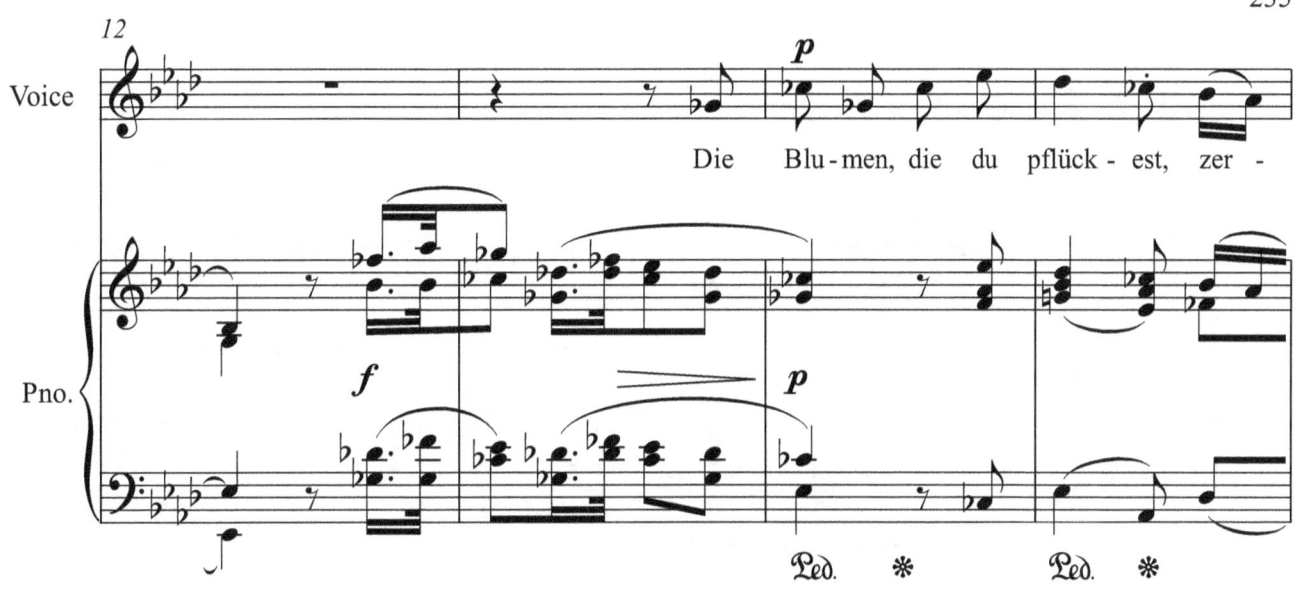

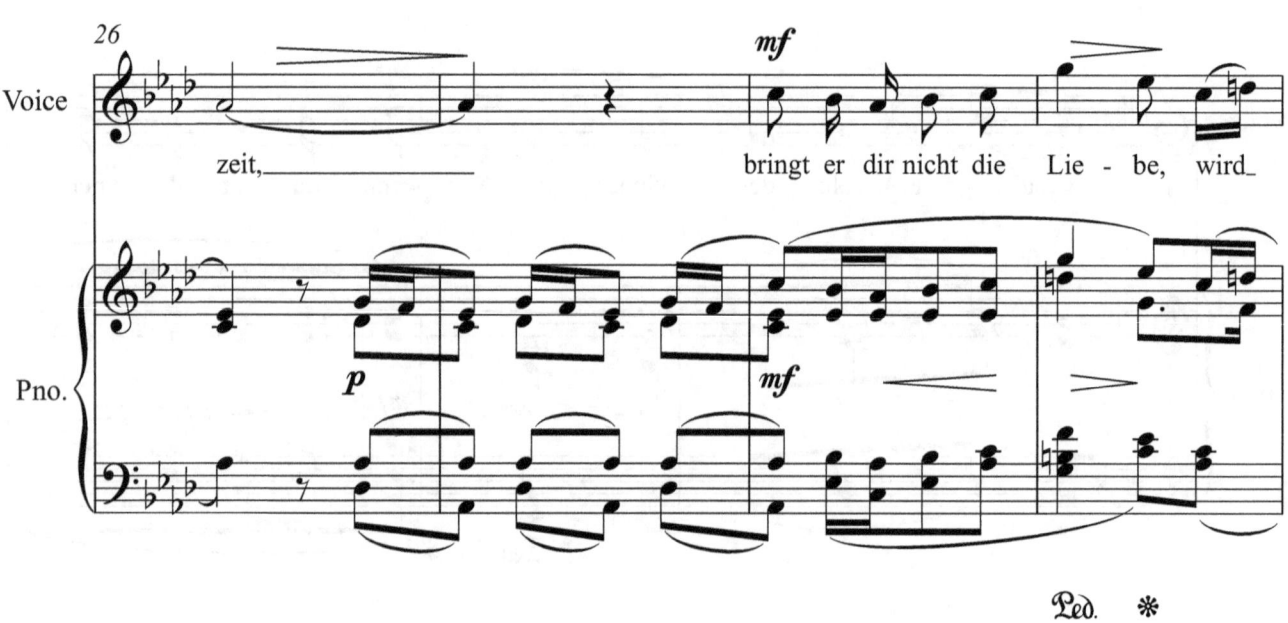

Fräulein Anna Volkmann zugeeignet
Wenn ich's nur wüsste!

Wilhelm Osterwald

Robert Franz, Op. 26 No. 1

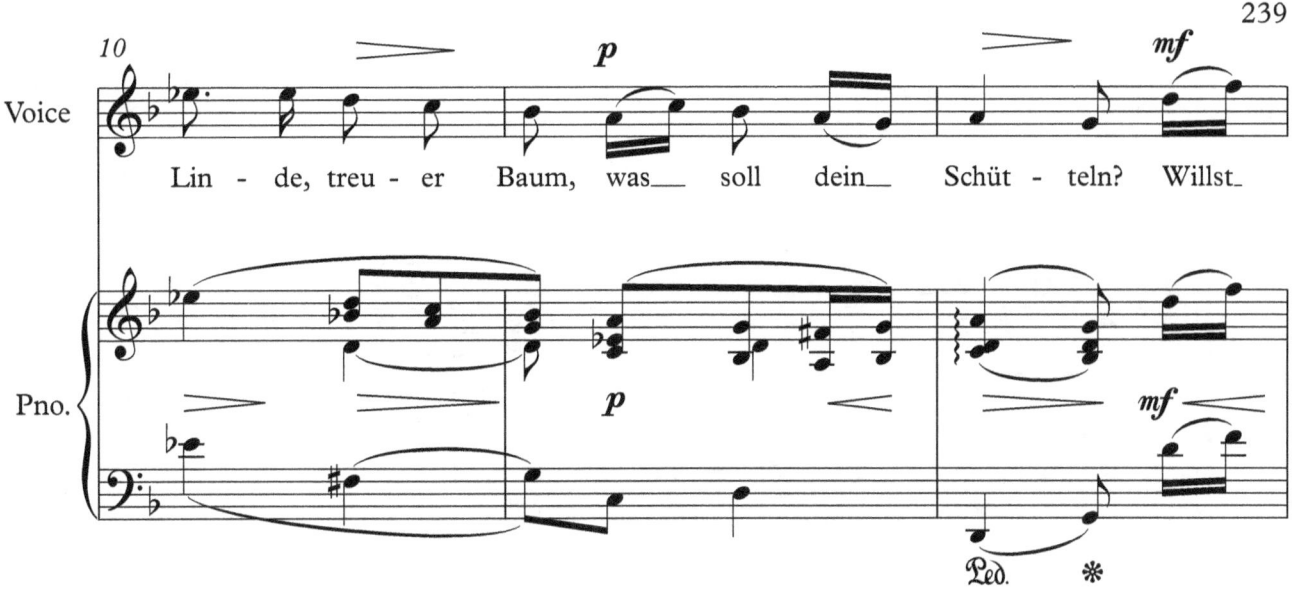

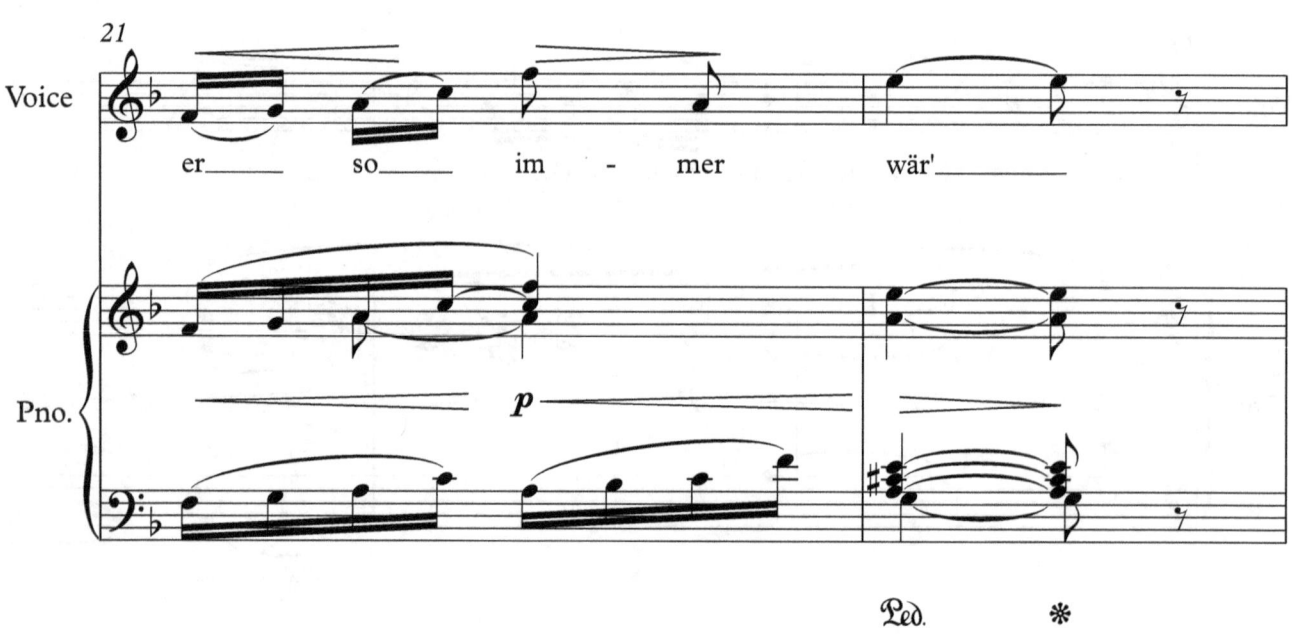
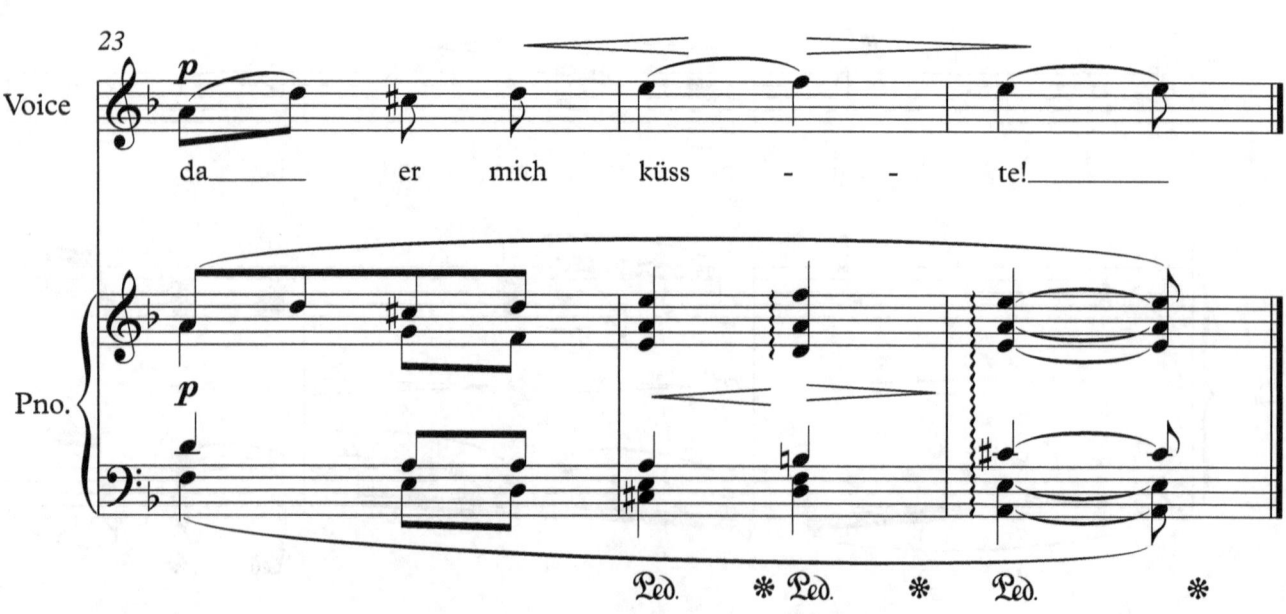

Lieber Schatz, sei wieder gut mir
(Im Volkston)

Wilhelm Osterwald

Robert Franz, Op. 26 No. 2

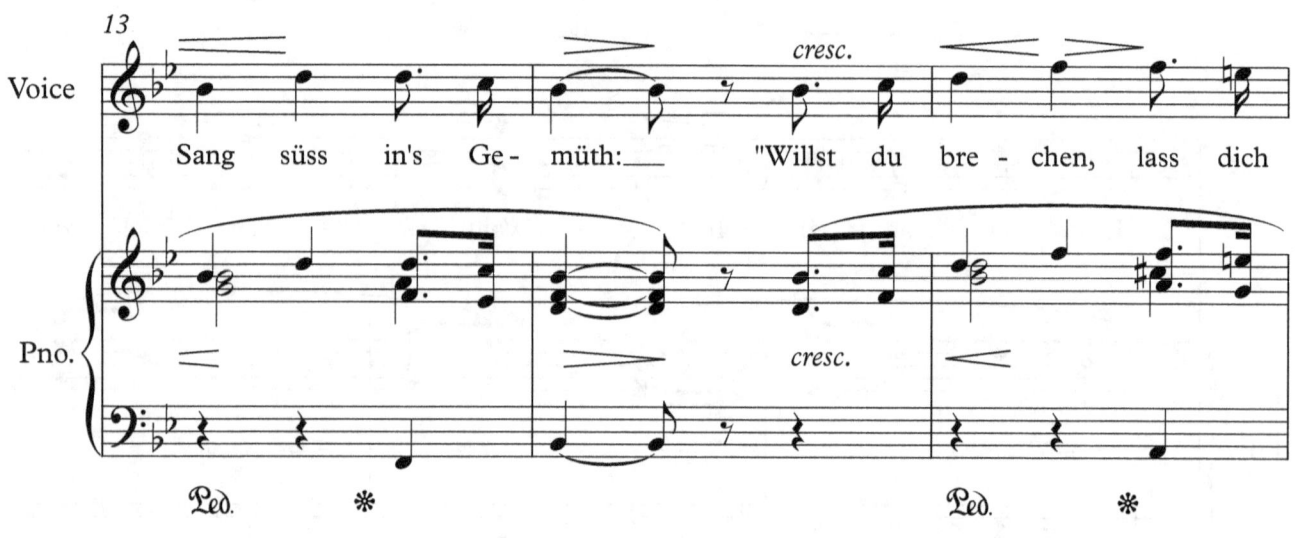
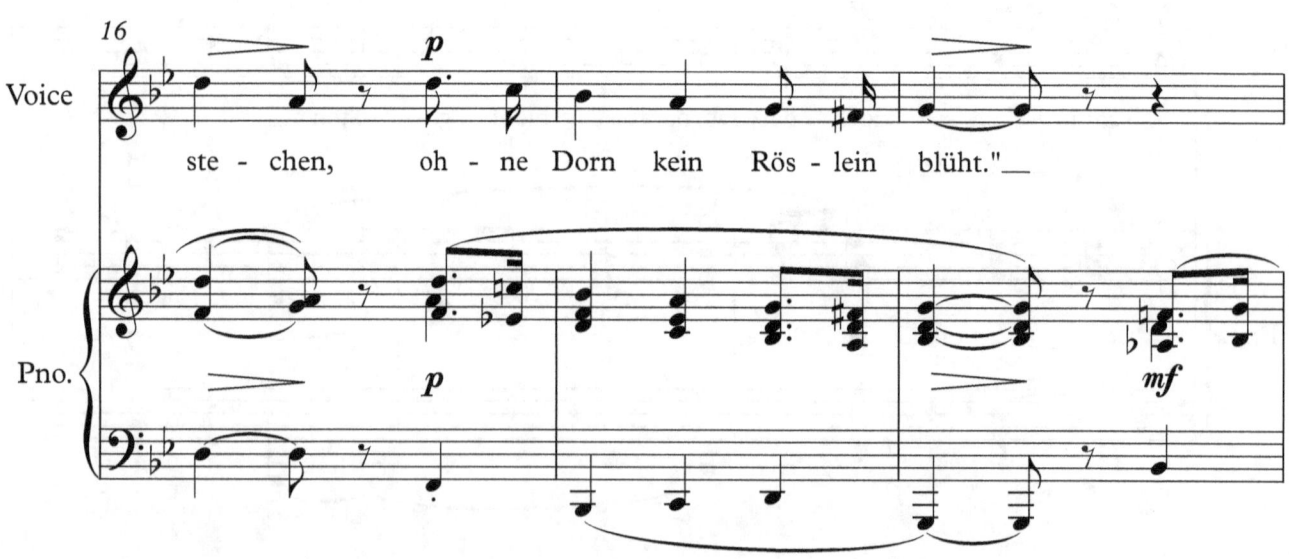

Vergiss mein nicht!

Wilhelm Osterwald

Robert Franz, Op. 26 No. 3

Copyright © Iain Sneddon 2019

245

Fräulein Marie Bretschneider zugeeignet
Schöner Mai, bist über Nacht

Wilhelm Osterwald

Robert Franz, Op.30 No. 4

Copyright © Iain Sneddon 2019

August Saran zugeeignet
Dort unter'm Lindenbaume

Wilhelm Osterwald   Robert Franz, Op. 31 No. 1

Ade denn, du stolze!

Wilhelm Osterwald

Robert Franz, Op. 31 No. 2

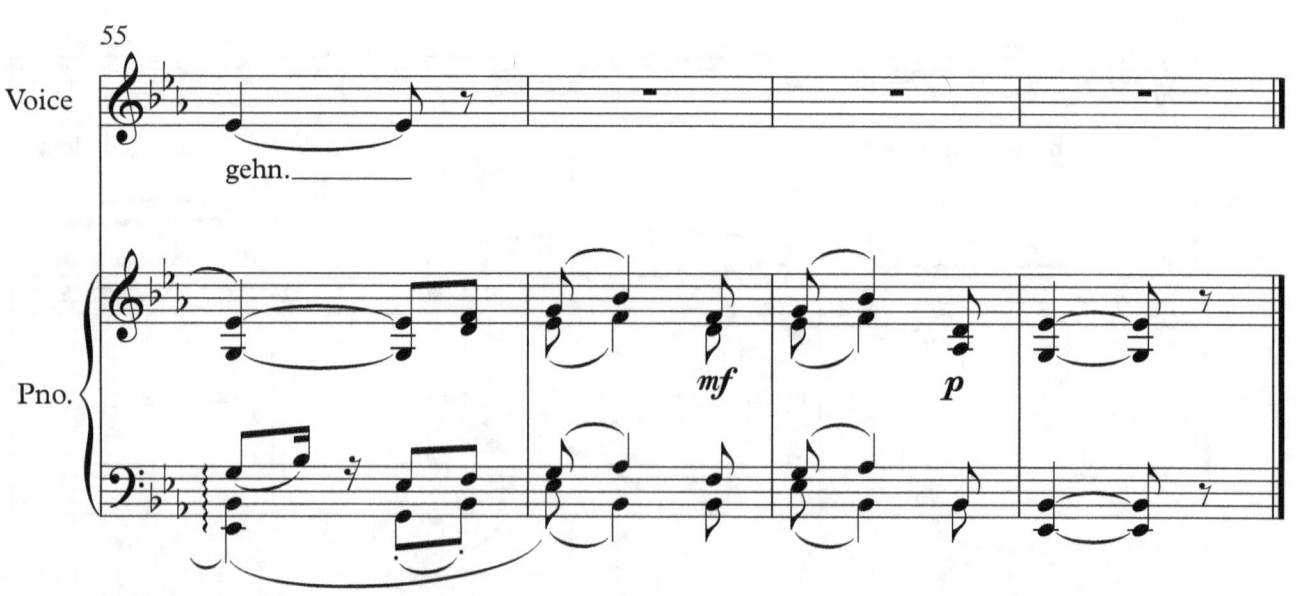

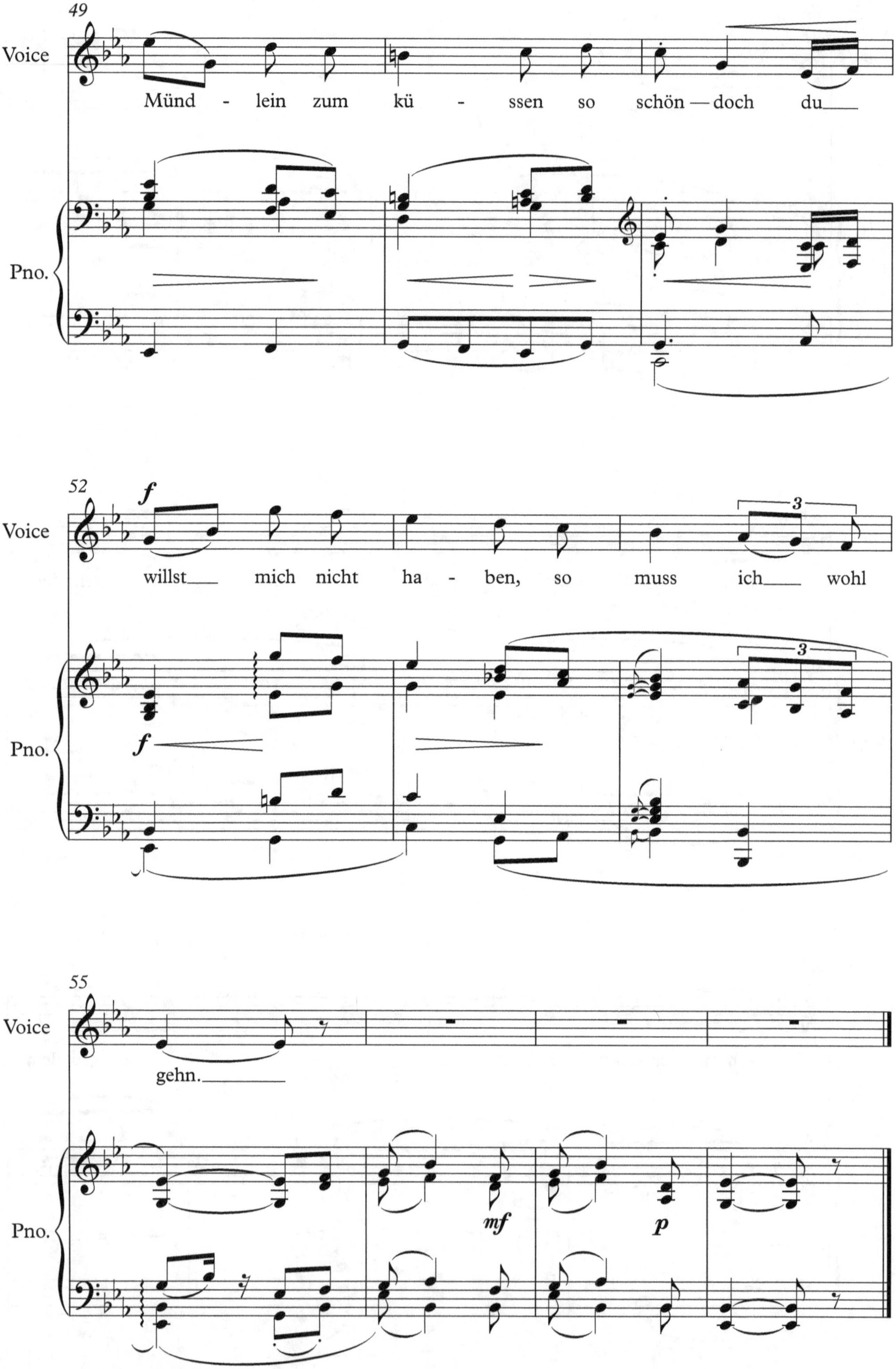
49
Voice
Münd - lein zum kü - ssen so schön — doch du
Pno.
52
Voice
f
willst mich nicht ha - ben, so muss ich wohl
3
Pno.
f
55
Voice
gehn.
Pno.
mf
p

Die Harrende

Wilhelm Osterwald

Robert Franz, Op. 35 No. 1

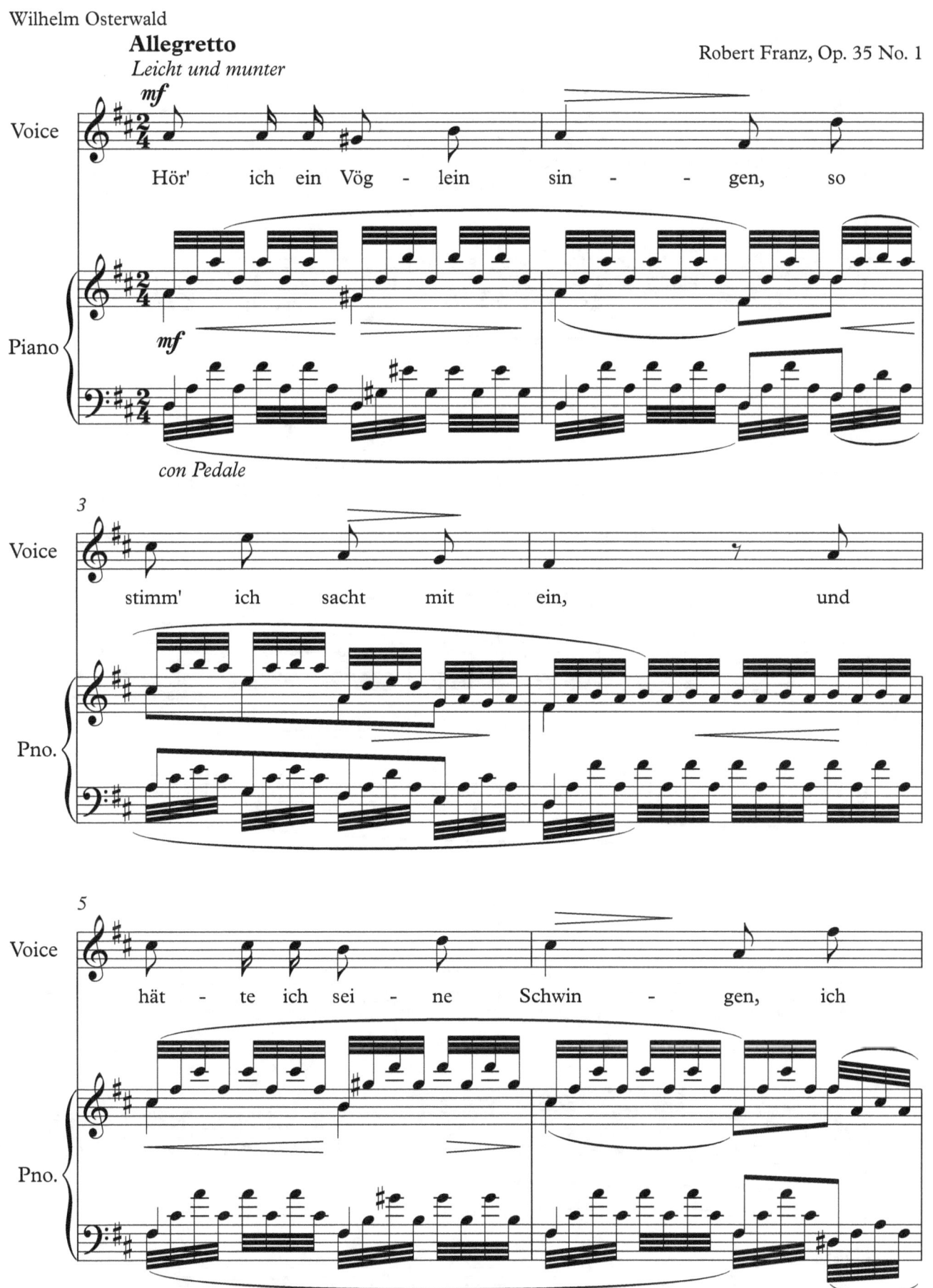

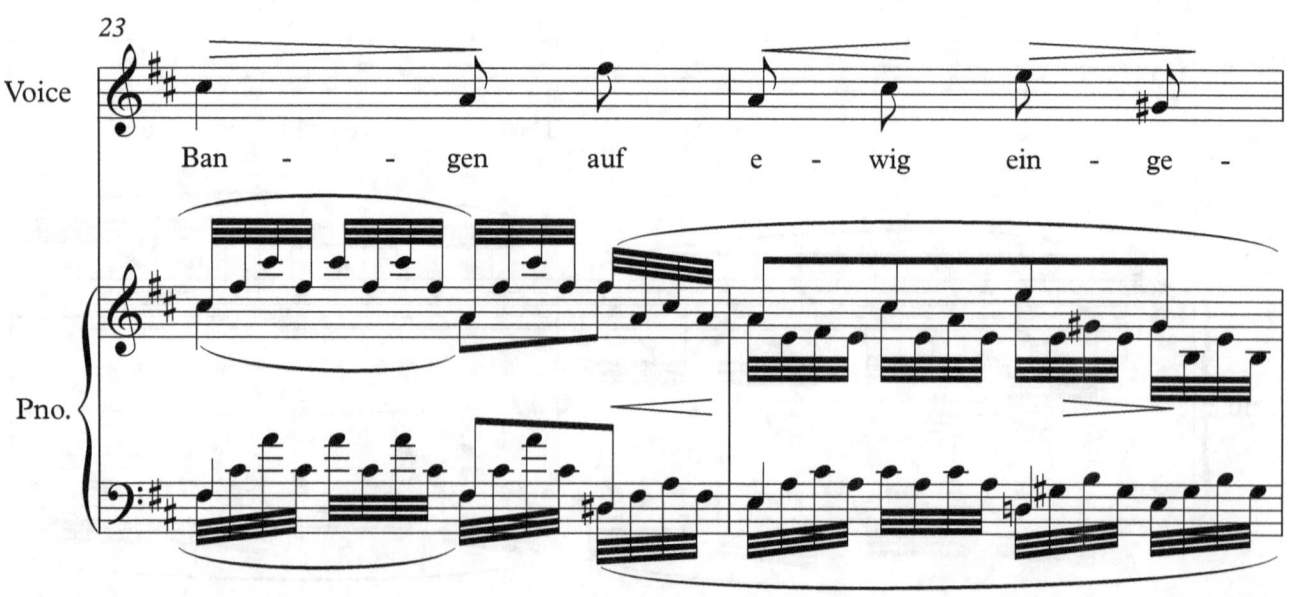

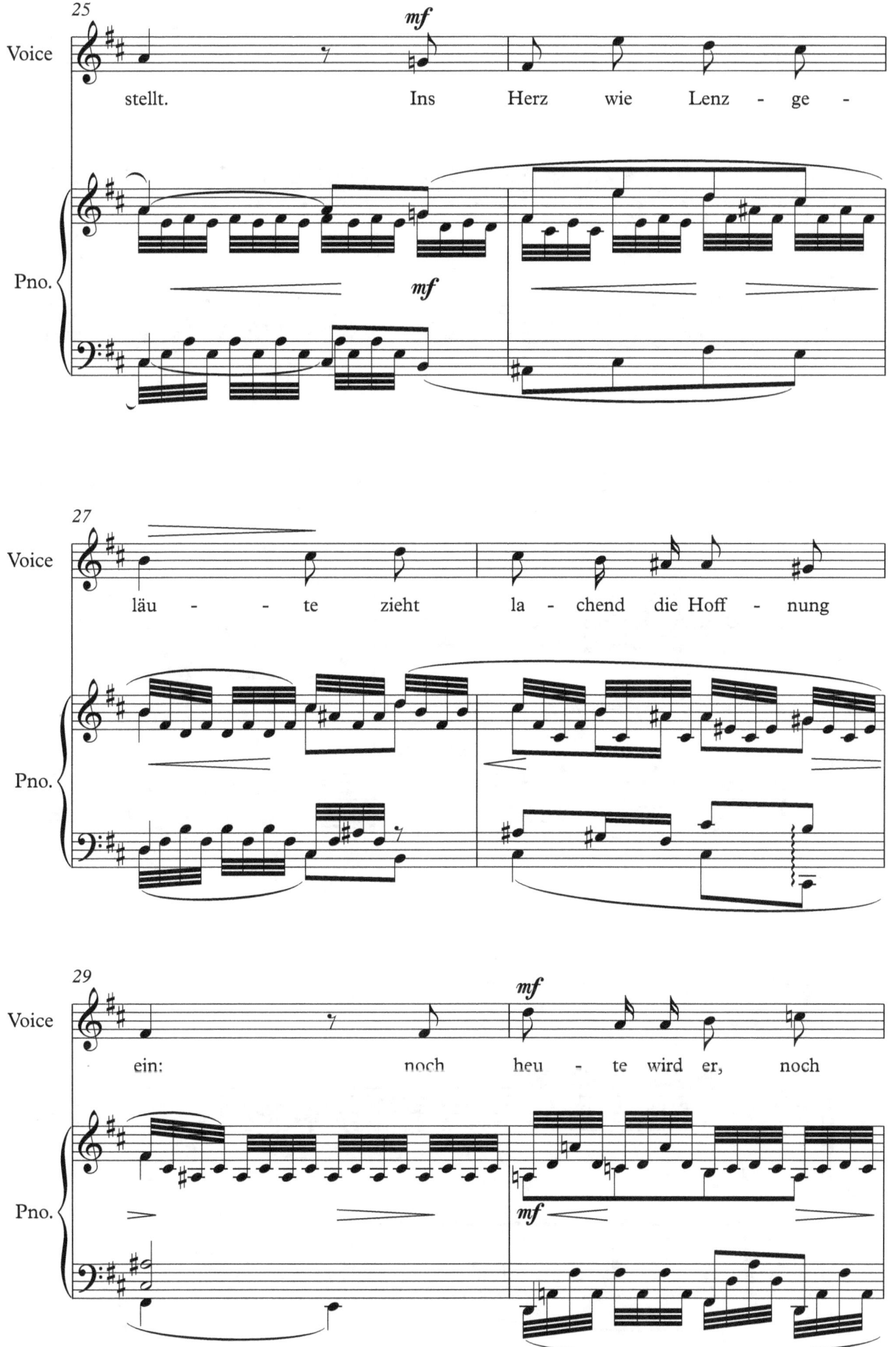

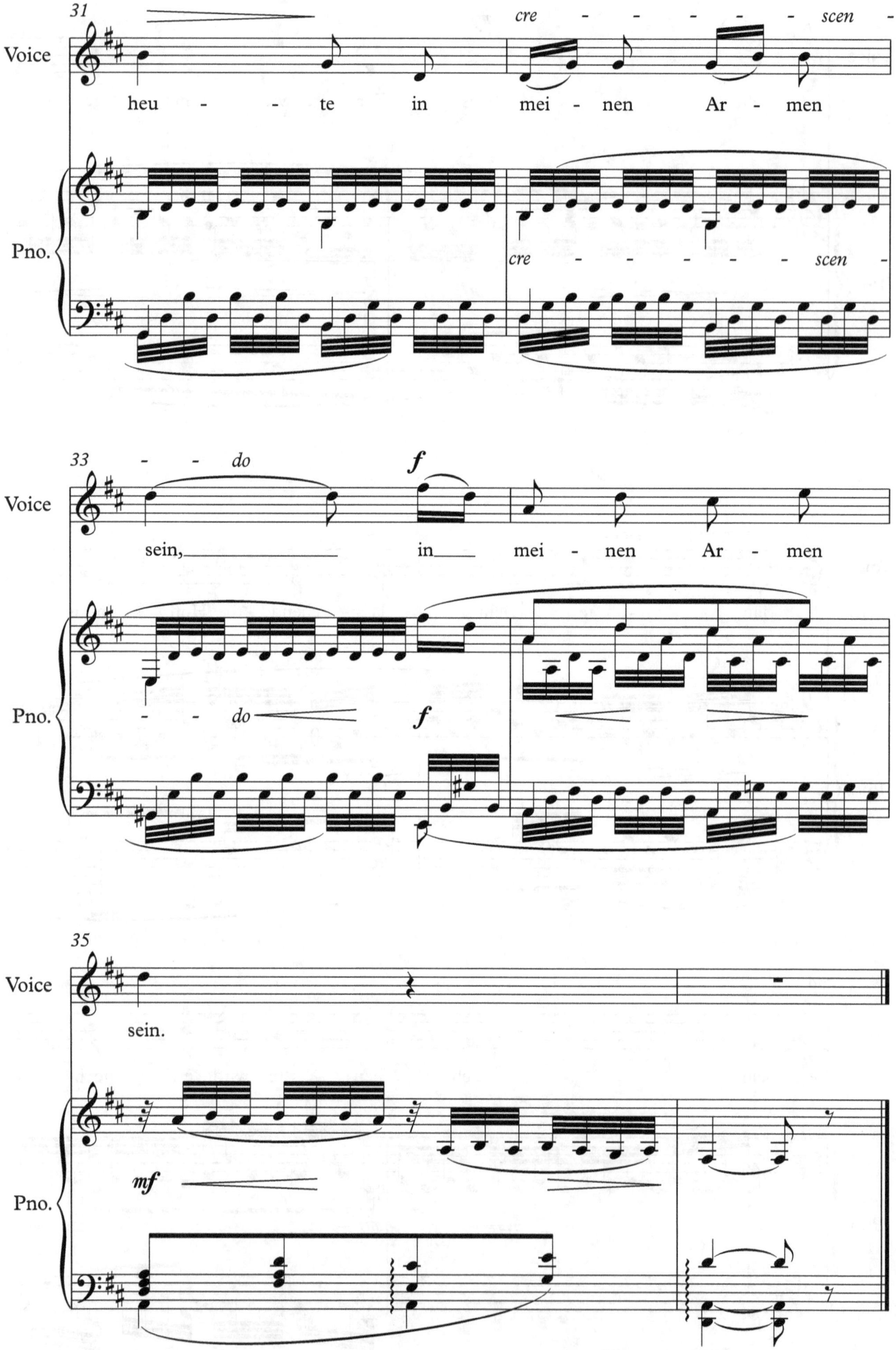
31
cre - - - - - scen -
Voice
heu - - te in mei - nen Ar - men
Pno.
cre - - - - - scen -
33
- do
f
Voice
sein, in mei - nen Ar - men
Pno.
- do
f
35
Voice
sein.
Pno.
mf

Aufbruch

Wilhelm Osterwald
Robert Franz, Op. 35 No. 6

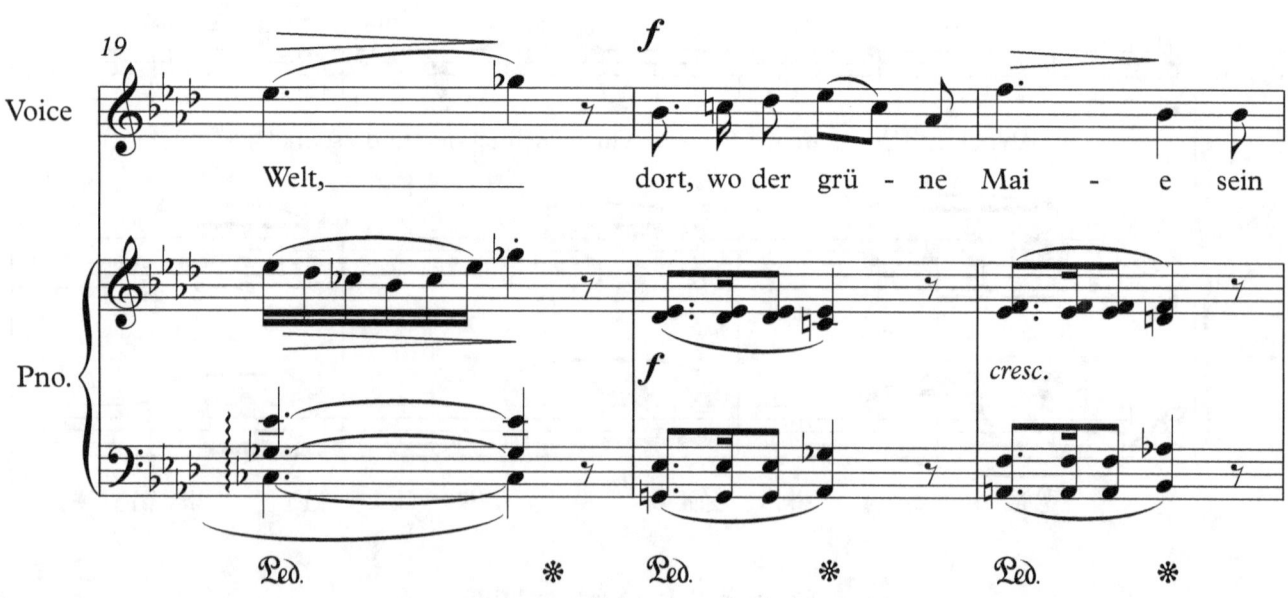

Erster Verlust

Wilhelm Osterwald
Robert Franz, Op. 36 No. 2

271

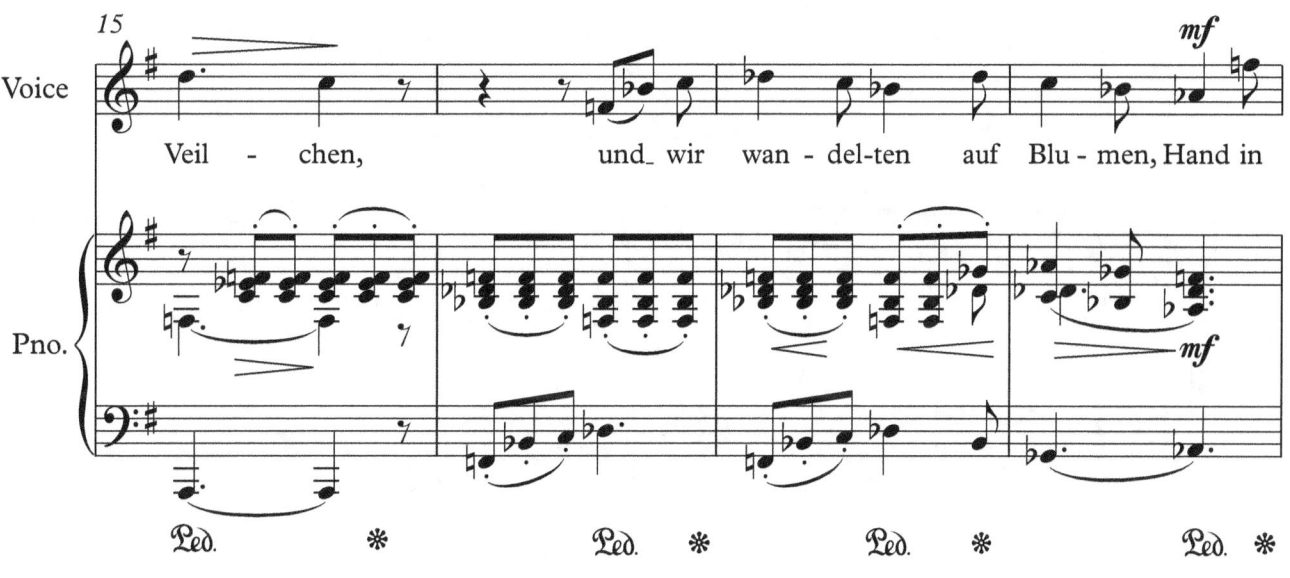
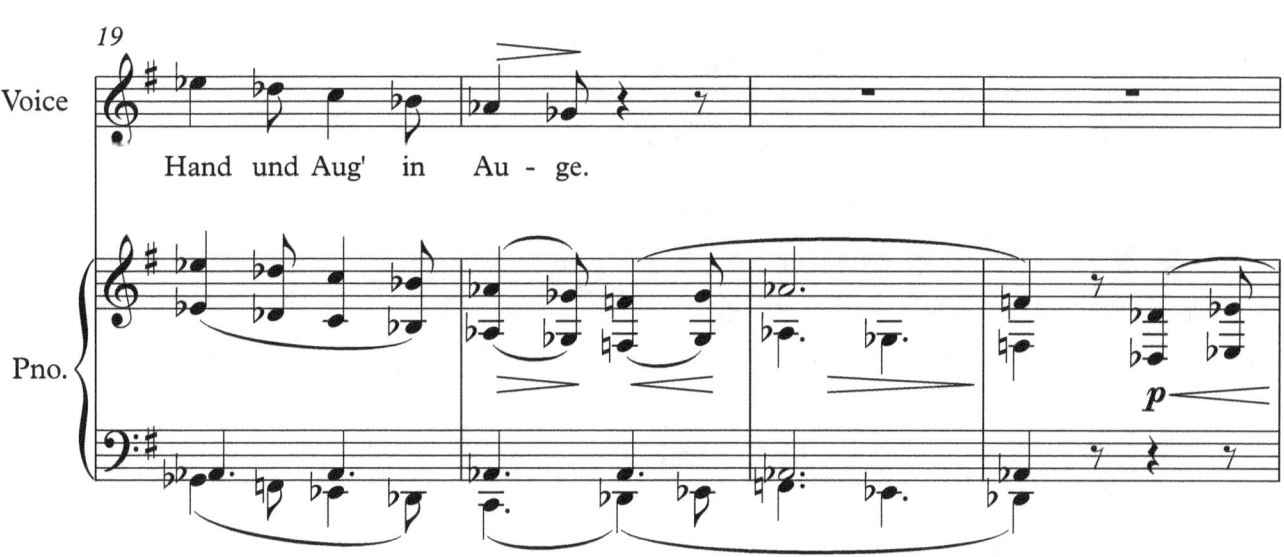

34
Voice
mf
Denn es ist ein Schnee ge - fal - len
Pno.
mf
Ped. * Ped. * Ped. *
36
Voice
ü - ber Nacht auf al - le Blu - men,
Pno.
Ped. * Ped. * Ped. *
38
Voice
und die Veil - - chen sind ge-stor - ben,
Pno.

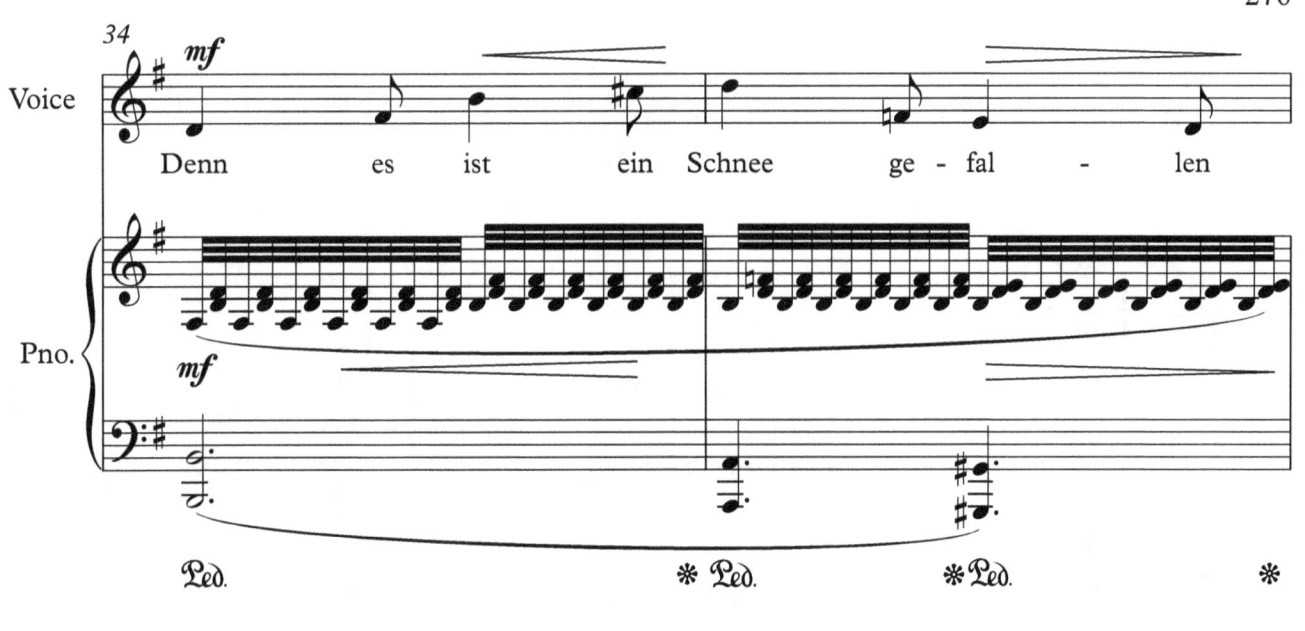

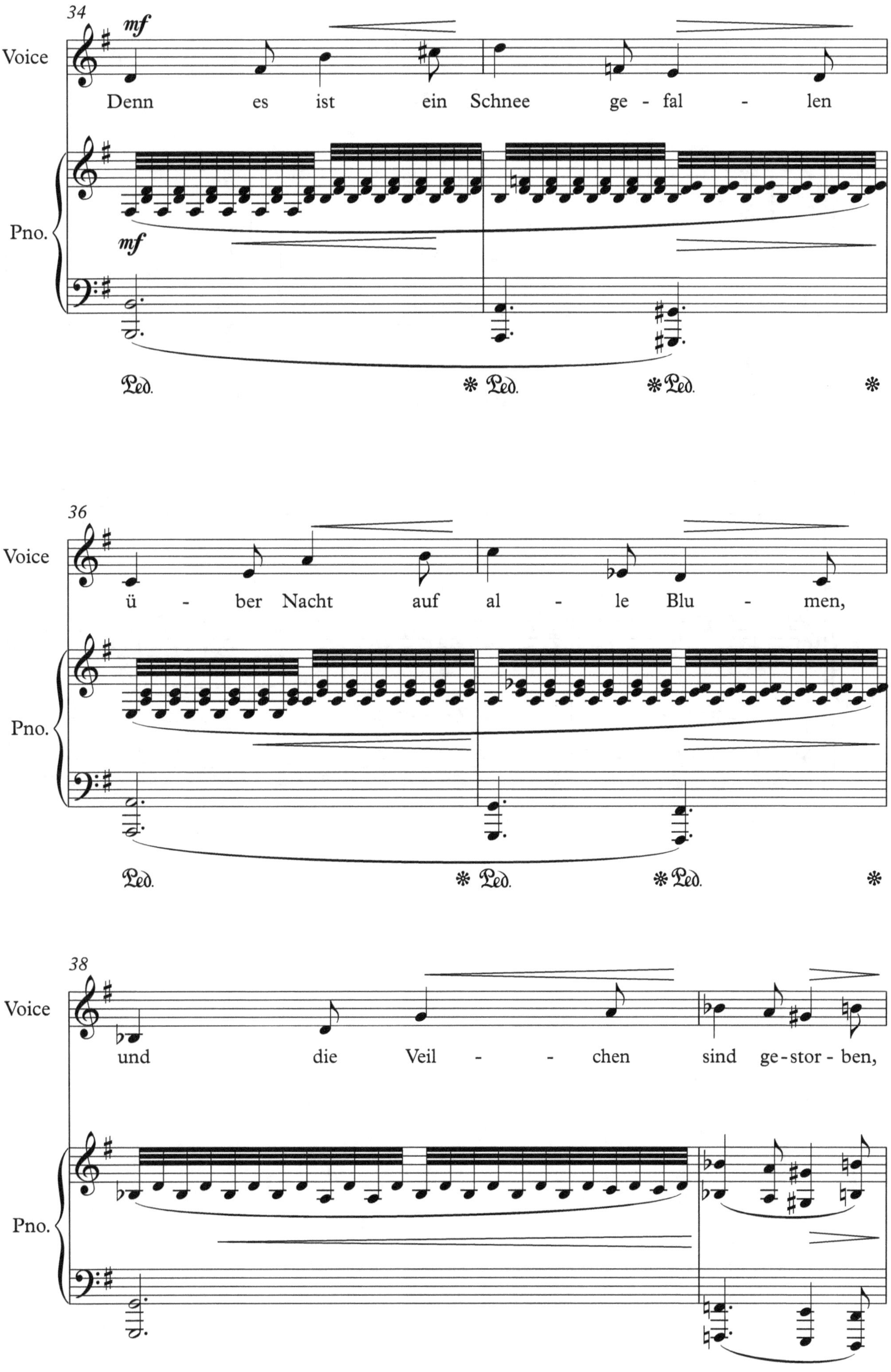

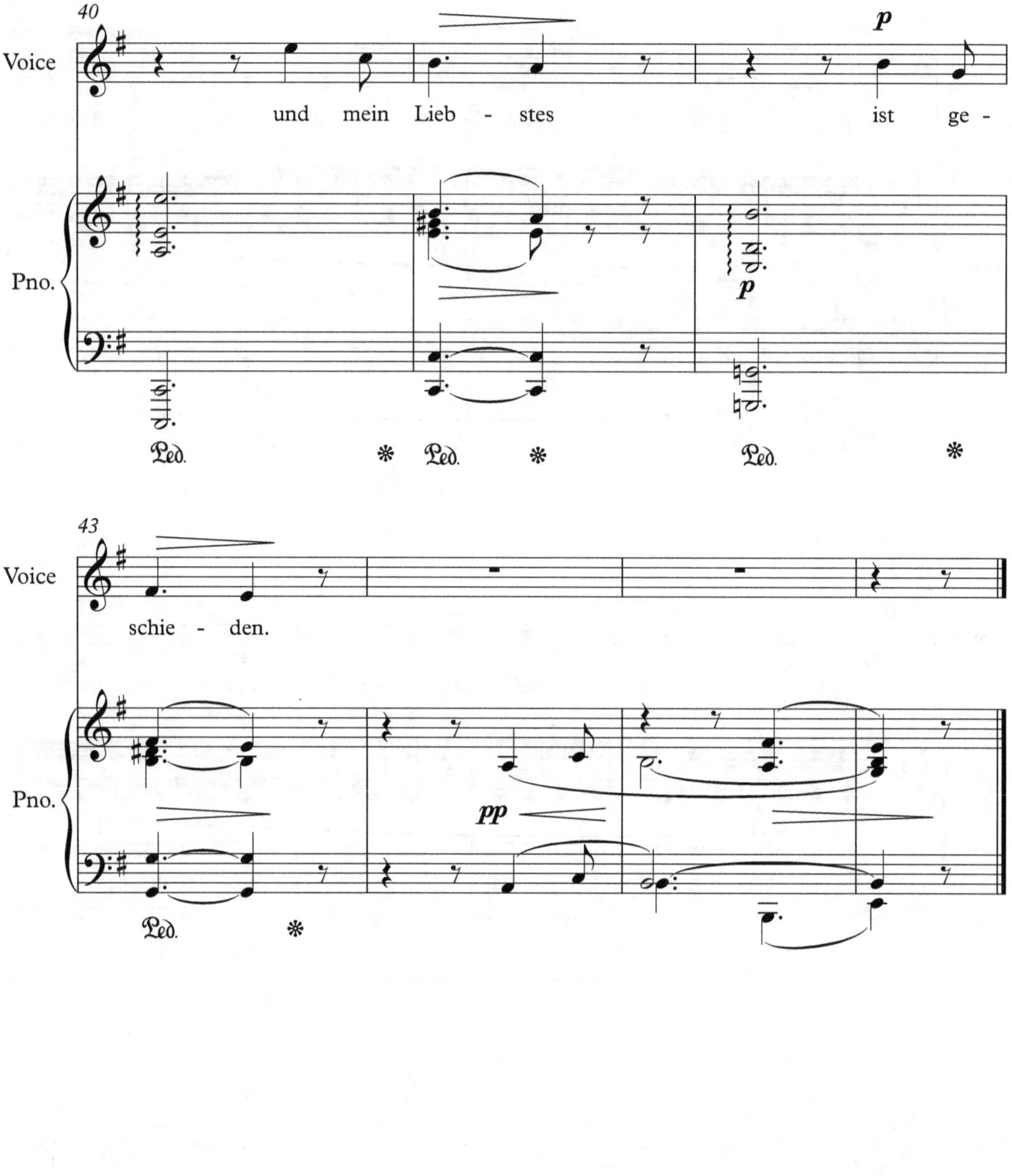
40
Voice
und mein Lieb - stes ist ge -
p
Pno.
p
Ped. * Ped. * Ped. *
43
Voice
schie - den.
Pno.
pp
Ped. *

Bei der Linde

Wilhelm Osterwald

Robert Franz, Op. 36 No. 4

Nun hat mein Stecken gute Rast

Wilhelm Osterwald

Robert Franz, Op. 36 No. 6

280

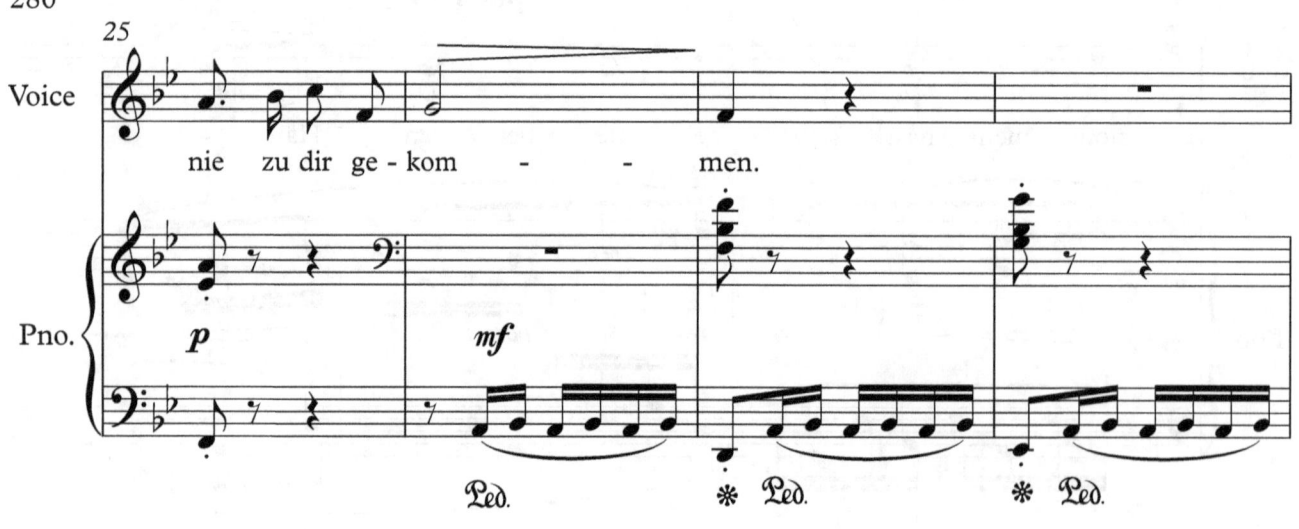

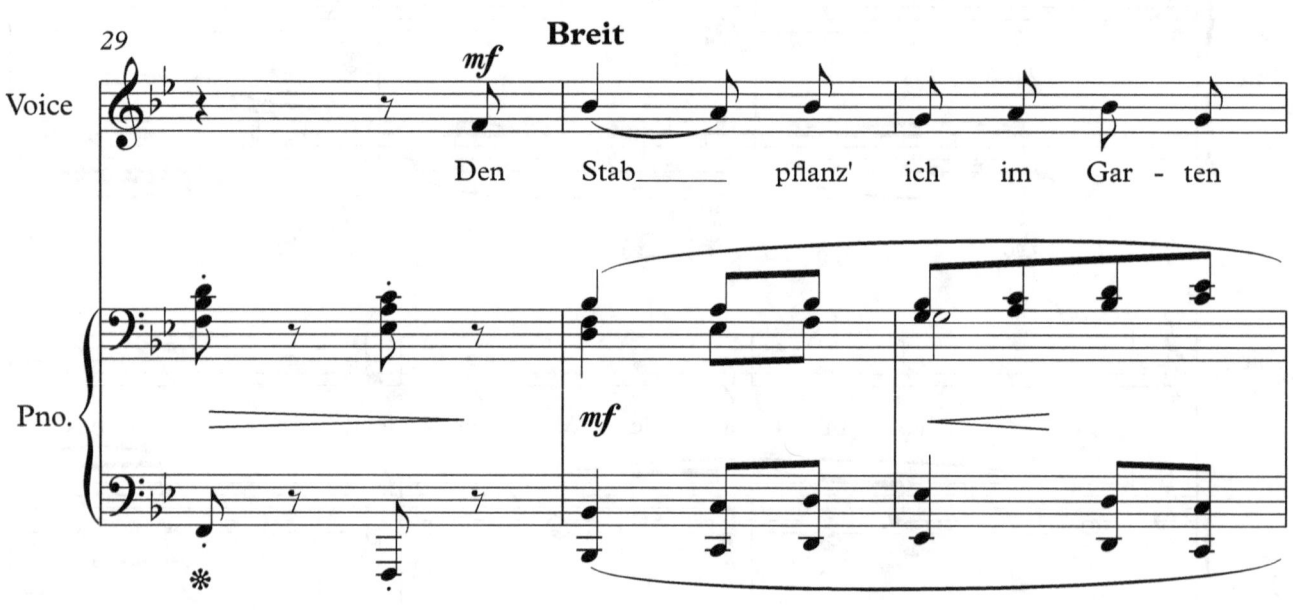

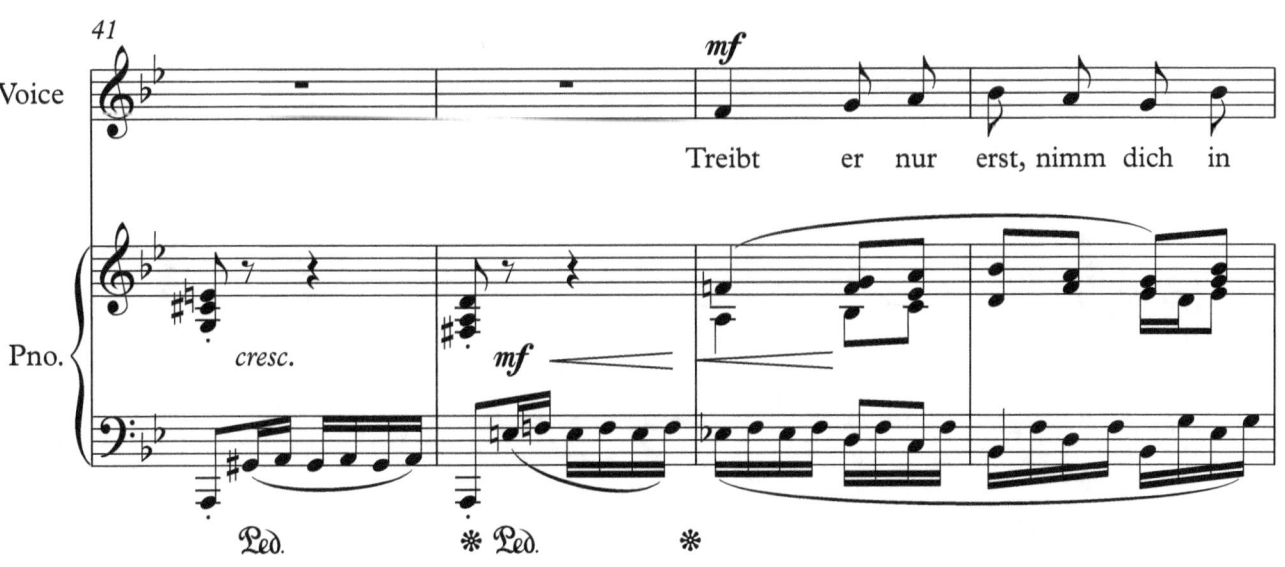

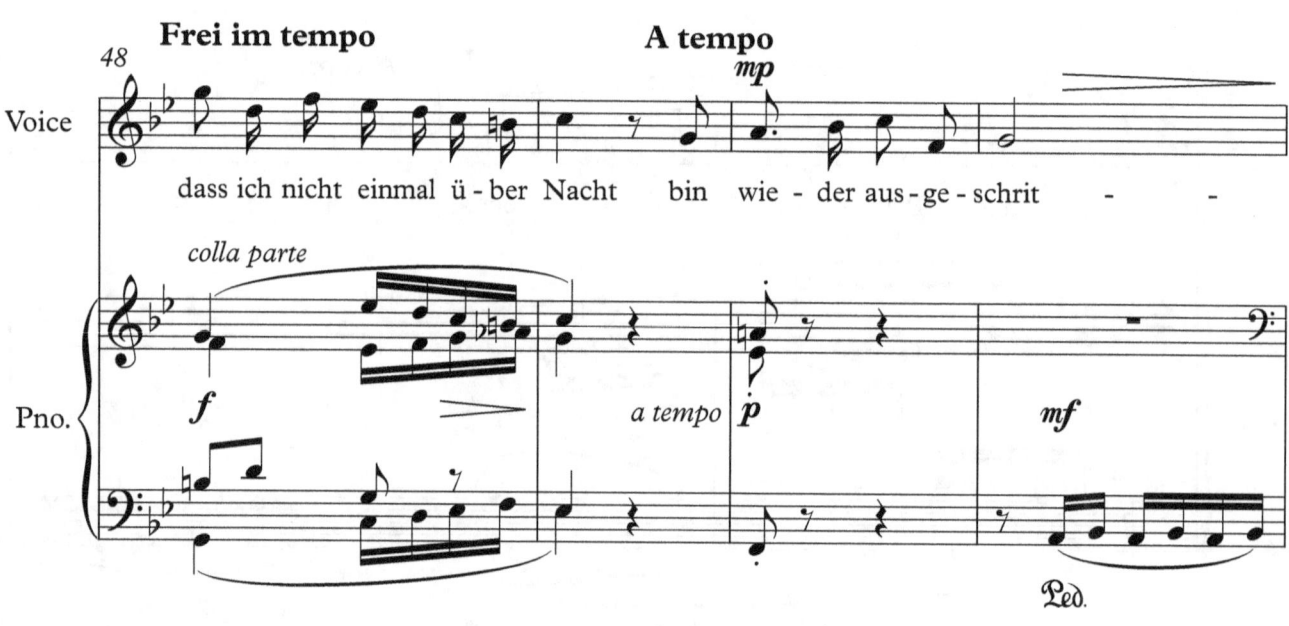

Zu spät

Wilhelm Osterwald
Robert Franz, Op. 37 No. 2

Copyright © Iain Sneddon 2019

Sonnenwende

Wilhelm Osterwald

Robert Franz, Op. 37 No. 5

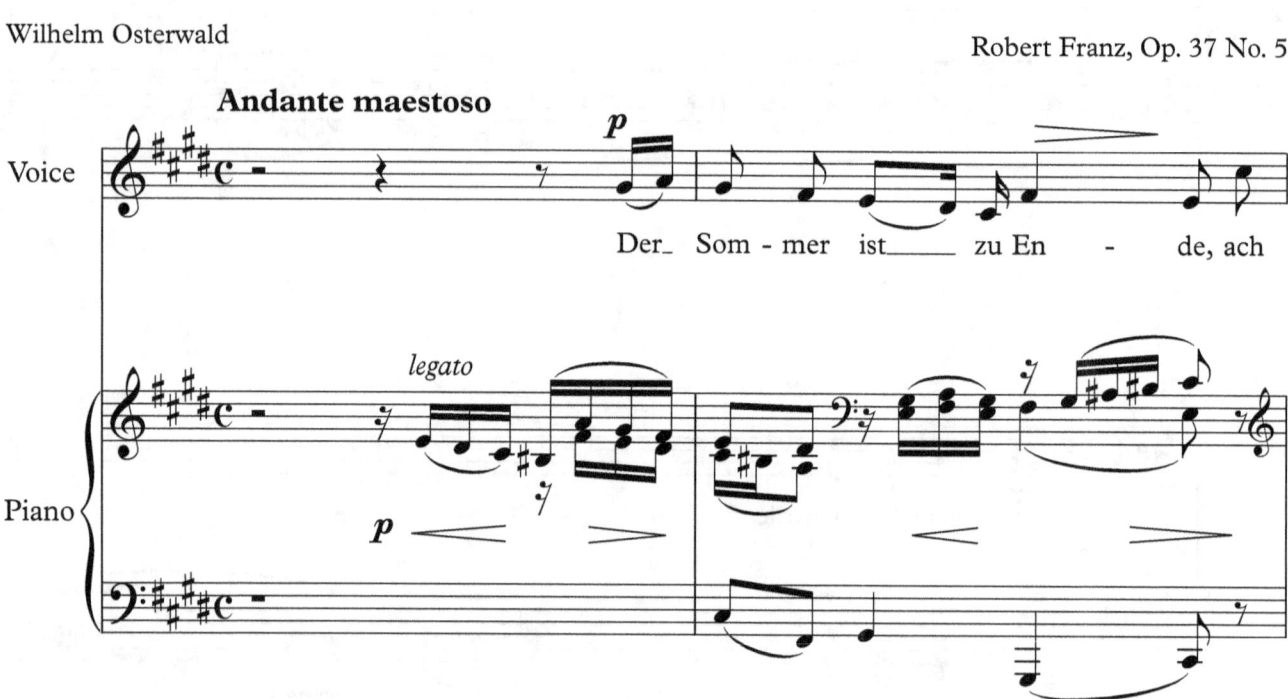

Copyright © Iain Sneddon 2019

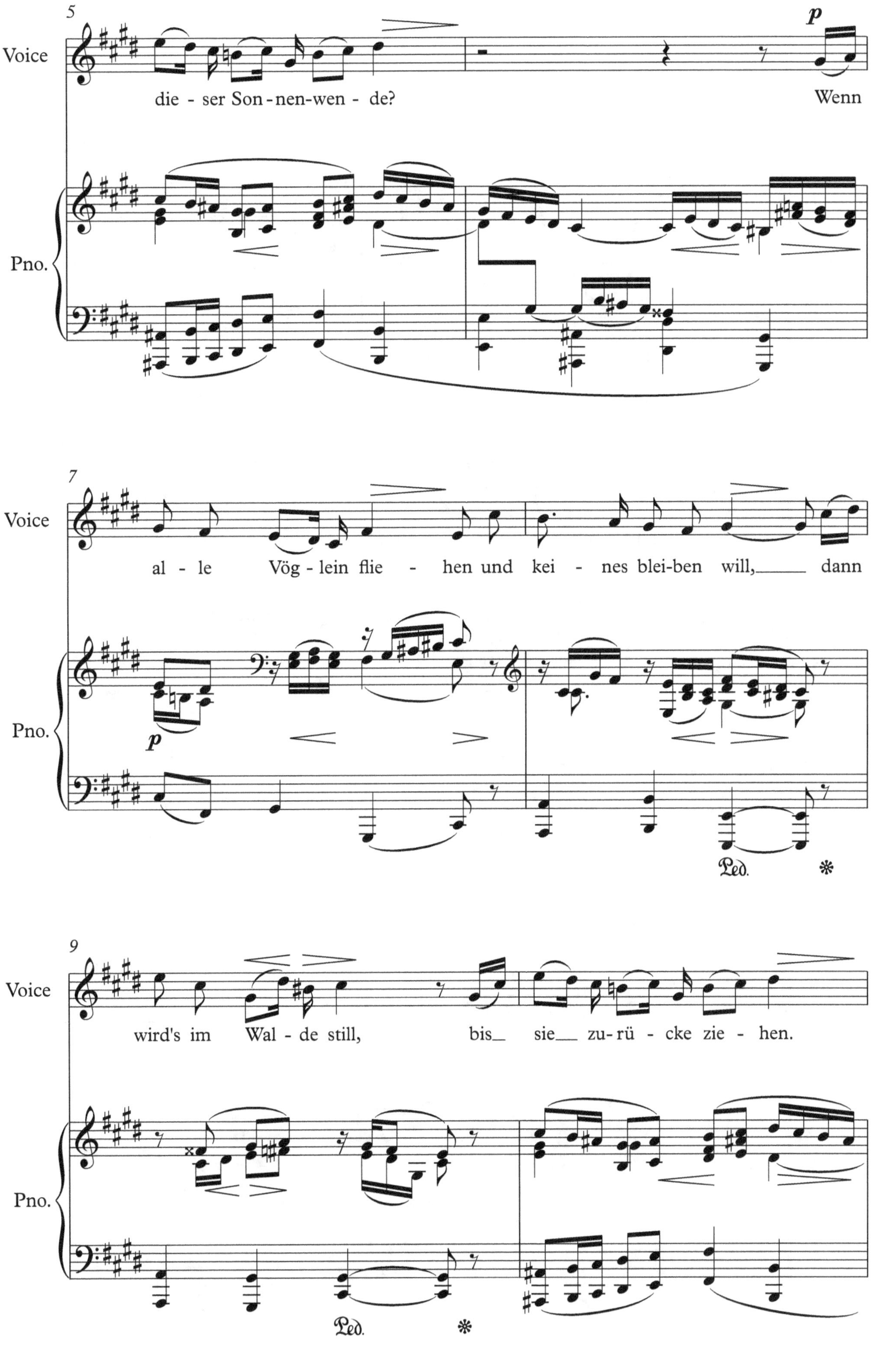
5
Voice
p
die - ser Son - nen - wen - de?
Wenn
Pno.
7
Voice
al - le Vög - lein flie - hen und kei - nes blei - ben will, dann
Pno.
p
Ped.
9
Voice
wird's im Wal - de still, bis sie zu - rü - cke zie - hen.
Pno.
Ped.

Herrn Baron von Keudell zugeeignet
Mein Schatz ist auf der Wanderschaft

Wilhelm Osterwald

Robert Franz, Op. 40 No. 1

Copyright © Iain Sneddon 2019

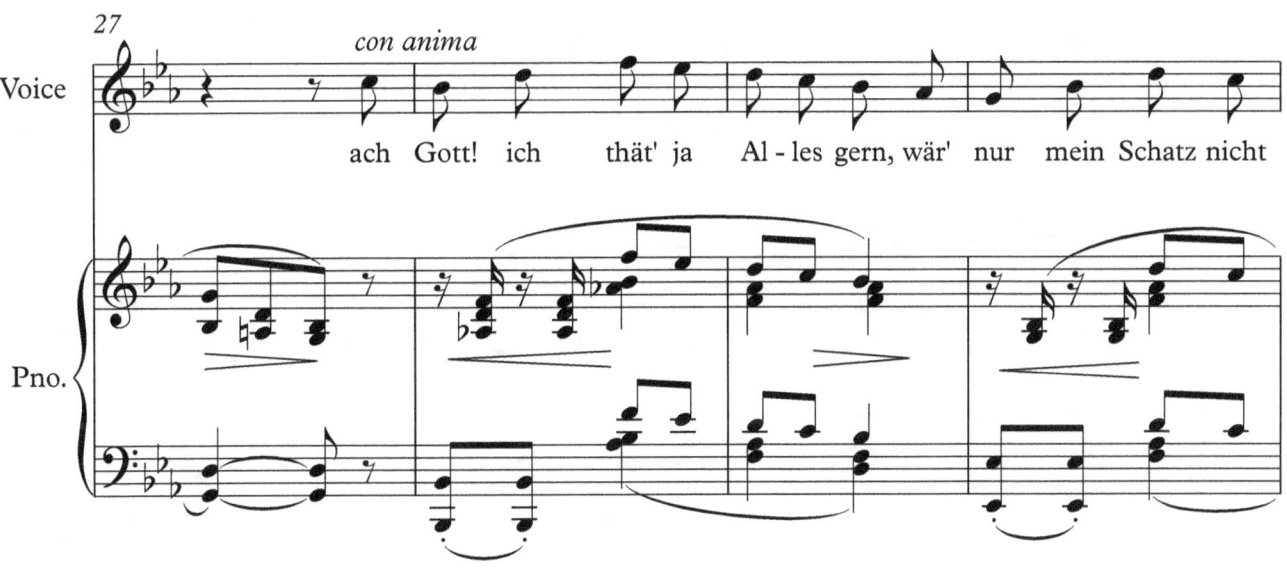

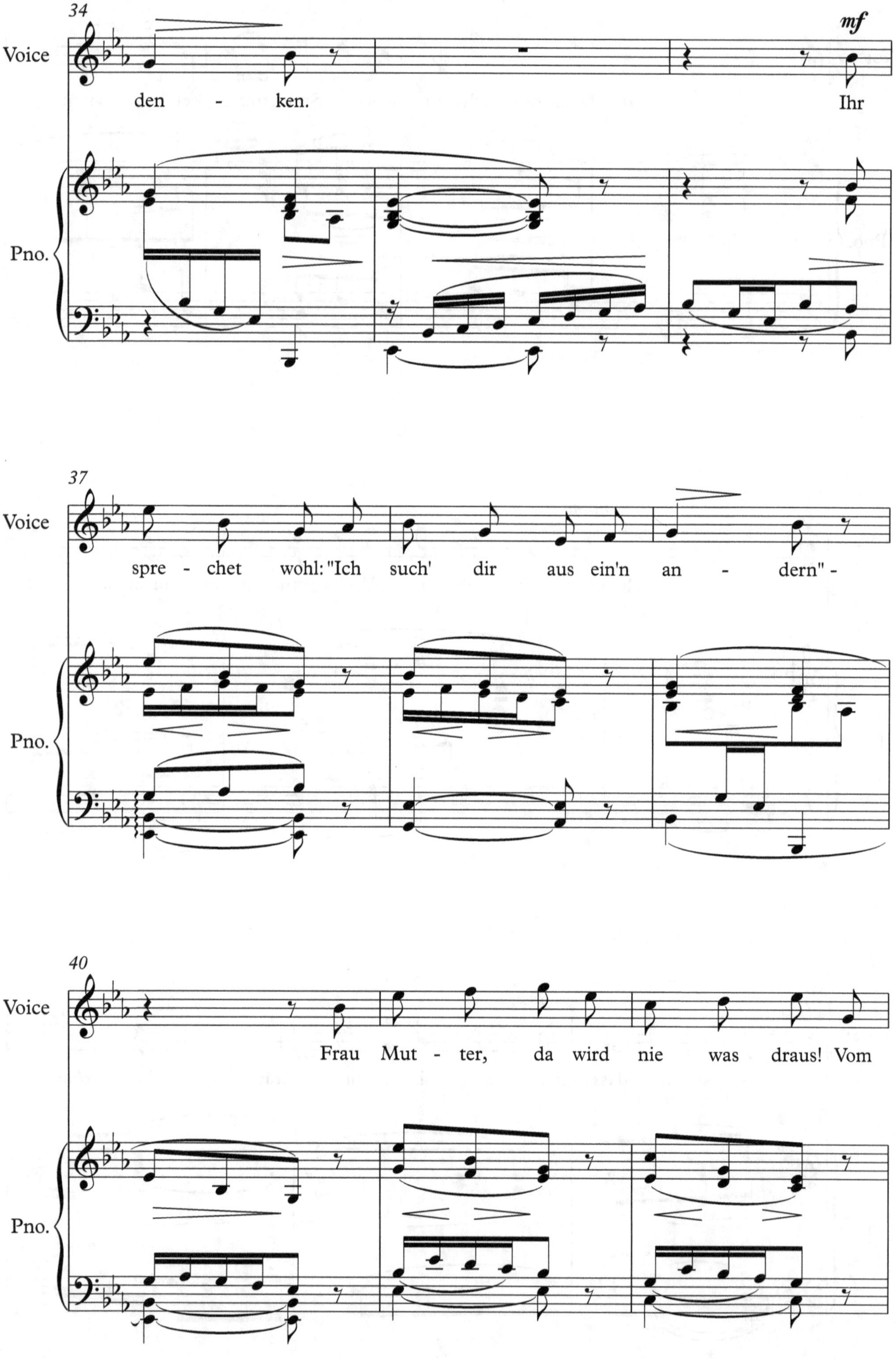
34
Voice
Pno.
mf
den - ken.
Ihr
37
spre - chet wohl: "Ich such' dir aus ein'n an - dern" -
40
Frau Mut - ter, da wird nie was draus! Vom

Du grüne Rast im Haine

Wilhelm Osterwald
Robert Franz, Op. 41 No. 6

296

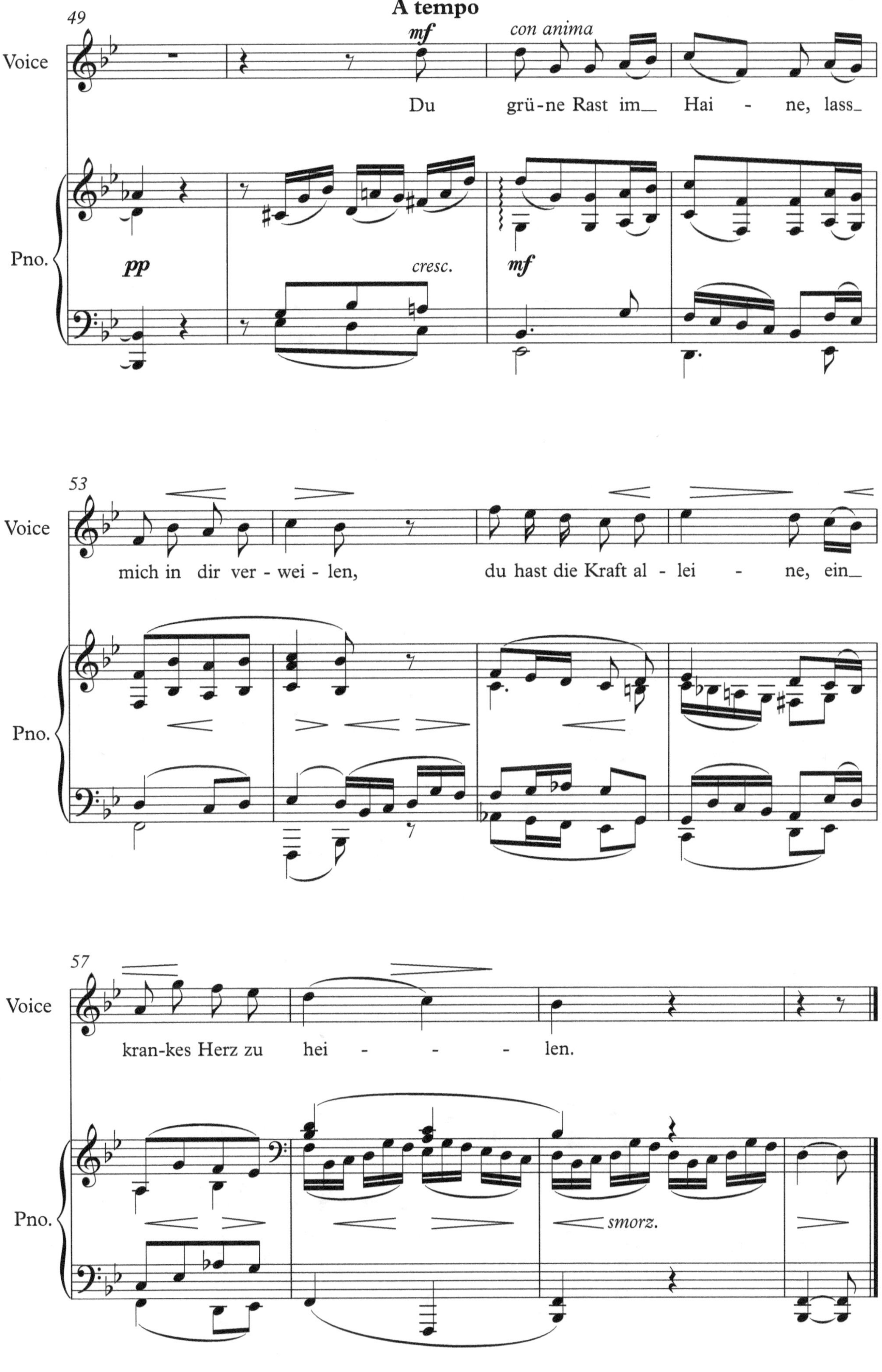
49
A tempo
con anima
Voice
Pno.
pp
cresc.
mf
Du grü-ne Rast im Hai - ne, lass
53
mich in dir ver - wei - len,
du hast die Kraft al - lei - ne, ein
57
kran-kes Herz zu hei - - - len.
smorz.

Träume

Wilhelm Osterwald
Robert Franz, Op.43 No. 1

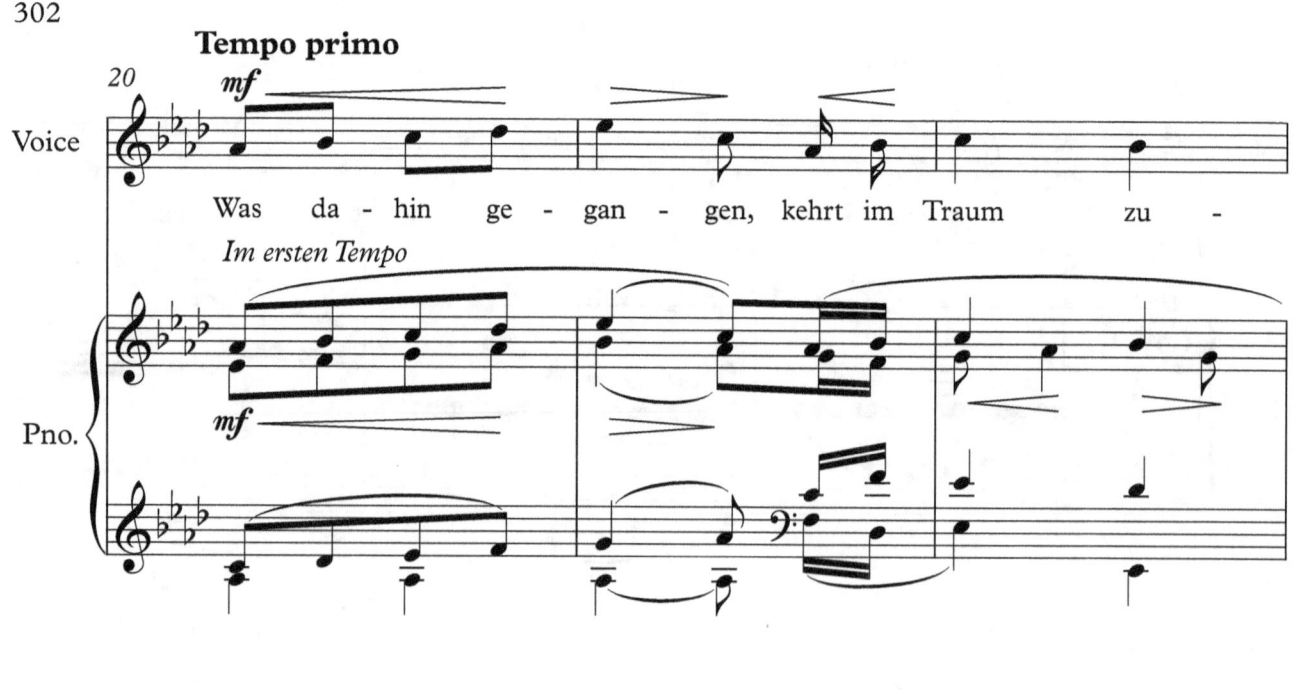

Gleich wie der Mond so keusch und rein

Wilhelm Osterwald

Robert Franz, Op. 43 No. 2

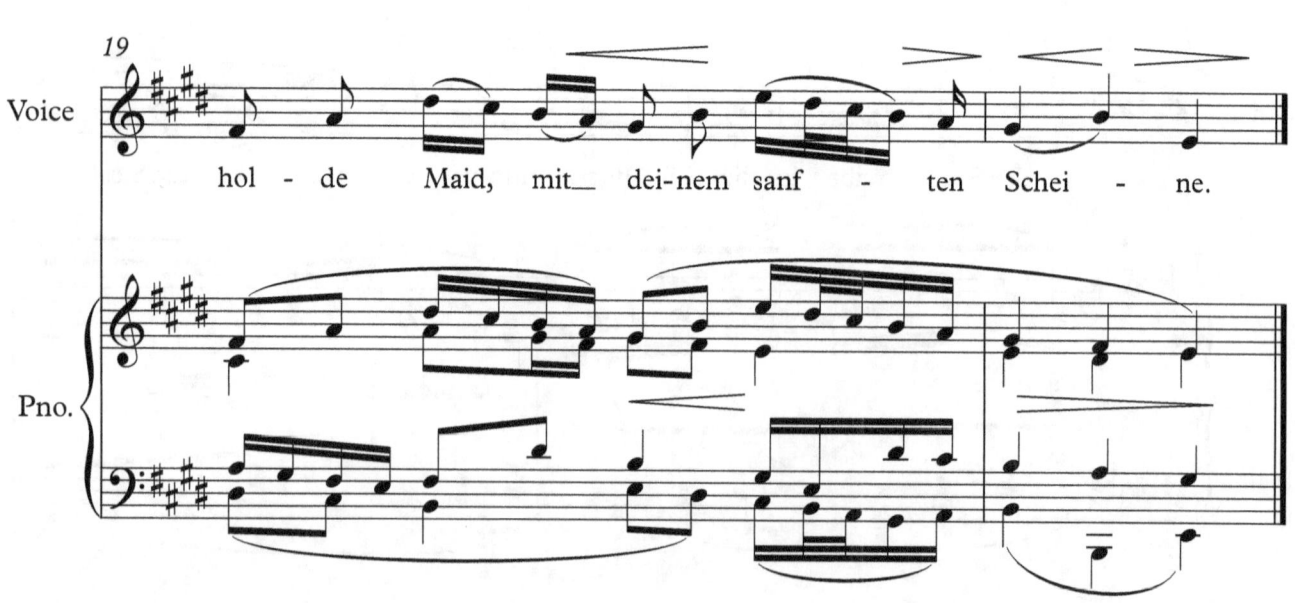

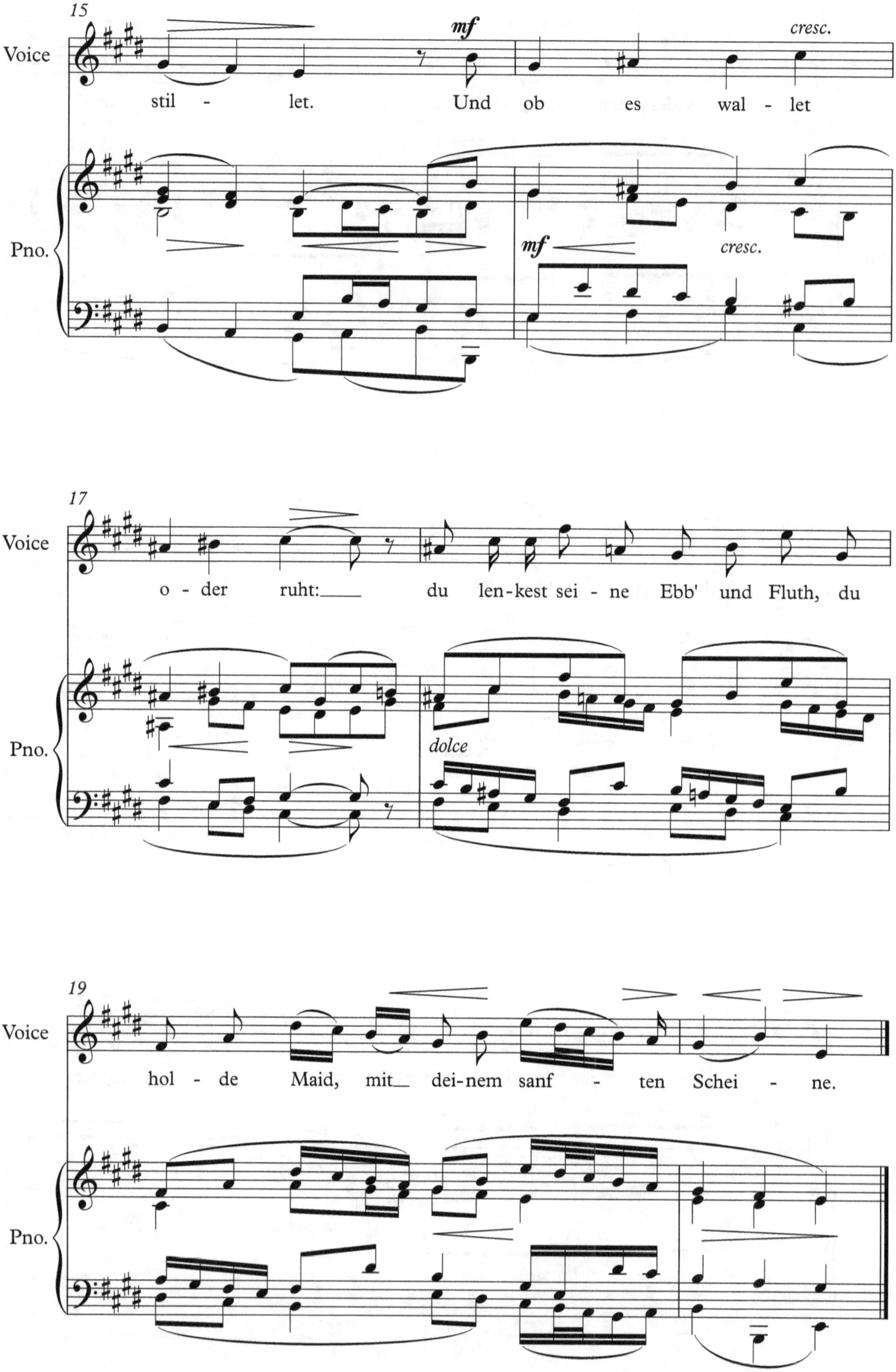
15
Voice
mf
cresc.
stil - let. Und ob es wal - let
Pno.
mf
cresc.
17
Voice
o - der ruht: du len-kest sei - ne Ebb' und Fluth, du
Pno.
dolce
19
Voice
hol - de Maid, mit dei-nem sanf - ten Schei - ne.
Pno.

Entschluss

Wilhelm Osterwald

Robert Franz, Op.43 No. 3

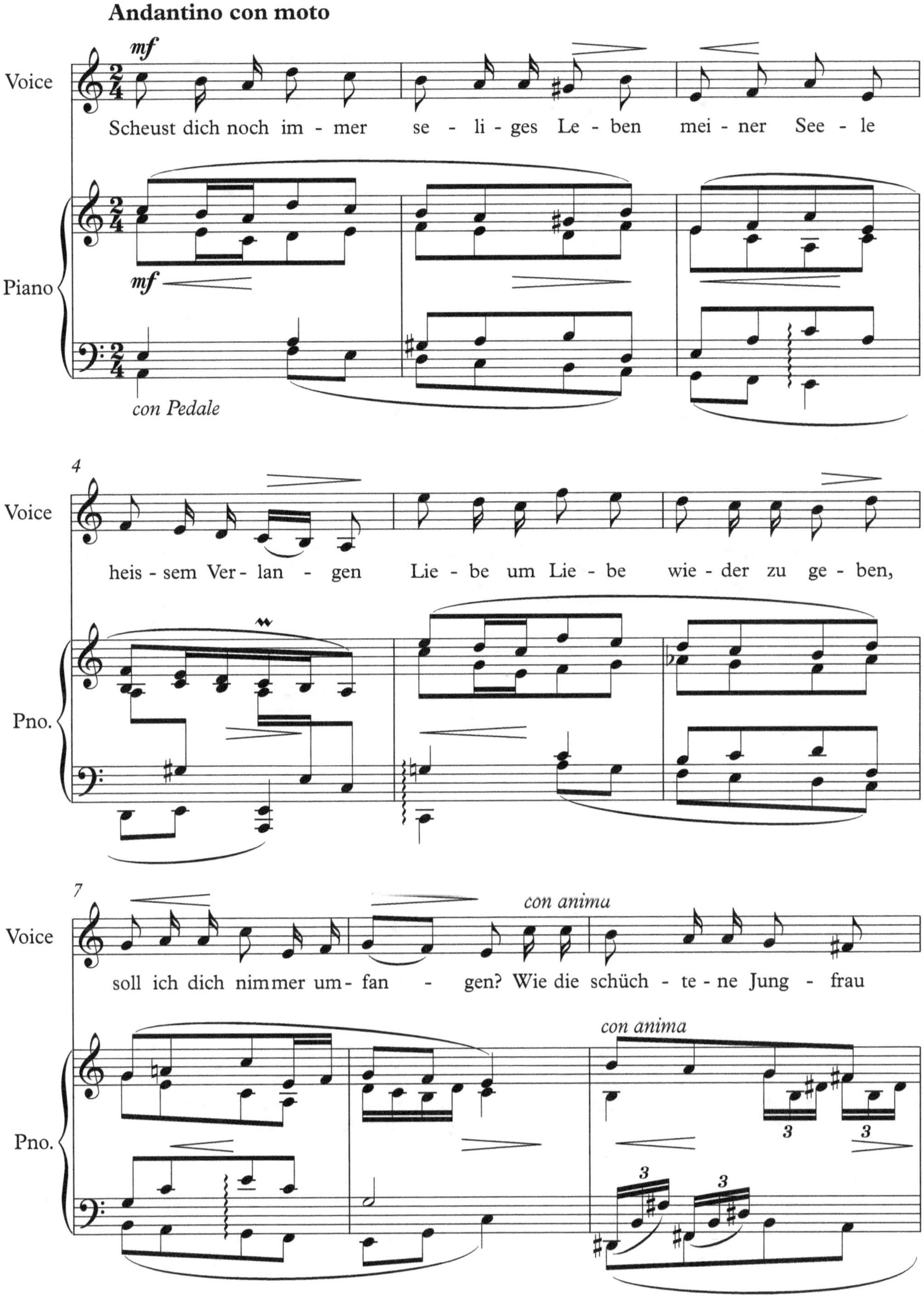

Andantino con moto
Voice
Piano
mf
Scheust dich noch im - mer se - li - ges Le - ben mei - ner See - le
con Pedale
4
Pno.
heis - sem Ver - lan - gen Lie - be um Lie - be wie - der zu ge - ben,
7
con anima
soll ich dich nimmer um - fan - gen? Wie die schüch - te - ne Jung - frau
3

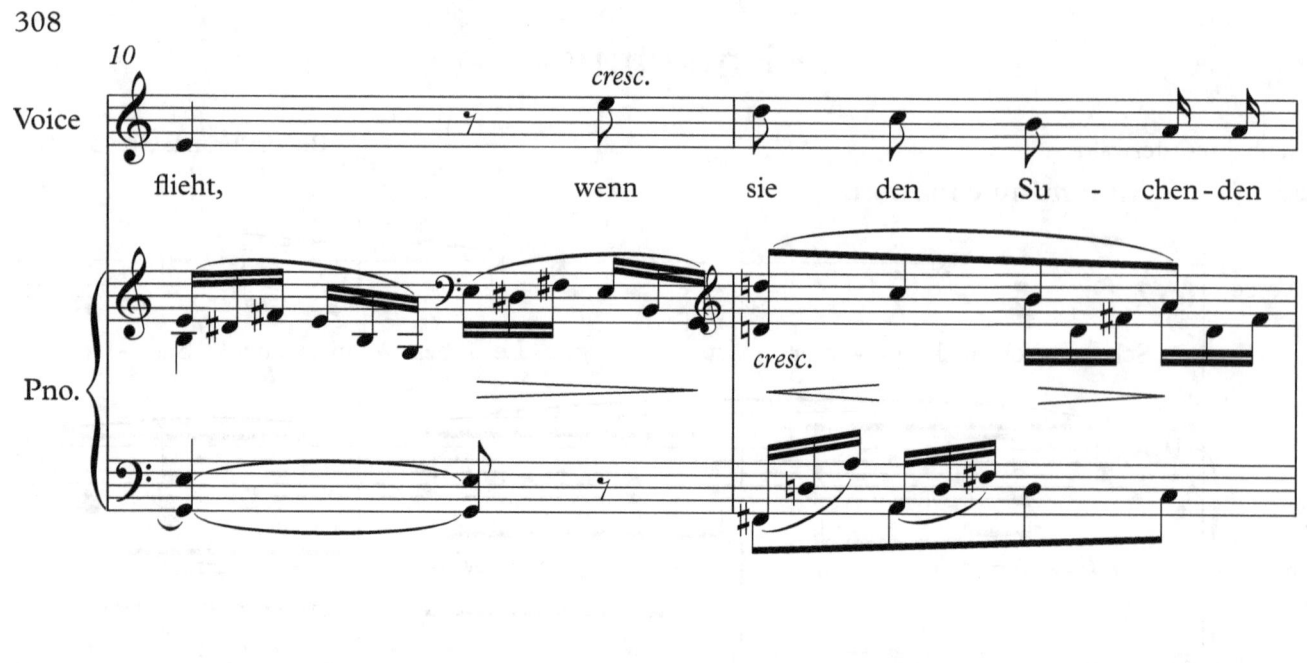

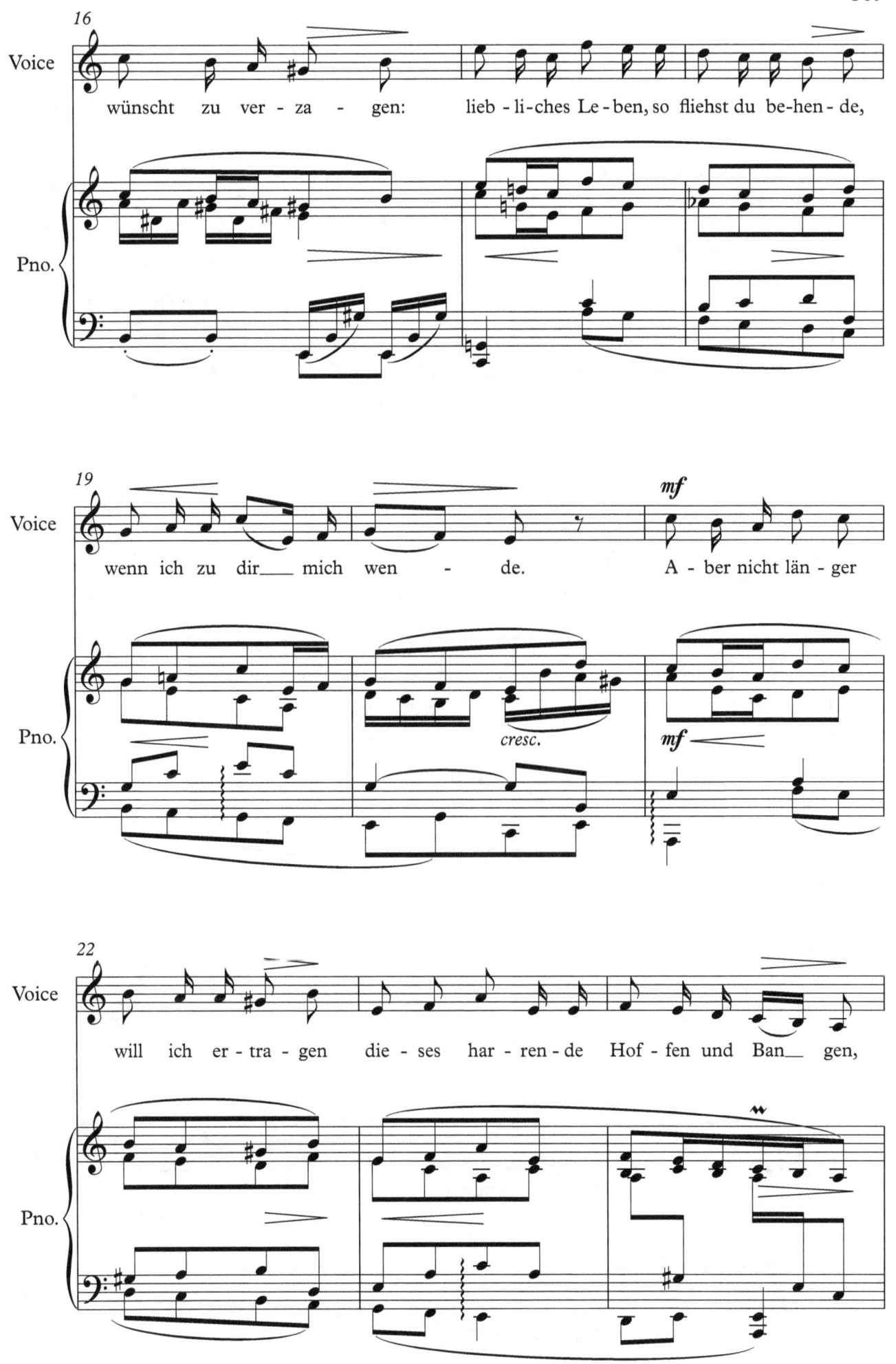

In Blüthen

Wilhelm Osterwald

Robert Franz, Op. 43 No. 6

313

Herrn S. B. Schlesinger in Boston gewidmet

Aprillaunen

Wilhelm Osterwald Robert Franz, Op.44 No. 2

Copyright © Iain Sneddon 2019

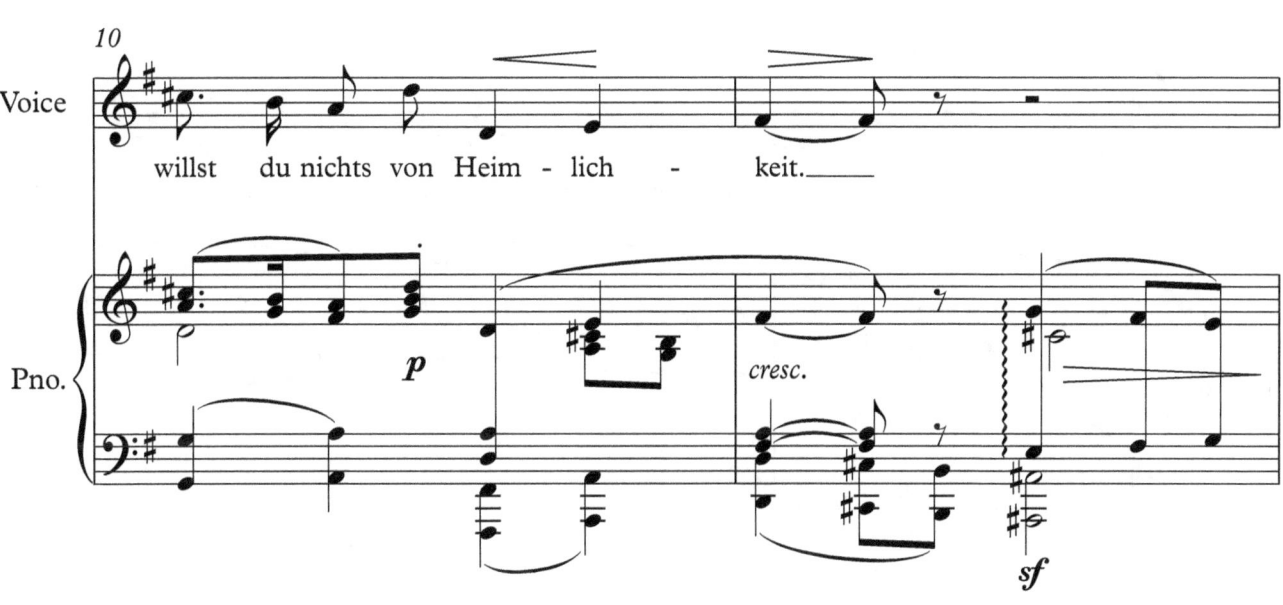

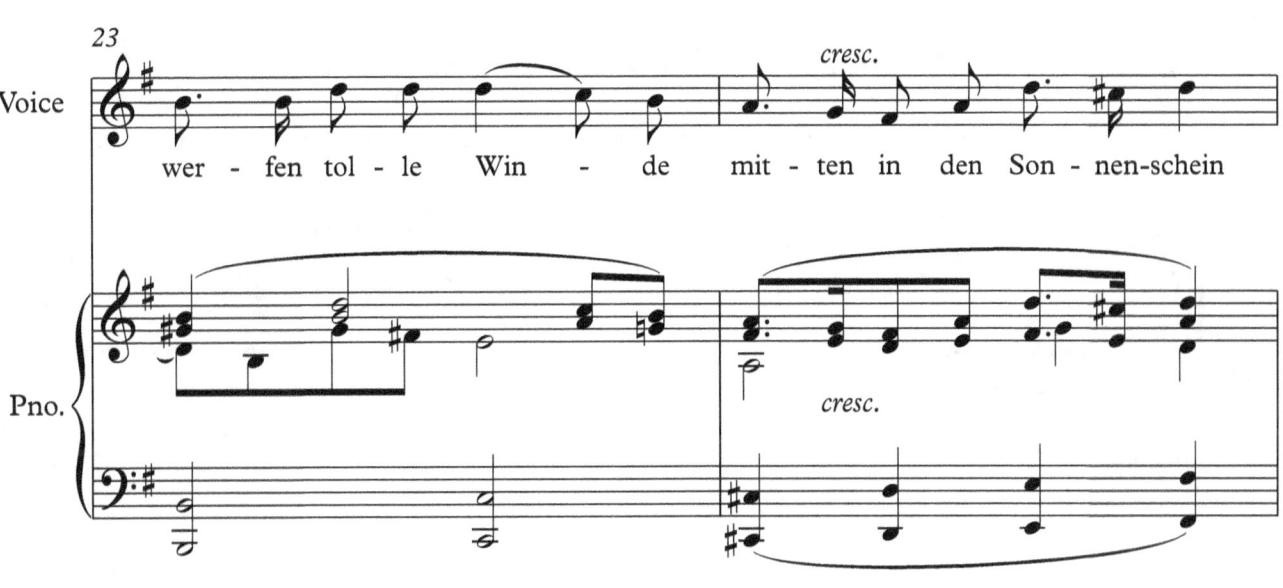
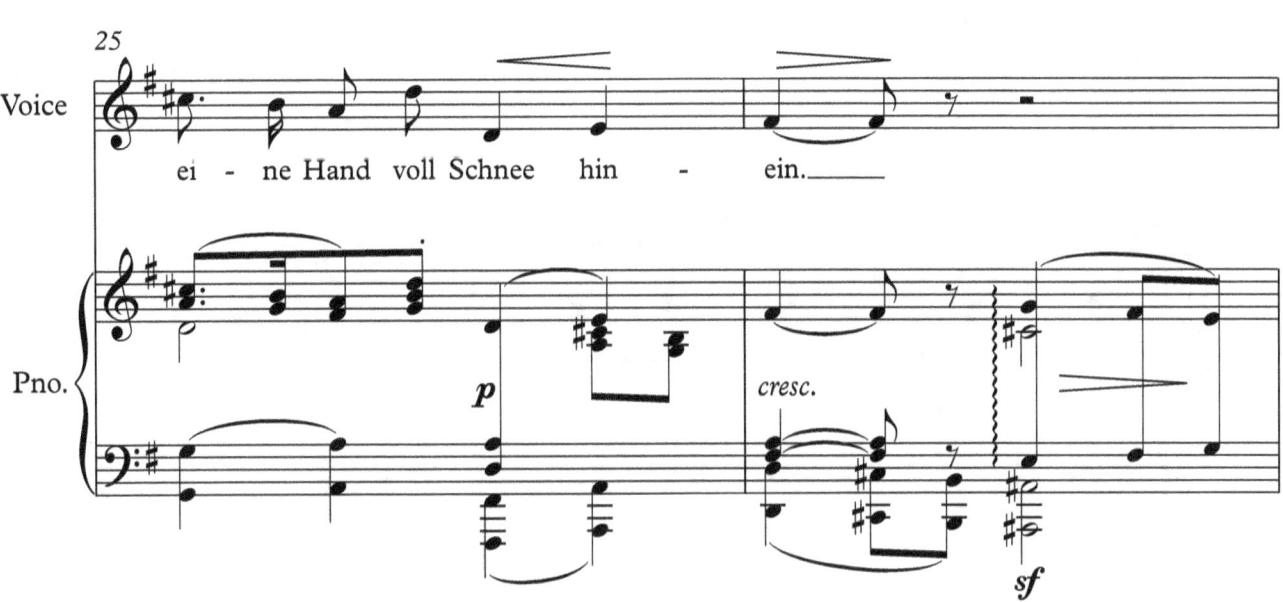

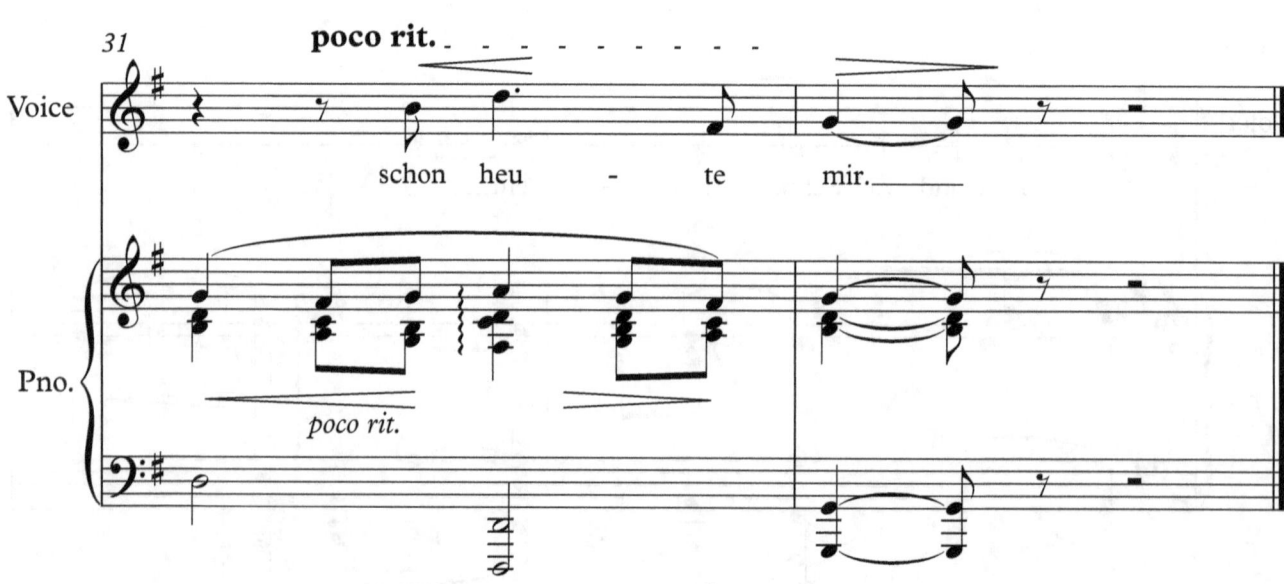

Seiner Majestät Dem Könige von Bayern Ludwig II in tiefster Ehrfurcht gewidmet
Dornröschen

Wilhelm Osterwald Robert Franz, Op. 51 No. 3

Copyright © Iain Sneddon 2019

322

Erinnerung

Wilhelm Osterwald

Robert Franz, Op. 51 No.10

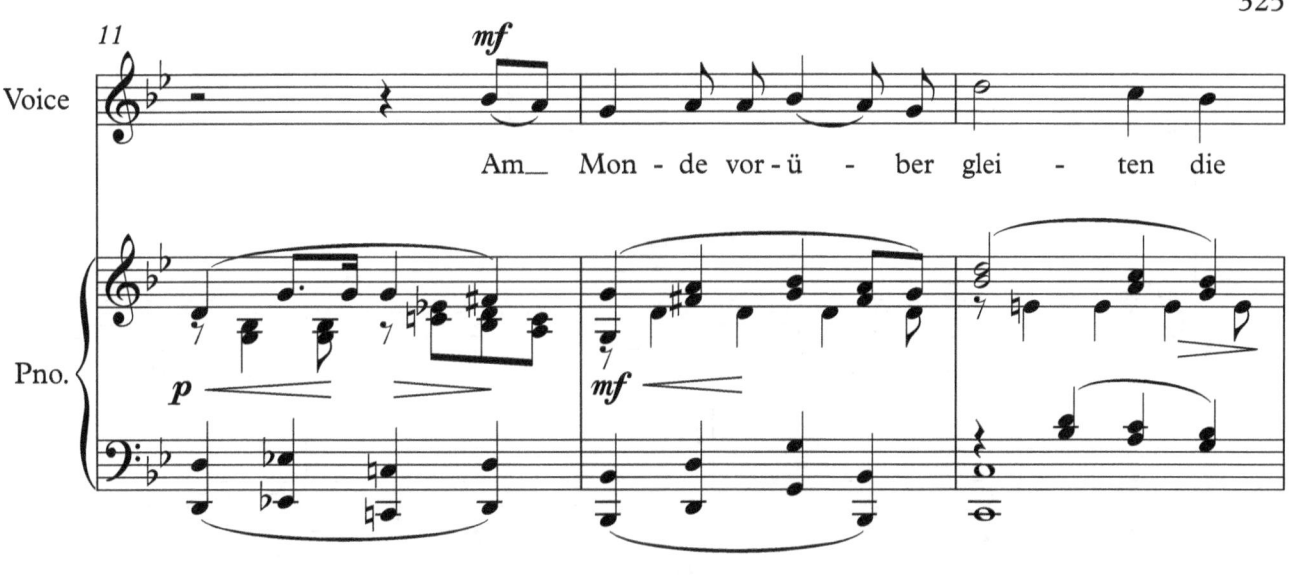

Albumblatt

Robert Franz, ohne Opus

Copyright © Iain Sneddon 2019

Original title: *Entsagung* (Renunciation)

Appendix

The five Robert Franz settings included in this appendix have considerable input from Wilhelm Osterwald. The texts are not considered original poems by Osterwald and were not therefore included in the Franz Catalogue as part of the 51 Osterwald Lieder.

Herziges Schätzle Du! - Op. 50 No. 1

Key:	A major
Time signature:	2/4
Duration:	56"
Vocal range:	G#4-A5
Median pitch:	C#5

The first verse is a Swabian folksong from the south of Germany, an area now largely comprised of the state of Baden-Württemberg. The Swabians are still proud of being a distinct group within Germany with a recent advert proclaiming:

>Wir können alles. Außer Hochdeutsch (We can do anything. Except speak High German)

Verse 1 is traditional. Verses 2 and 3 are by Osterwald closely following the lead of the first and do not add many new ideas. Osterwald also maintains many of the characteristic Swabian dialect in his verses.

Franz's setting is largely strophic. A notable diversion comes in bar 20 where the accompaniment eases out allowing warmth in the phrase *"sich freundli mi an"* (so kindly upon me).

Herziges Schätzle du,	Darling of my heart,
hast mir auch all' mei Ruh'	you have also stolen my peace
g'stolen, du loser Dieb,	you careless thief
hab' di doch lieb!	I do love you!
Wenn dir in's dunkelblau,	When you're in the dark blue of night,
funkelhell Schelmaug' schau,	your naughty eyes sparkle brightly,
mein' i, i säh' in mein	I mean, I see with mine
Himmelreich 'nein,	into the Kingdom of Heaven,
in mein Himmelreich hinein.	with mine into kingdom of heaven.
Aber wann du bist fern,	But when you are away,
hab' i kei Sonn', kei Stern,	I have no sun, no star,
der mir die dunkel Welt	for me the dark world
freundli erhellt!	gently brightens!
Hab' ein Erbarmen dann,	Have a mercy then,
Schatz, mit mir armen Mann,	Sweetheart, on me, a poor man,
funkelhell Schelmaug' du,	your naughty eyes sparkle brightly,
sich freundli mi an,	so kindly upon me,
sich freundli mich an!	so kindly upon me!

Wann mir dei' Schelmaug' lacht,	When your naughty laugh,
ist mir die Erdennacht,	for me makes the earthly night,
ist mir das Jammerthal	for me makes the valley of tears
hell auf einmal!	brighten once again!
Auch, und wenn du mich liebst,	Also, if you love me,
mir a süss Busserl giebst,	Give me a sweet kiss,
spring' i gleich lebig	I'll ascend right now
in's Himmelreich 'nein,	into the kingdom of heaven,
in's Himmelreich hinein!	into the kingdom of heaven!

Sechs deutsche Lieder aus dem 15. und 16. Jahrhundert

The *Six German Songs from the 15th and 16th Centuries* for solo voice and piano were published in Leipzig by F. E. C. Leuckart in 1875. Choral arrangements of all six songs were published in 1879, suggesting that the solo songs had proved popular.

In his book *Robert Franz and the German folk song and hymn (1875)* August Saran noted:

> "A closer investigation amongst the known old German songs, especially in the *Ott Collection* published by the Society for Music Research, likewise gave the most surprising results. There were melodies in it that are so strikingly similar to Franz's songs in tone and mood that we arrived at the unexpected conviction that Franz's song was in the deepest sense nothing more than, with the means of modern art, enriched and idealized German folk song. Consider for example, the four numbers reworked by Franz from the *Ott'sche Sammlung* but do not forget that the editor will, until very recently, have had as little idea as the listener of how the accompaniment forms, which Franz uses here, are as naturally adapted to the old melodies as if they had come into being with the melodies at the same time. And yet they are forms that are as natural and necessary as they are to the Franz songs, where you can surely find them on every page; a significant sign of his close affinity with ancient art."

Osterwald adapted the texts of *Scheiden und Meiden* and *Far' hin!* (Numbers 1 and 2) from songs in the *Lochamer Liederbuch* compiled around 1460 by Jodocus von Windsheim, which is one of the most important collections of fifteenth-century German music. The title of the collection relates to a later inscription in the book made around 1500:

> *Wolflein von Lochamr ist das gesenngk büch* (Wolflein of Lochamr made this book)

The title does not, therefore, directly relate to the town of Lochheim in Bavaria, as suggested by the name "*Lochheimer Liederbuch*" given in the published edition of the Robert Franz's settings.

Osterwald's task would have been both to modernise the middle German of the original texts and ensure that they would be entertaining for a Victorian parlour. The cover of the first edition, although published in Leipzig, indicates it was also available in London, an important market.

The texts for the four remaining German songs have their origins in the *Ott'sche Sammlung* (The Ott Collection) the short name for:

> *Ein hundert fünfzehn weltliche und einige geistliche lieder mit deutschem, lateinischem, französischem und italienischem text zu vier*

compiled by Johann Ott and published in Nuremberg in 1544. A modern edition in three volumes was published by subscription in Berlin in 1876, the year after the publication of the Franz settings, suggesting that Osterwald may have had to access the original part books as his source.

The *Ott Collection* consists of 115 polyphonic settings for 4 to 6 voices including compositions by Senfl, Crequillon and Isaac. All four songs from the *Ott Collection* selected by Osterwald and Franz had previously been set by Ludwig Senfl (c. 1490 - 1543).

Osterwald preserved only the title, the meter and the general theme of the two songs to the extent that his creations might be considered original poems on a traditional theme. This can be clearly seen by comparing an original text with Osterwald's adaptation:

As set by Senfl in the Ott Collection	**As "adapted" by Osterwald**
Ich armer Mann, was hab ich g'than,	Ich armer Mann, was focht mich an,
dasz ich ein Weib hab gnommen!	als ich die Junge freite,
Ich hätt es wol unterwegen lan,	die nun mit mir lebt für und für
ich wär sein noch wol kommen;	in leid'gem Wilderstreite!
wie oft es mich gereuet hat,	Wenn ich möcht weinen, lachet sie,
das kann ich wol ermessen!	und lach' ich möcht' sie weinen,
Allzeit musz ich im Hader stan	ich seh' wohl: mit der Jungend nie
zum Bett und auch zum Essen.	Ist sich das Alter einen.
Wenn ich des Nachts will schlafen gan	Wenn ich mit ihr, einmal spazier',
und freundlich mit ihr scherzen,	hat sie stets Lust zu laufen,
mit mir facht sie ein Hader an,	ich, müd' und schwer, trott' hinterher
der bringt mir heimlich Schmerzen.	und kann mich kaum verschnaufen;
Sprich ich zu ihr: Ruck her zu mir,	wenn sich dann gar 'ne Fiedel rührt,
sie thut sam sei's entschlafen.	wo ich's nicht kann vermeinen,
Will ich viel Kurzweil mit ihr han,	und sie zum Tanz ein Lüstchen spurt,
so musz ichs von ihr kaufen.	dann Gnade meinen Beinen.
Den Kauf treib ich so lang im Jahr,	Ich arme Gauch, was musst' ich auch
damit bleib ich bei Hulden	das Junge Weibchen nehmen,
mit meiner Frauen, sag ich fürwahr,	da sich nicht will zu Tanz und Spiel
die Hand musz ich ihr vergulden:	das Alter mehr bequemen?
guldn Ketten und Schauben will sie han,	Drum wenn ihr wollt ein junges Weib
merkt auf, ihr jungen Kanben!	zu eurer Freude haben,
Also geschicht eim alten Mann,	freit jung mit frischem Sinn und Lieb,
der ein junges Weib will haben.	merkt's wohl, ihr jungen Knaben.

Scheiden und Meiden –
Sechs deutsche Lieder aus dem 15. und 16. Jahrhundert No. 1

Key:	A major
Time signature:	6/8
Duration:	2'02"
Vocal range:	D4-G5
Median pitch:	B4

The melody used by Franz is easily recognised as the one in the *Lochamer Liederbuch*. In the opening phrase, Franz adds an up beat for the word "Ach" to allow "fällt" to come on a strong beat and the falling phrase.

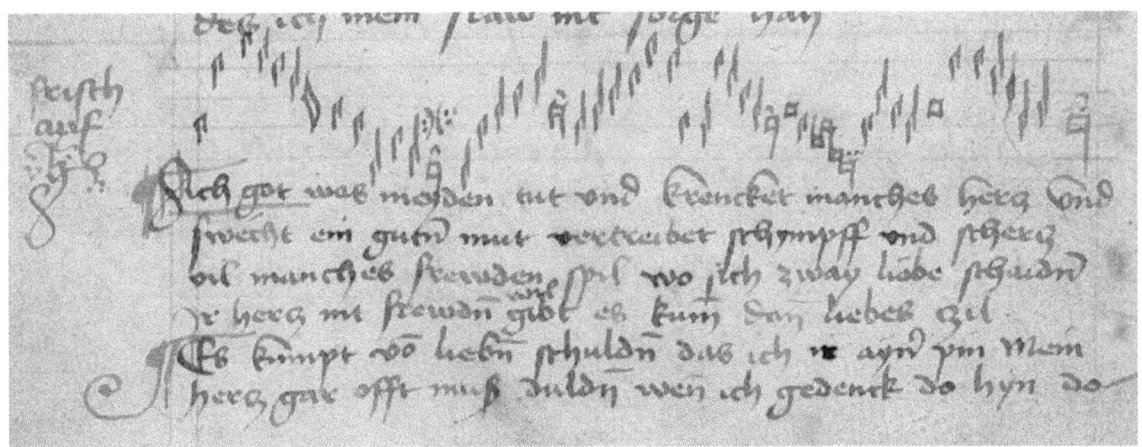

Figure 1: Extract from the Lochamer Liederbuch Page 25

Scheiden und Meiden

Ach Gott! wie fällt
das Meiden den jungen schwer!
Es giebt so bitt'res Leiden
auf Erden sonst nicht mehr,
als wenn in heisser Pein
sich wo zwei Liebe scheiden,
und müssen ach! allein
fern von einander sein.

Was hilft der Blumen Blühen
in voller Frühlingspracht?
Was frommt der Sonne Glühen
in Schöner Sommernacht?
Sie sind ohn' Duft und Glanz,
wenn in des Herzens Mühen
der Freudensel'ger Kranz
hinsiecht und welket ganz.

O schein' o sonne, scheine
uns zwei zusammen neu,
verein' auf's neu, vereine,
was sich geliebt so treue
und liebt bis in den Tod,
o liebe Sonne scheine,
dass schmilzt auf dein Gebot
der Trennung Winternoth.

Separation and restraint

Oh God!
how hard restraint is for the young!
There is not on earth
such bitter suffering,
as the searing pain
where two loves part,
and must be apart
from one another.

What helps the flowers bloom
in full splendour of spring?
What makes the sun glow
on a beautiful summer night?
They are without fragrance and lustre,
when in a heavy heart
the wreath of blessed joy
withers in there and wastes away.

Shine, O sun, shine
on us both afresh,
unite us anew, unite
those who love so faithfully
until death.
O dear sun shine
so that winter's cold separation
melts at your command.

Fahr' hin! –
Sechs deutsche Lieder aus dem 15. und 16. Jahrhundert No. 2

Key:	F major
Time signature:	Common time
Duration:	1'42"
Vocal range:	F4-G5
Median pitch:	A4

The melody used by Franz is closely related to the one in the *Lochamer Liederbuch*.

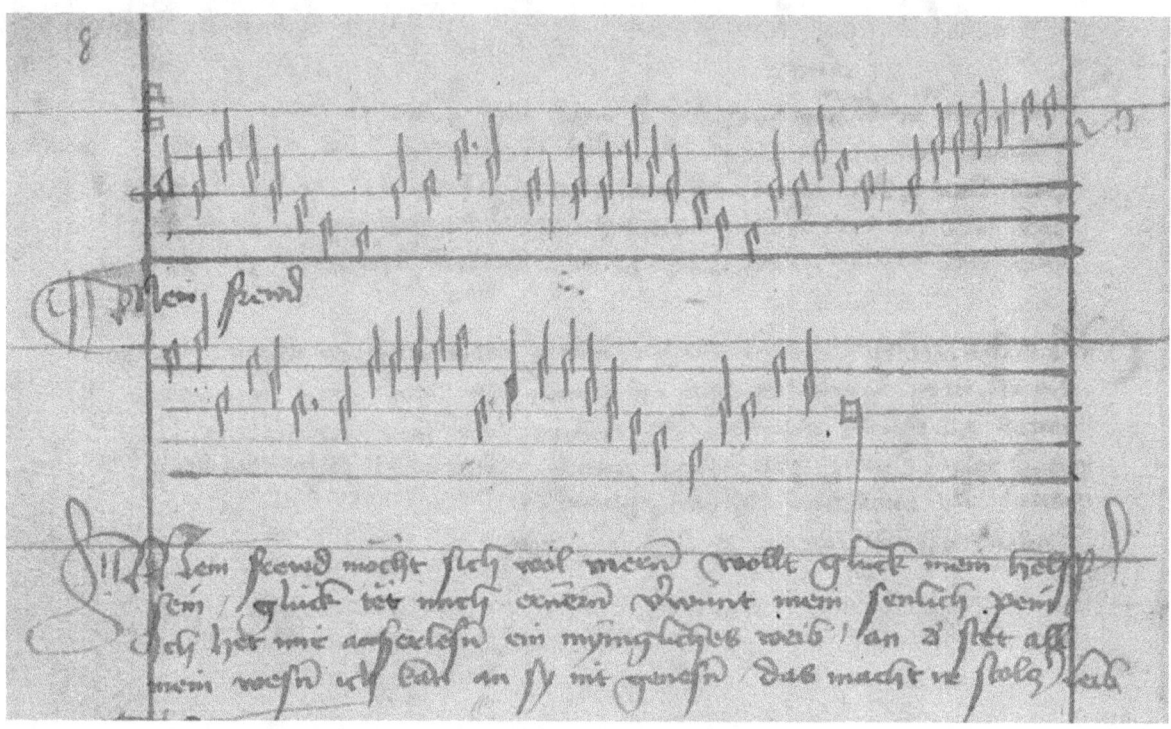

Figure 2: Extract from the Lochamer Liederbuch Page 7

The repeated rising c to f crotchets in the left hand of the piano seem to represent the limp of the partially lame horse. In the third verse (bar 32) Franz adds additional bass notes to reinforce his sweetheart receiving an emphatic farewell. The final diminuendo (bars 39 and 40) has horse and master limping off into the distance.

Fahr' hin!

Mein Pferd das ist am Huf so schwer,
dass ich's nicht bring' zum Traben mehr,
als wär' ihm 's Korn verhagelt gar,
als wär' ihm 's Korn verhagelt,
es lahmt, als litt's an Spat und Hack,
das macht des Schmeides Schabernack,
der hat mir's Pferd vernagelt.

Farewell!

My horse is so slow on the hoof
that I can no longer make it trot,
    it is as if he is the worse for drink,
    as if he is drunk,
he is as lame as if he suffers from housemaid's knee
and looks like a joke from a smithy
    who has shod him badly.

Ich will mit ihm zu Markte ziehn	I'll to go to market with him
und will's vertauschen mit Gewinn,	and exchange him for a profit,
der Schmeid soll mein nicht spotten mehr,	the Blacksmith shouldn't mock me,
der Schmeid soll mein nicht spotten,	the Blacksmith shouldn't scoff at me,
den alten Gaul den geb ich fort	I'll give up the old nag
und bring' ein junges Füll'n von dort,	and bring home a young filly
das soll fein lustig trotten.	that can trot happily.
Mein Liebchen ward mir ungetreu	My sweetheart was unfaithful to me
und wählt' sich einen Buhlen neu	and has chosen a new lover
beim Tanz wohl unt'r der Linden dort,	they're dancing under those linden trees,
beim Tanz wohl unter der Linden;	dancing under the lindens;
fahr' hin, du ungetreuer Schatz!	Farewell, unfaithful sweetheart!
Ich weiss mir wohl an deinem Platz	I know full well that in your place
ein bessres Lieb zu finden.	I'll find a better love.

Ich armer Mann – *Sechs deutsche Lieder aus dem 15. und 16. Jahrhundert* No. 4

Key:	F minor
Time signature:	Common time
Duration:	1'10"
Vocal range:	E♭4-E♭5
Median pitch:	A♭4

Franz follows Senfl's original melody from the *Ott Collection* throughout with only minor variations to accommodate Osterwald's new words.

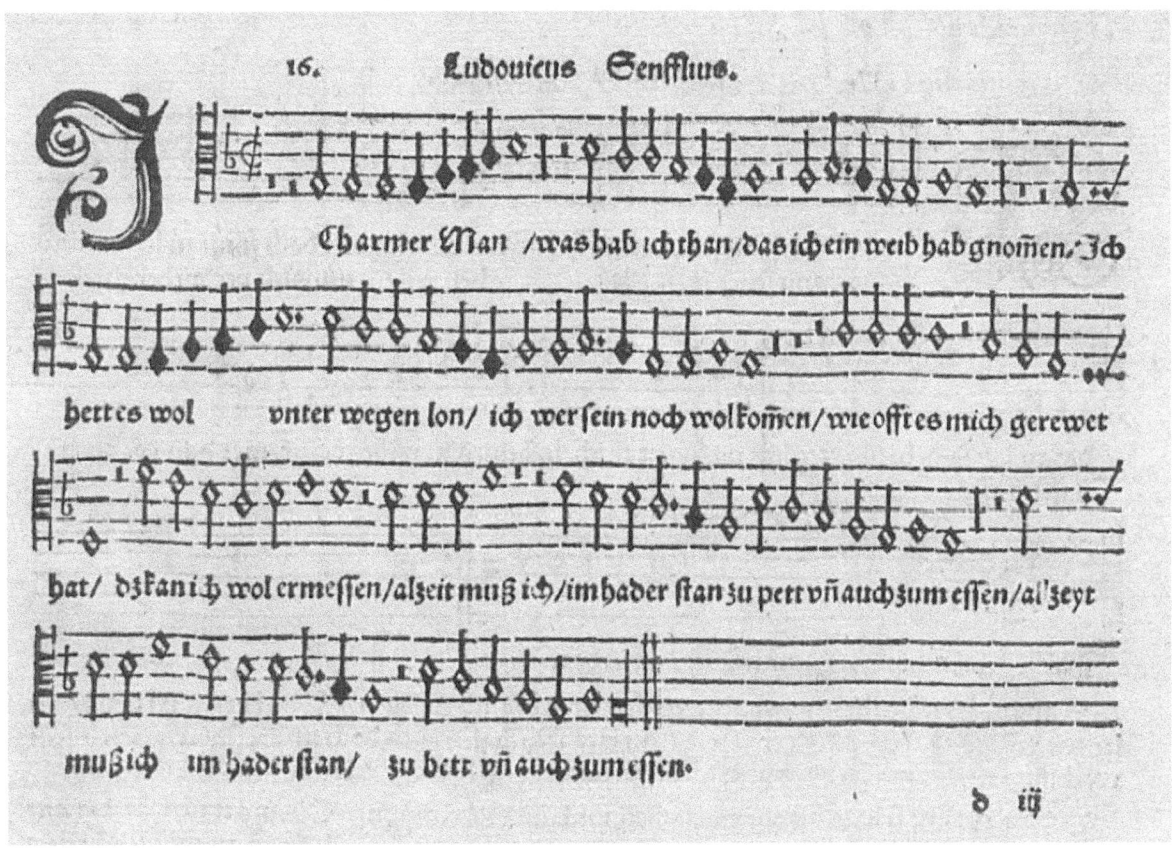

Figure 3: Extract from the Ott Collection, Tenor book, item 16

Ich armer Mann / I, a poor husband

Ich armer Mann	I, a poor husband
Ich armer Mann, was focht mich an,	I a poor husband, what did I care
als ich die Junge freite,	when I courted the maiden,
die nun mit mir lebt für und für	who now lives with me for ever and ever,
in leid'gem Wilderstreite!	in sorry wild strife!
Wenn ich möcht weinen, lachet sie,	If I want to cry, she laughs,
und lach' ich möcht' sie weinen,	and if I laugh she wants to cry.
ich seh' wohl: mit der Jungend nie	I see well, an old person is not
Ist sich das Alter einen.	to be with a young one.
Wenn ich mit ihr, einmal spazier',	Whenever I stroll with her,
hat sie stets Lust zu laufen,	she always wants to run,
ich, müd' und schwer, trott' hinterher	I'm tired and plodding, trotting along behind
und kann mich kaum verschnaufen;	and I can barely catch my breath;
wenn sich dann gar 'ne Fiedel rührt,	if a fiddle strikes up
wo ich's nicht kann vermeinen,	where I can't hear myself think
und sie zum Tanz ein Lüstchen spurt,	and she feels the urge to dance,
dann Gnade meinen Beinen.	then pity my legs.
Ich arme Gauch, was musst' ich auch	I poor fool, why did I have to
das Junge Weibchen nehmen,	take a young wife,
da sich nicht will zu Tanz und Spiel	since not wishing to dance and play
das Alter mehr bequemen?	makes old-age more comfortable?
Drum wenn ihr wollt ein junges Weib	So if you wish have a young wife
zu eurer Freude haben,	to please you,
freit jung mit frischem Sinn und Lieb,	go courting in youth with fresh mind and body,
merkt's wohl, ihr jungen Knaben.	mark this well, you young lads.

Dich meiden –
Sechs deutsche Lieder aus dem 15. und 16. Jahrhundert No. 6

Key:	D minor
Time signature:	Common time
Duration:	3'09"
Vocal range:	D4-G5
Median pitch:	B♭4

Franz follows Senfl's original melody from the *Ott Collection* only for the last verse.

Figure 4: Extract from the Ott Collection, Tenor book, item 11

For the third verse Franz adds a modulating bar (No 29) raising the pitch of the melody by a minor third into Senfl's original key but does not change the key signature. This gives the feeling that the melody of the third verse is a descant to the previous verses.

Saran explains this fortunate accident:

> "These pieces are also in the form of the modern song: a singing voice accompanied by the pianoforte. In some the transposition took place into keys other than the original, a freedom that will hopefully not meet with too much contradiction. Now and then, as with a song from the Lochheimer Manuscript, it was necessary for slight modifications of the melody. Whoever does not mind the trouble of comparing [Franz's versions] with the originals will find that they may not be more of a transformation than those which the old composers frequently allowed in their contrapuntal adaptations. Only the keys of the song *Dich Meiden* require an explanation: As a result of an oversight, this melody was notated in the alto clef instead of the tenor clef and this is how it came into the hands of the editor [Franz]. Fortunately, the text not only allowed for a twofold treatment of the melody, but even seemed to demand it, leaving the first two verses in D minor and modulating to F major in the third verse, as the original dictates. Those who take offence at this for historical reasons may delete the D minor part, as well as the prelude to the last verse - the rest essentially corresponds to the form of the originals." (August Saran, Halle, 1875)

Dich meiden

Dich meiden – nein, ach nein!
die Pein trägt meine Seele nicht,
wenn du – nicht mein kannst sein,
mein armes Herz, mein armes Herz bricht.
Dich sehn ist Morgenroth,
dich meiden Nacht und Tod.

Die lange Nacht, die Nacht
durch wacht mein Auge thränenschwer,
die Sternenpracht, die Pracht
entfacht mein heisses Leid, mein Leid noch mehr,
wenn mir von Hoffnung nicht
ihr leuchtend Prangen spricht.

Du süsses Lieb, du süsses Lieb,
o gieb mir wieder neuen Muth.
Was fort dich trieb, was fort dich trieb,
vergieb, und sei, o sei mir wieder gut,
nur du, du bist, ob nah', ob fern,
ja doch mein einz'ger, mein einz'ger Stern.

Avoid you

Avoid you? –no, oh no!
My soul cannot bear the pain,
if you cannot be mine,
my poor heart breaks.
To see you is sunrise,
to avoid you is night and death.

The long night, the whole night
through, my eyes stay awake heavy with tears,
the starry splendour, the splendour
kindles my ardent suffering, my suffering increases,
if her bright resplendence
does not speak of hope.

You sweet love, sweet love,
Oh, give me new courage.
What drove you, what drove you away,
forgive, and be, oh, be well again,
only you, you are, whether near far,
yes, my only one, my only star.

Notes and Translations Copyright © Iain Sneddon 2019

Frau Helene von Hornbotstel-Magnus gewidmet

Herziges Schätzle Du!

Verse 1: Traditional Swabian
Verses 2 and 3: Willhelm Osterwald

Robert Franz, Op. 50 No. 1

Copyright © Iain Sneddon 2019

Scheiden und Meiden

From the *Lochamer Liederbuch* (c. 1460)
adapted by Wilhelm Osterwald

Robert Franz, Sechs deutsche Lieder
aus dem 15. und 16. Jahrhundert No. 1

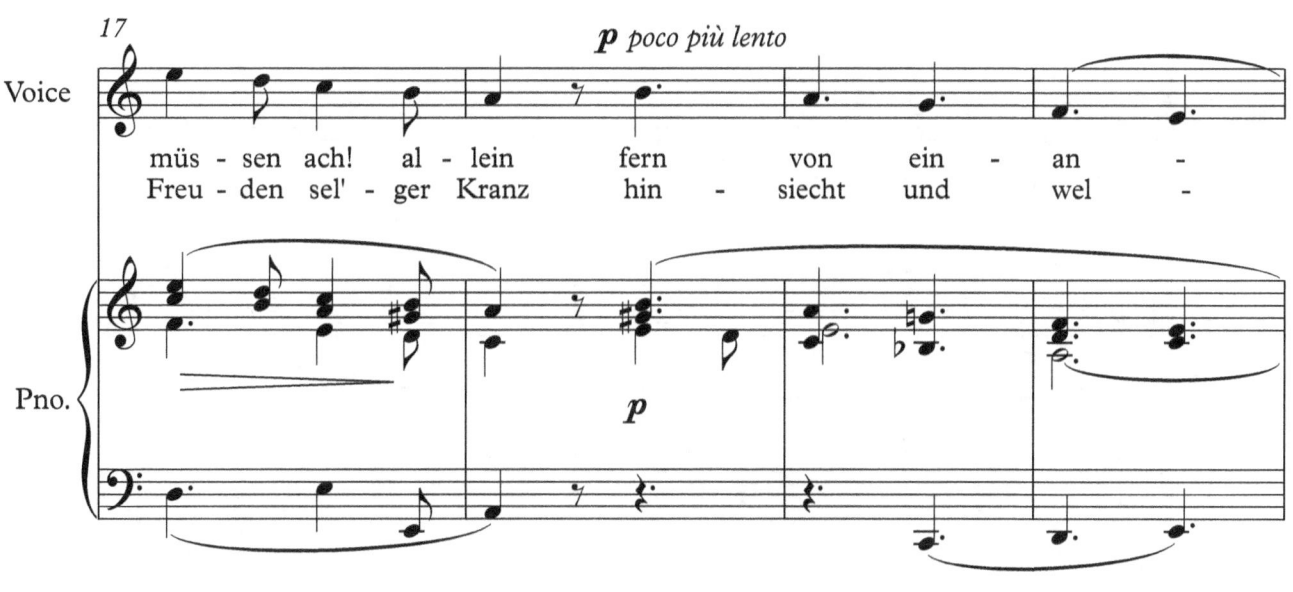
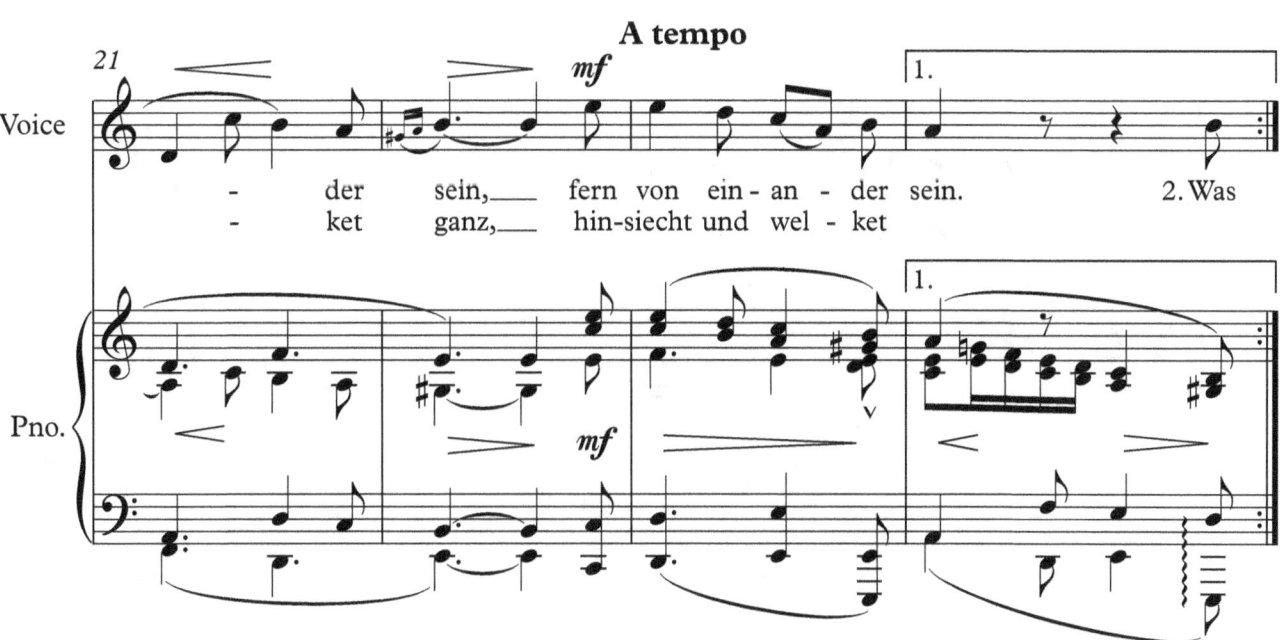

Fahr' hin!

Lochamer Liederbuch (c. 1460)
adapted by Wilhelm Osterwald

Robert Franz, Sechs deutsche Lieder
aus dem 15. und 16. Jahrhundert No. 2

Copyright © Iain Sneddon 2019

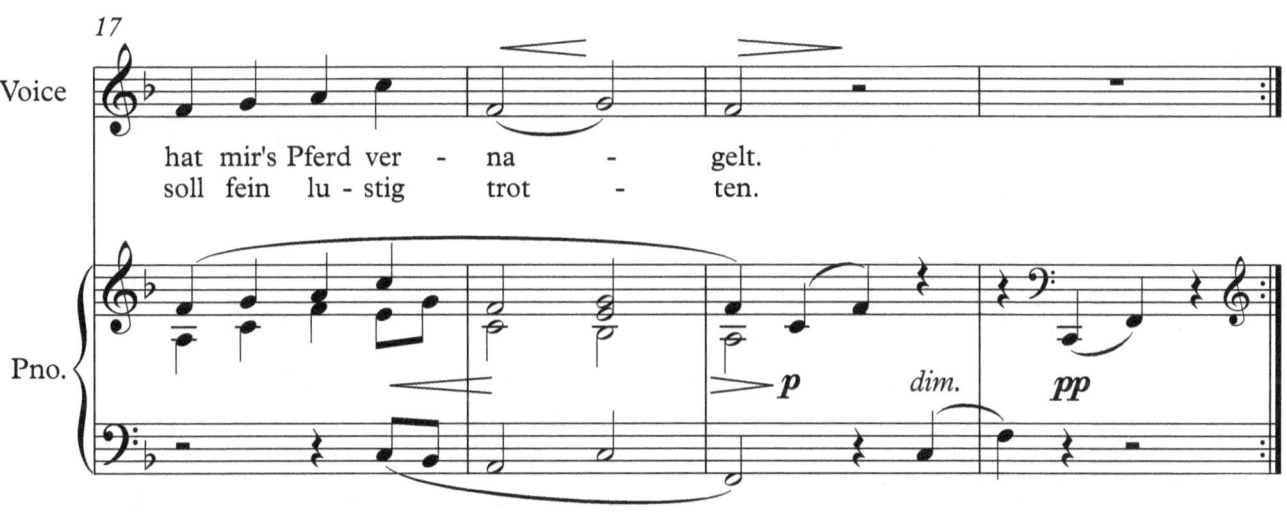

Ich armer Mann

From the *Johannes Ott Collection*
Adapted by Wilhelm Osterwald

Robert Franz, Sechs deutsche Lieder
aus dem 15. und 16. Jahrhundert No. 4

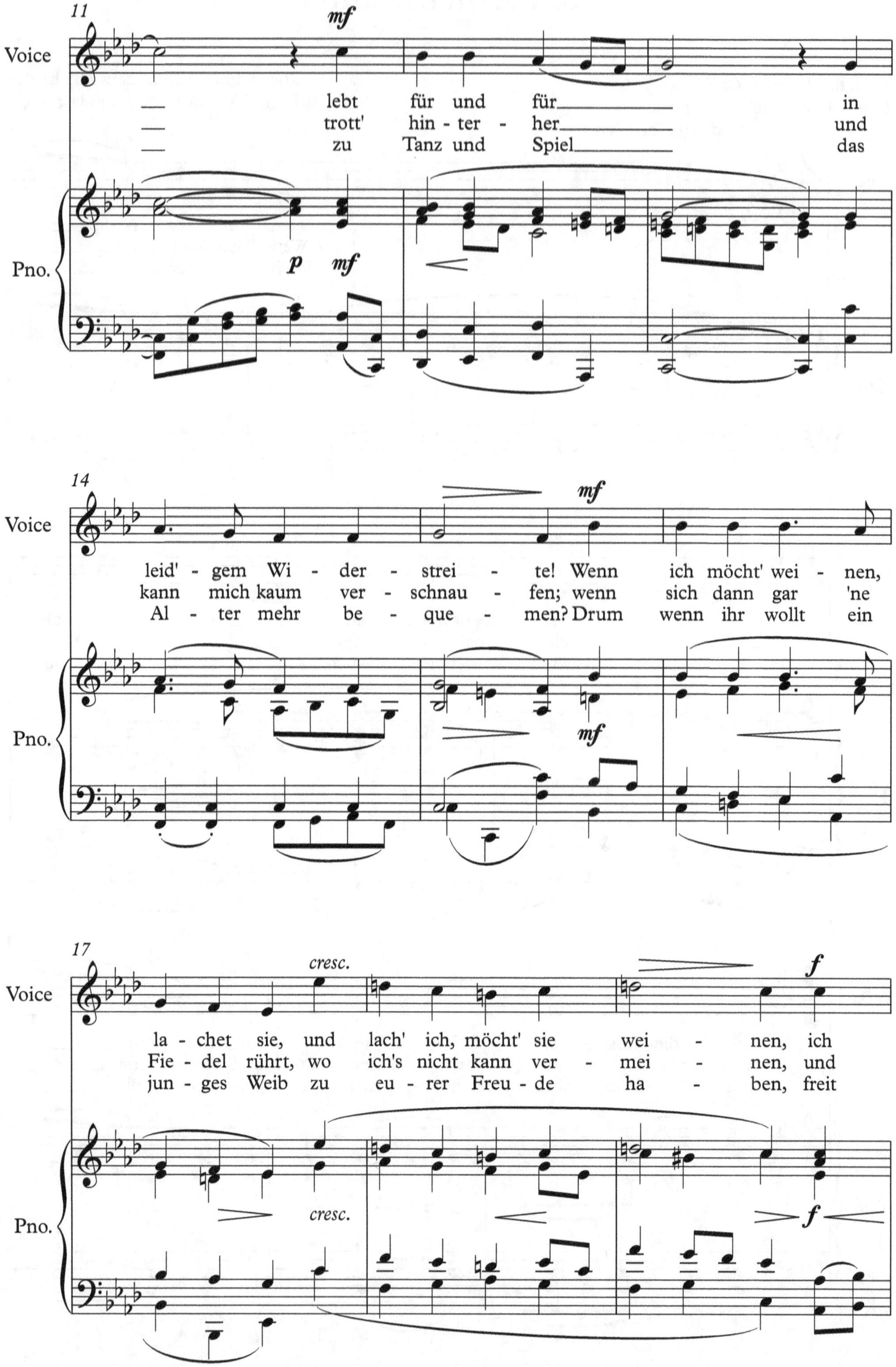
11
mf
Voice
— lebt für und für in
— trott' hin - ter - her und
— zu Tanz und Spiel das
p mf
Pno.
14
mf
Voice
leid' - gem Wi - der - strei - te! Wenn ich möcht' wei - nen,
kann mich kaum ver - schnau - fen; wenn sich dann gar 'ne
Al - ter mehr be - que - men? Drum wenn ihr wollt ein
mf
Pno.
17
cresc.
f
Voice
la - chet sie, und lach' ich, möcht' sie wei - nen, ich
Fie - del rührt, wo ich's nicht kann ver - mei - nen, und
jun - ges Weib zu eu - rer Freu - de ha - ben, freit
cresc.
f
Pno.

Dich meiden

From the *Johannes Ott Collection (1544)*
adapted by Wilhelm Osterwald

Robert Franz, Sechs deutsche Lieder
aus dem 15. und 16. Jahrhundert No. 6

*) First edition has C♮

Copyright © Iain Sneddon 2019

*) First edition has C♮

356

*) First edition has D♯ and B♭

Acknowledgements

With grateful thanks to Graham Johnson for his introduction to this volume, his encouragement and his insights into the songs.

Picture Credits:

Stiftung Händel-Haus, Halle, Germany. For:

- the engravings of Robert Franz and Wilhelm Osterwald;
- the photograph of Franz's birth house; and
- the photograph of Robert Bethge.

The Salt Worker in traditional ceremonial dress is licensed from INTERFOTO/Alamy Stock Photo.

All other photographs © Victoria Edge 2019.

Thank you also to:

Marc Verter for proofreading the typeset songs.

Hannah Whale for her editing of the cover photo.

Dr Marc Jarzebowski, DMJ Genealogie, Ahrweilerstraße 3, 14197 Berlin, for resourceful research and new findings.

Dr Konstanze Musketa, Stiftung Händel-Haus, Halle an der Saale, Germany, for her generous assistance.

Stephan Bächtold: German language consultant, for his unfailing interest, support and expert knowledge.

Jonas Demelt for the Digital Robert Franz Library (RobertFranz.org).

Juliet Carberry for her invaluable editorial assistance.

Michael Edge for his sponsorship of the project and finance.

The staff at the British Library.

Biographies

Graham Johnson OBE is one of the world's leading vocal accompanists and a world expert on German Romantic Lieder, particularly those of Franz Schubert. His CD booklet notes and the three volume *Franz Schubert: The Complete Songs* set new high standards.

Graham Johnson was awarded an OBE in the 1994 Queen's Birthday Honours list and was created Chevalier in the *Ordre des Arts et Lettres* in 2002. He is also an Honorary Member of the Royal Philharmonic Society.

Iain Sneddon specialises in the works of Betty Roe, Isaac Nathan, Carl Loewe and Vaclav Tomašek. His articles about Betty Roe have been published in Musical Opinion and the British Music Society Newsletter. He is the chief editor for Robish Music and published the collection *The Silver Hound and Other Songs* to accompany a recording of Betty Roe's songs on Métier Records (MSV 28566), which he also co-produced.

Victoria Edge is an Associate of the Royal College of Music for Singing Performance and a graduate in German from London University. She has devised and presented many programmes of German poetry and song. She wrote *The Winter Journey of Wilhelm Müller;* a treatise on the autobiographical elements of *Die Winterreise,* the basis of Schubert's song cycle, which was published in Musical Opinion. She is the Originator and Project Developer for the recording of the Complete Osterwald Lieder and Songs, released on MPR/Willowhayne Records (MPR 106).

Index of Titles and First Lines

Title/*First Line*	Page number	Opus	No.
Abends	220	20	4
Ach dass du kamst	129	4	12
Ach Gott! wie fällt	342		
Ach wenn ich doch ein Immchen wär'	107	3	6
Ach! daß du kamst, ach, daß du kamst	129	4	12
Ach! musstest du denn scheiden	112	4	8
Ade denn, du stolze!	254	31	2
Albumblatt	328		
Als die Linden trieben	275	36	4
Aprillaunen	316	44	2
Aufbruch	265	35	6
Aus bangen Träumen	283	37	2
Aus der Ferne schallen Gesänge	231	22	4
Bei der Linde	275	36	4
Da der Sommer kommen ist	189	11	4
Da die Stunde kam	159	7	3
Den Strauss den sie gewunden	244	26	3
Der junge Tag erwacht	155	7	1
Der Mond ist schlafen gegangen	207	17	2
Der Schnee ist zergangen	152	6	5
Der Sommer ist zu Ende	286	37	5
Der Tag beginnt zu dunkeln	220	20	4
Des Waldes Sänger singen	182	10	6
Des Waldes Wipfel rauschen	147	6	4
Dich melden	352		
Die Harrende	259	35	1
Die Liebe hat gelogen!	147	6	4
Die Lüfte werden heller	265	35	6
Die Schwalbe zieht, der Sommer flieht	224	21	6
Die Sterne flimmern und prangen	324	51	10
Dornröschen	321	51	3

Title/*First Line*	Page number	Opus	No.
Dort unter'm Lindenbaume	251	31	1
Du grüne Rast im Haine	294	41	6
Durch säuselnde Bäume	118	4	9
Entschluss	307	43	3
Erinnerung	324	51	10
Erster Verlust	270	36	2
Far' hin!	346		
Frühe Klage	231	22	4
Gestern hielt er mich im Arme	270	36	2
Gewitternacht	164	8	6
Gleich eines Herzens bangen Fieber-träumen	122	4	10
Gleich wie der Mond so keusch und rein	304	43	2
Grolle lauter, zürnend Gewitter	164	8	6
Herbstsorge	122	4	10
Herziges Schätzle Du	338	50	1
Hör' ich ein Vöglein singen	259	35	1
Ich arme Mann	349		
Ich lobe mir die Vögelein	137	5	8
Im Frühling	211	17	5
Im Grase lieg' ich manche Stunde	211	17	5
Im Mai (*Musst nicht allein im Freien*)	234	22	5
Im Mai (*Nun grünt der Berg*)	184	11	3
Im Sommer	189	11	4
In Blüthen	312	43	6
In dem Dornbusch	241	26	2
Jetzt steh' ich auf der höchsten Höh'	175	9	5
Kurzes Wiedersehen	112	4	8
Liebchen, was willst du?	316	44	2
Lieber Schatz, sei wieder gut mir	241	26	2
Lieblich blüh'n die Bäume	300	43	1
Mein Pferd das ist am Huf so schwer	346		
Mein Schatz ist auf der Wanderschaft	289	40	1
Musst nicht allein im Freien	234	22	5

Title/*First Line*	Page number	Opus	No.
Nun da die Bäum' in Blüthen	312	43	6
Nun grünt der Berg, nun grünt das Thal	184	11	3
Nun hat das Leid ein Ende	216	18	3
Nun hat mein Stecken gute Rast	278	36	6
O banger Traum, was flatterst du	141	5	10
Scheiden und Meiden	342		
Scheust dich noch immer, seliges Leben	307	43	3
Schöner Mai, bist über Nacht	248	30	4
Sonnenwende	286	37	5
Ständchen	207	17	2
Träume	300	43	1
Treibt der Sommer seinen Rosen	162	8	5
Um Mitternacht	198	16	6
Umsonst	182	10	6
Und die Rosen, die prangen	179	10	5
Und kommt der Frühling wieder her	126	4	11
Und welche Rose Blüthen treibt	193	12	1
Vergessen	141	5	10
Vergiss mein nicht!	244	26	3
Verlass' mich nicht!	224	21	6
Vom Berge	175	9	5
Vor meinem Fenster regt	238	26	1
Wanderlied	126	4	11
Wenn ich's nur wüsste!	238	26	1
Will über Nacht wohl durch das Thal	134	5	4
Zu Spät	283	37	2

www.ingramcontent.com/pod-product-compliance
Lightning Source LLC
Chambersburg PA
CBHW080811010526
44113CB00013B/2359